50 SEASONA

For Ann

50 Seasonal Sketches

NEIL PUGMIRE

EASTBOURNE

ISBN 1 84291 042 6

Published by
KINGSWAY COMMUNICATIONS LTD
Lottbridge Drove, Eastbourne BN23 6NT, England.
Email: books@kingsway.co.uk

Book design and production for the publishers by
Bookprint Creative Services, P.O. Box 827, BN21 3YJ, England.
Printed in Great Britain.

Contents

PART 2: SPECIAL SERVICES AND OTHER EVENTS

Acknowledgements

Over the past 15 years, I've had the privilege of working with some excellent actors and great friends. It's no exaggeration to say that I couldn't have written this book without their inspiration, input and creativity. Thanks to all those in TOAST (The Oxford Area Schools Team); the drama group at St Aldate's Church, Oxford; friends who've acted at St Margaret's Church, Burnage; the drama group on the Abersoch Holiday Mission; members of Bench Theatre Company in Havant, and members of Top Cat Theatre Company in Portsmouth. Thanks also to my dad, Alan Pugmire, and to David MacInnes, John Byrne and all the other church leaders who let me try to illustrate their services with sketches.

Thanks particularly to Diana Nairne, Andy Poole, Richard Pheasant, Fudge Fordyce and members of Top Cat Theatre Company, who suggested improvements to individual sketches; and to Lucy Moore and Malcolm Stewart, who both read through the manuscript and made excellent comments.

My biggest thanks, of course, go to my wife Ann, whose willingness to become the chief breadwinner in our household enabled me to give up the day job and become a professional writer. She continues to be a constant inspiration and great encourager.

Performance and Copyright

The right to perform any of the sketches within this book is included within the cover price, so long as those performances are in an amateur context, for example in church or school. Where any charge is made to the audience, permission in writing must be obtained from the author, who can be contacted through the publishers. A fee may be payable for the right to perform sketches in such circumstances.

The book is copyright, and no part may be copied without permission in writing from the publisher. Where multiple copies of a sketch are required for those playing the parts, it is generally simpler and cheaper to buy extra copies of the book.

Foreword

This collection of sketches from Neil Pugmire is an invaluable resource for the church at this time. With so many in our society who have minimal knowledge of the New Testament and little incentive to find out about the Christian faith, there is a greater need than ever to find points of contact and ways of arousing interest among ordinary people. Simple dramatic pieces such as these can achieve just that. The good communicator knows that entertaining presentation, rightly used, is effective in imparting truth.

It was the ballet dancer Moira Shearer who, on being asked to explain the meaning of a dance that she had performed, replied, 'If I could have said it, do you think I would have danced it?' Some things in life require actions as well as words if they are to make a full impression on the hearer. The great Christian statesman, Stanley Jones, made this comment about Jesus: 'On the Mount of Beatitudes, he opened his mouth and taught the people; on the Mount of Calvary, he opened his heart and showed the people.' The message of the cross is not only a proposition about the justice of God in forgiving sin, it is a dramatic presentation of the lengths to which God will go in his love for us. The sheer drama has riveted men and women down the centuries. No wonder thousands flock to Oberammergau.

In the Middle Ages, before the printed Bible became

available to all, the common people got their understanding from miracle and mystery plays performed in the streets. More recently, in the 1970s, Paul Burbridge and Murray Watts pioneered the early work of the Riding Lights Theatre Company, with light-hearted sketches based on parables and biblical stories. David Watson, of St Michael-le-Belfrey in York, used them to great effect in his city missions and many other churches began to do the same.

Neil Pugmire is in this tradition. As a gifted undergraduate and lay assistant at St Aldate's, Oxford, as well as on missions and in school assemblies, he proved to have flair, not only as a performer but as a scriptwriter. He produced the popular series for children called *Toastenders* (since revamped as *Southsea-Enders*), while his *Salty Towers: Cana Branch* was premiered at my own son's wedding! Over the past 10 years, his fluent pen has continued to pour out sketches, of which this volume provides a sample.

The value of such sketches is often underestimated. Good ones hold the attention, make you laugh, connect with human experience and punch home a simple message. They can lighten the atmosphere, bring biblical facts alive, challenge people's lifestyle and, above everything else, implant nuggets of Christian truth firmly in the memory. In a day when people's attention span is short and ignorance of the gospel is widespread, this is needed. These sketches are not a substitute for preaching and teaching, but as a way of catching the attention, illustrating a point and challenging people to respond, they are a powerful tool.

After a mission team had visited a Northern Ireland prison, a terrorist wrote words to this effect: 'The message of the gospel was too familiar to make an impact on me, but the sketch made me suddenly realize that I must get right with God.' I warmly commend this book to all those seriously trying to bring the good news of Christ to this generation.

Canon David MacInnes, St Aldate's, Oxford

How to Use This Book

Looking for a funny sketch to jazz up the Christmas carol service? Need something challenging for your youth group to discuss? Desperate for material to bring a Bible story to life within a family service? Look no further: *50 Seasonal Sketches* can help. This book includes sketches to be performed throughout the church's year as well as those written for special occasions such as weddings, baptisms, school assemblies and even the anniversary of your church building. There are monologues, duologues, sketches with narrators, funny sketches, moving mimes and even a one-act play. So there should genuinely be something for everyone, whatever the state of your drama group or the liturgical position of your church.

The idea of compiling a book of sketches to perform at various points in the church year is not a new one, but it is worth revisiting because so much of what we do as Christians depends on the calendar. Christmas, Lent and Easter come round every year, and people are always interested in something that helps them to look at those seasons in a new light. This book also provides sketches for other special occasions that don't depend on the calendar. Although many sketches for family services, evangelism, street theatre and school assemblies have already been published, few have been written particularly for weddings, baptisms or healing services. And as churches become more open to the use of the arts within worship, it is helpful to have a resource to cater for all sorts of occasions.

I have been fortunate to work with some excellent actors and actresses in a variety of church, mission, school and street theatre settings. A whole string of vicars and church leaders have been receptive to suggestions for weekly children's serials, extravagant plays and sketches with ridiculously over-the-top costumes. If you are in a similar situation, you will find challenging sketches and a one-act play within these pages that should stretch you as they stretched us. But not every church has a tradition of performing theatrically, or any kind of drama group to speak of. You may get a sinking feeling every time you see any script with more than a couple of lines to learn. You may only have a couple of days in which to prepare something with your youth group before Sunday's big service. There should be something in this book for you as well.

Planning services

I'm a firm believer that drama within church services shouldn't be used as an end in itself, but should be an effective illustration of what the preacher or service leader wants to say. Sketches such as the ones within this book can make their jobs much easier – indeed, many of them were written to help illuminate a preacher's point. It's important, however, that all those planning a service are singing from the same hymn sheet, not just in terms of theme, but also in the tone used. There's no point a fire-and-brimstone preacher building up to a climax about how the story of Noah illustrates God's terrifying judgement on the human race, to be followed by two members of the drama group doing a hilarious sketch in a camel outfit.

The best way to use this book is to talk to the preacher or

service leader about the overall theme, what sketch would be most suitable, and how it would slot into the order of service. Sketches within sermons do work well, so long as they are introduced properly and the preacher picks up on the theme of the sketch afterwards. Many sketches also work well as a prelude to a sermon, or to introduce the theme at the start of a service. The best preachers can adjust what they want to communicate where necessary so that the sketch fits seamlessly into what they are saying. Sometimes they may even ask to see the sketch before preparing their sermon so that they can work around it. As always, communication is vital.

Of course, there are churches where drama is still slightly frowned upon as at best a distraction and at worst a dangerous irrelevance. Introducing some drama into services in that kind of situation can be difficult. Here you need to combine sensitivity with good communication and effective planning. If you start with relatively simple and uncontroversial sketches, both your church leaders and your congregation should realize that drama can be effective. The door might then start to open for something more adventurous. Be gracious, however: don't assume that you are right and the rest of the congregation is wrong if they don't immediately take to it. Perhaps your approach, the content of the sketch, or the way it was performed left something to be desired and detracted from the worship.

Key to symbols

This book includes symbols to make it easier for you to use. The following key should help you find what you are looking for.

Funny sketches

 Many sketches have potentially comic moments, but some are designed to be laugh-out-loud funny. Often the comedy value lies as much in the characterization or the situation as in any blatant gags.

Sketches to be followed up by preacher

Although many of these sketches are written for performance within a church context, some of them will *only* work effectively if someone is able to draw out the point afterwards or make the connection between what the audience has just seen and some Christian teaching. Sketches without this symbol should speak for themselves and could be performed without explanation.

Complex sketches that need a director

Ideally there should always be someone who is 'directing' – i.e. not acting, but commenting on what your sketch looks like. That's not always possible. It may be best, however, not to attempt sketches with this symbol unless there is a director available.

Monologues

Sketches that can be performed by one person alone.

Bible-based sketches

 All of the sketches in this book could be used to help illustrate various parts of the Bible, but those with this symbol are more directly based on particular passages.

Child-friendly sketches

It's not just the sketches in the family service section that might be suitable for performing to children. Look out for this symbol in other sections of the book.

Teenager-friendly sketches

 Something that might work well with an older church congregation might seem irredeemably naff to a teenager. Sketches with this symbol should be more suitable for 13–20-year-olds than others.

Sketches with minimum rehearsal time

 These are the sketches you want if you are short of time or if you are using actors who have difficulty learning lines.

Controversial sketches

These sketches are on hot topics, might cause complaints or need to be handled sensitively. Check with your church leader before using!

Sketches that focus on the world

These are sketches that veer away from traditional church territory to look at the world in which we live. Some may even be suitable for performance in a totally secular venue.

In addition, each sketch includes details of the following:

Aim

 This is the bit the preacher or service leader could also read. It also tells you what you are hoping to achieve by using the sketch.

Cast

This tells you how many people you will need and gives a brief pen-portrait of each character, as well as possible costume requirements.

Props

 This tells you what else you will need to perform each sketch.

Costumes and props

It is tempting to assume that you can make it easier to perform sketches in church by skimping on costumes or props. In fact, pulling out all the stops to make a costume believable or even over the top enhances many sketches. In some sketches in this book, the visual element is the basis for much of the comedy. This can be particularly important for sketches you hope to perform in front of children. If you are blessed with people within your church who are good at making costumes out of cardboard or elaborate outfits from bits of old material, treat them well – you never know when you will want to use them! If not, keep on the lookout for decent costumes or props. Store them in a convenient place at home or at church, or draw up an inventory of who owns what useful items within the congregation. One option, especially for Santa outfits or first-century Palestinian costumes, is to hire them from specialist theatrical costume shops or fancy-dress shops. They are only likely to cost a few pounds and are normally worth it for the amount of extra credibility you gain with an audience.

If you want to ask any questions about any particular sketches, it's possible to contact me through the Top Cat Theatre Company website: www.topcattheatre.com. And if you can't find precisely what you require in this book, I also write sketches to order for a small fee. Visit the website for details.

Working with a Drama Group

Unless you plan to spend all your time performing monologues, at some point you will have to work with a team of people! This has advantages and disadvantages. The major advantage is that it is much easier to be creative with other people, as each person adds his or her own suggestions and ideas or brings an individual personality to a particular character. The disadvantage is that someone has to organize this disparate group to make sure they get to rehearsals on time, collect the right props and feel valued and involved. In other words, 'people' skills become important. Christians should be good at this kind of thing, but we shouldn't assume that church drama groups will automatically be creative, encouraging and well organized just because the actors are Christians! What follows are some tips that should help you run such a group within your church.

What drama group?

You may think that 'drama group' is a slightly pretentious label to pin onto your tiny band of reluctant teenagers. In many churches there are few people willing to act something out during a church service, and you may find volunteers hard to come by. Any volunteers you do find may lack confidence, acting skills, mobility, the ability to learn lines, or a

combination of all of those things! You may find that
churchgoers assume that drama is just 'something for the
youth group to do'. It's a shame if they do, because older
people can add richness and an experience to drama that the
youth group may not be able to get across (imagine, for
instance, a genuine Second World War veteran acting as the
narrator in 'No Greater Love' on page 178. They may also
not have the self-consciousness of teenagers, who can end up
dissolving into fits of laughter at inappropriate times.
Sometimes you may need to start with something simple,
allow people to see that it is effective and encourage others
to get involved. Churchgoers often lack confidence in the
gifts they can bring to worship, but there are often smaller,
non-speaking parts people can play that will ease them
gently into it. This is where your skills of encouragement and
gentle persuasion will be needed most!

Leadership

Even if you are only planning to perform one two-minute
sketch once in every blue moon, it is helpful to have someone
in charge. It may be that you appoint someone to lead the
drama group as a whole, who can liaise with the church
leaders about when and how sketches are performed. It may
be that you find several different people – one to 'direct' the
actual drama and watch what the actors are doing, another
to cope with the administration of collecting props and costumes, and another to organize the dates of rehearsals.

It helps if the person who is in charge has some experience
of performing, as they can impart useful tips, encourage
nervous first-timers and will know where to look for decent
sketches. That's not always possible, however. Sometimes it's
helpful to see the drama group as similar to a Bible study
group or home group. Members will, after all, be learning
more about God, making themselves feel vulnerable and dis-

covering new gifts. If you imagine that you are appointing a leader for such a group, with all the experience and people skills necessary, you won't go far wrong.

Discipline

It may seem odd to talk about discipline within the context of drama groups. After all, isn't drama fun? Don't people perform drama in church because they enjoy it? Well, yes, but – as any youth or children's worker will tell you – it's important to set boundaries within which people can express themselves. Drama groups are no different. Anyone who has been involved with amateur dramatics knows the frustration of waiting for half the cast to turn up, watching a show-off monopolize the rehearsal process, or dealing with an actor who thinks he or she knows better than the director.

Good leadership should help that sense of discipline to come naturally. Don't hit first-timers with a photocopied list of rules, because that may put them off. If problems begin to appear, however, it's worth laying down a few ground rules. Here's some that I've found helpful:

Punctuality is vital

The rehearsal process often can't start until everyone is there. If someone has difficulty getting there on time, talk to them in private about why that is and try to help them, if you can, by rescheduling rehearsals. If, however, someone is being just plain lazy, stress that they will not be performing with you if they are late next time. If necessary, give actors a rehearsal schedule which includes clear dates and times so that no one can be in any doubt about when you are getting together.

Everyone's opinion is important

One of the great things about rehearsals is that you can try umpteen different ways of performing a sketch until you reach a consensus about what works best. If someone suggests something that sounds ridiculous, don't waste time arguing about it: try it out! If people think it works, keep it in. If it doesn't, it should be obvious even to those who suggested it. People should always feel that their suggestions are taken seriously, even if ultimately one person has the final say on whether they will be taken up.

Respect for the person directing the sketch is also important

It may be that someone who wouldn't normally direct is asked to do so to give them some experience. Make sure that you all listen to what they say and then do it. Stress to others that this person is in charge, and – for the time being – what they say goes. If they are not actually performing within the sketch, they are in the best position to see whether something works.

Respect for the actors is important too

If someone is putting their heart and soul into a performance, that actor is making himself or herself very vulnerable. Even in comedy sketches, there may be an element of that person's own character coming through. If the director or other actors are laughing at the acting (rather than the character or the lines), that person's self-confidence may be taking a knock. If other actors are not listening, popping in and out or chatting among themselves, it may be difficult for that person to concentrate. All members of the drama group will feel freer to express themselves if they know that no one will make fun of their efforts. The other actors will benefit – and may even learn something – if they also watch what is going on.

Make it clear what your expectations are regarding line learning

My view is that lines should always be learnt, as looking at scraps of paper during a performance usually destroys the mood that the sketch has created. If that is your approach, make sure the actors know you have a deadline by which lines should be learnt – and stick to it! If that means that your actors have to be continually prompted during a particular rehearsal, so much the better – it shows what they still have to do. You may, of course, have a newly formed group or members who lack confidence in their acting skills, and you may decide that insisting that they learn vast quantities of lines will not encourage them to take drama any further. If so, choose a sketch with minimal line learning, or be clear about who you think should learn lines and who doesn't need to, to avoid confusion later.

Delegate responsibilities to others

If you are the person who is leading the group, don't take on everything yourself. There is usually a huge variety of jobs (making costumes, photocopying scripts, finding props, liaising with the person in charge of the church PA system) that need doing, and it is ultimately much less stressful if you can delegate some of these. You may be in the fortunate position of knowing someone who can make costumes or create elaborate sets. Invite them to your meetings and involve them in the creative process.

Acting in church

If actors were asked to name the worst place to perform drama, church buildings would probably be top of their list! You know the kind of thing: draughty old buildings, with regimented pews that can't be moved, pillars blocking the view, and altars or music groups taking up all the space at the front. Bear this in mind when choosing sketches to perform. You may be elated at having staged something hilarious, spiritually moving and challenging, only to discover that half the congregation couldn't hear a word or see anything that happened below waist level.

Depending on the sight lines within your church, it might be worth experimenting to find the best position for performances. If not everyone can see what's happening at the front, what about performing in the middle of one aisle, or in the balcony at the back? Why not perform a monologue in the pulpit, or get your characters to stand up on pews within the congregation itself? Ultimately, you may decide that you would rather not perform in church at all. You may want to stage a series of sketches or a full-length show in a hall or theatre where you can control the sound system and lighting, and put up some kind of set and leave it there – rather than hastily having to assemble tables, chairs, telephones and lampstands during a convenient hymn.

Spiritual growth

You may be surprised to learn that drama can help people grow spiritually. Newcomers can feel accepted into the church by feeling that they belong to a small group, nervous people can grow in confidence, and directors can understand more about the Bible and Christian teaching as they work closely with the vicar or pastor. Many of the points made earlier about leadership and discipline are just as relevant in the wider Christian community as in a drama group. Someone who nurtures those people skills in a smaller group will be in a better position to use them in a wider social situation. Someone who practises leadership, even if it is just directing one simple sketch, will learn something about the value of encouragement and constructive criticism which they can also use in other contexts.

Prayer is another key element in the process. It does concentrate the mind to think that you will be called on to remember eight pages of complex lines from a moving monologue within the next five minutes. Drama is a risky business, and seeing God answer the prayers of the nervous or the self-conscious can be a great boost to someone's spiritual life.

It's no exaggeration to say that people can blossom before your very eyes as gifts and talents that they never thought they had come to the fore. That's not to say that drama is for everybody – there are some who will never feel comfortable being up front – but for those who want to take part, it can raise self-esteem, promote confidence and help them understand more about God.

Rehearsals and Workshops

Others with more experience have written at greater length and with more insight about the rehearsal process and the kind of theatrical exercises that help you get the most out of your actors, but the following hints and tips should be helpful if you are just starting the process.

Warm-ups

Warming up is important, not just in the physical sense of moving around and using your muscles, but in a psychological way as well. If you have been lounging around on sofas chatting and drinking coffee while you discuss which sketch to perform, you may feel less like throwing yourself into a demanding physical sketch. If you're already on your feet after playing silly games and taking part in some improvisations, you're more likely to be in the mood.

Groups vary as to what kind of warm-ups they prefer. With children and even teenagers, playing some kind of *game* that involves running around frantically is often helpful. Other groups, and those without so much energy, may prefer to do some *gentle physical exercises* to loosen up reluctant muscles. That might involve shaking your hands, rotating arms, stretching legs and even bending double. The idea is to improve the blood circulation and get your limbs working rather than to do a full aerobic workout. Some professional actors swear by *vocal exercises* in which they repeat complicated tongue twisters at the top of their voice, sing scales or manipulate the muscles around the face to make sure that they can project their voice. It may also be helpful with beginners to do an exercise that encourages them to speak loudly and clearly, as that can be the biggest problem with those who aren't used to performing. Split them into pairs, and give one person (A) in each pair a sentence. Put all the As at one end of the room and all the Bs at the other end. Ask all the As to speak simultaneously and to keep repeating their sentences until their partners understand them.

Emotions

If the essence of drama is the characters, then the essence of character is emotion. It's important, therefore, to be able to convey a sequence of different emotions – even within a short sketch – that will convince the audience. One method is to ask people to portray certain *named emotions* in turn. The idea is to get them to use their whole bodies rather than just their faces to portray 'happiness', 'anger', 'boredom', 'shock', 'disappointment' and so on. Another is to give them a *scenario* (e.g. 'an old person walking to the bus stop in a rough area late at night', 'a starving man crawling through the desert who suddenly sees water . . . only to discover it's a mirage', 'a girl whose dad has been away for a year who sees him coming up the drive') and ask them to move from one side of the room to the other in a way that also expresses the emotions they might feel. This should lead on to a greater understanding of how movement can also express how characters are feeling.

Mime

Many people feel uncomfortable performing any kind of simple movement because they feel that mime skills are beyond them. In fact, it only takes a little practice to become convincing enough for the kind of sketches performed in church. One way to encourage people to develop this skill is to divide them into groups and ask them to put together some kind of tableau or *frozen picture*. You might give each group suggestions such as 'milking a reluctant cow', 'at the dentist', 'proposing to your girlfriend', 'telling off a disobedient child' or 'celebrating the winning goal'. The important thing is that they should form themselves into a position and then hold it there. Others should be able to distinguish the emotions from their body postures and guess what is going on. You might then move on to groups miming well-known *fairy stories or nursery rhymes*, and again ask others to guess which one each group is performing. Encourage people to be somewhat 'larger than life' to help convey their character or emotion – and remind them of that principle when rehearsing sketches later.

Characters

These kinds of exercises provide some of the building blocks for creating characters. Once people have grasped those essentials, it should be easier to do. One method you can use is called the *train carriage exercise*. Allow people to relax (perhaps by lying on the floor) and give them a whole series of different types of people, attributes and situations from which to choose. The types of people might include 'schoolgirl', 'member of the royal family', 'foreign tourist', 'tramp' and 'celebrity'. Their attributes might include 'worried about going bald', 'sensitive about their wooden leg', 'very forgetful', 'extremely intelligent' and 'has an irritating habit of breaking into song'. The situations in which they find themselves might vary from 'just won the lottery', 'a close relative has just died' and 'on the way to a job interview' to 'completely lost' or 'someone has just asked you to marry them'. Once they have chosen one item from each list, they imagine how that person might be feeling, how they might walk around the room (which they can try), how they might speak, and so on. When they are ready, introduce them one at a time into a 'train carriage' (two sets of chairs facing each other) and see how they react with each other. The leader should be able to guess who has chosen what. The exercise should help people as they think about the characters they are due to play in sketches or plays.

Creating sketches

If you're trying to create your own sketches, some of the above is probably necessary before you reach this stage. Creating characters and watching them interact is only a couple of steps away from devising your own sketches.

One of those steps involves deciding on the *form* of the sketch. How will you present it? As a monologue? A mime? A dialogue? A useful exercise to help you here also involves nursery rhymes or fairy tales. Split into groups and give each group a well-known children's rhyme or fairy story. Then allow them to choose a TV format (quiz show, soap opera, documentary, news item) and present the story in that format. A breaking news story might be that hundreds of police have been mobilized to help find Little Bo Peep's sheep, or a quiz show entitled *Whose Slipper?* might be used to find out whether Prince Charming marries Cinderella or the Ugly Sisters. Once you've done that with one well-known story, you may be surprised how easily the same process works for Bible stories. So you can end up with a quiz show entitled *My God's Bigger than Your God* in which the prophets of Baal are pitted against Elijah on Mount Carmel and are both asked to invite their god to burn up the sacrifice (see 1 Kings 18:16–40).

Another form might involve mime or narration plus sound effects. Ask different groups to convey what happened in a nursery rhyme or Bible story using just sound effects made by the group itself, and you might stumble across an inventive way of telling the story. Ask different groups to tell a Bible story using only three frozen pictures, and then 'join the dots' – adding in more mime and narration only when absolutely necessary. You should be beginning to create something simple yet effective. Top Cat Theatre Company, for instance, used this last method to create 'Hats Off!' (see page 289). It could have been left as a mime, but the use of one word in a variety of ways helped to emphasize the point.

'Naturalism' (or real life) is the most difficult form to master, but it is possible to approach it with drama exercises. Find a nursery rhyme or Bible story and give each person in the group the chance to think about one of the people involved – their motivations, how they talk, how they interact with others, and how they move around the room. Put them in a train carriage, as before. Or use a 'hot-seating' method, where each actor is put on a chair in the centre of the room and asked questions about how their character feels. In the same way as the group may have created characters before, they may now start to come close to creating something that approximates to a real person. In passing, it should be said that this method is not a bad way of Bible study, opening new doors in the imagination. It may be that you decide that you want to tell the story from the point of view of someone who only appears fleetingly in the Bible story or not at all – Jairus's wife, the elder brother of the prodigal son, Noah's three sons, or even the whale that swallowed Jonah. The more unusual the character you pick, the more likely the audience are to discover something new about the passage.

The other thing you need to think about is the message or *theme* of the sketch. You may already be working within parameters set by the vicar or pastor if you have been asked to illustrate a particular point within the service. It may be, however, that he or she has simply asked you to dramatize a parable or a Bible story, rather than explicitly stating what message it should convey. Often the process described above of selecting characters and thinking about their reactions and feelings can throw up an unexpected teaching point or message. Like Jairus's wife, we may wonder why bad things have to happen in order for Jesus to show his power; or like the whale that swallowed Jonah, we may wonder how we fit into God's ultimate plan. This is where the liaison with the preacher or service leader is vital. It may be that the point you have discovered is the same as the teaching point they envisaged – but it may be nothing like it! You may have created something useful, but it might have to wait until another day.

Rehearsals

Perhaps you're not in the business of creating your own sketches. Perhaps you just want to use the ones in this book. That's fine! You may want to use some of the preceding exercises within your rehearsals anyway, to warm people up or keep them thinking creatively. Sometimes, however, you just need to get on with the script you already have. Drama groups will naturally vary in how they rehearse, but a good tip is to have your *first read-through* without moving (preferably standing, to keep people on their toes). If the actors haven't seen the script before, their initial reaction may be the same as that of a potential audience, so it's good to note any possible confusion or potential for laughs at this point.

Then you will need to do something called *blocking*, which involves working out who enters from where, where they move to on the stage, when they sit down and stand up, and where they go when they exit. Ideally this should be done in the part of the church where you will perform, and using as many of the props and costumes as you can get at that stage.

When people are generally happy about the blocking, you can then start running through the script properly, using both *words and movement*. This is where good directors come into their own, remembering the tips in the previous chapter about respecting actors' suggestions, but having an overall idea in their own mind about how the sketch might work. If you don't have enough people for a non-acting director, one person should still step out of the sketch at regular intervals and look at it from where the audience will sit. This is also where people skills come in handy. Some actors will need to be encouraged to speak up and make their movements larger and therefore easier to see. Others may need calming down.

Keep going until the director feels happy . . . and then have *one more run-through* to give everyone the satisfaction of having done it as it should be done at least once. If it's getting late, or the sketch is a complicated one, it may be necessary to ask people to go away and learn their lines, find some appropriate costume, or obtain some vital prop and come back for *more rehearsals* at a later date. Whatever you do, make sure that you have a *final run-through* at least one more time (and preferably in the performance space, in costume and with all the props), just before the service or event starts.

There's no great mystery about rehearsing: you just have to keep doing it until you get it right. However, if someone is having real difficulty in getting an accent right, or moving in the right way, or knowing their lines, think about a way round the problem. It may be that the troublesome part of the sketch is not vital and can be dropped or altered. It may be easier to ask someone else to take on that part, though such things should be handled sensitively. It may be that there is a way round the problem that involves entering from somewhere different or moving a line. These are the kinds of reasons why spouses, offspring and friends of the actors should not be allowed to come to rehearsals. Like a soufflé, drama can be an anticlimax or end up deflated if people look at it before it is ready.

Writing Sketches and Full-Length Plays

Sketches

You may be fortunate to have someone in your drama group with a gift for writing their own sketches, rather than devising them with a group of other actors. Or someone might develop that gift as they work with a group of actors over a long period of time: they end up visualizing the sort of thing that their group might do with certain material. If you have such a person, nurture them and help them to develop their talent.

If you think you might have that skill yourself, give yourself the chance to develop it. Go on writing courses, visit the theatre frequently, join a secular amateur dramatics group and perform in some classic plays, read some texts and analyse why they work . . . and above all, keep writing! It is very easy to have an idea one minute and forget it the next, so write things down to work on later. The other vital thing is time. Many of us lead such busy lives that we don't give ourselves the time to read a decent book, let alone try writing drama. Allocate a certain time every day to writing, and use it.

If you are working with a drama group, let them try out your material. Allow them to make suggestions that might improve your script. Watch them perform it and make notes about what seems to work and what doesn't. If you don't have that luxury, find people whose opinion you respect (if all else fails, find them in a secular writing course – they may be more honest than your Christian friends!) and ask them for constructive criticism.

Bear in mind that you probably only have time to make one clear, unambiguous point. Trying to do anything more can often cloud the issue and make your sketch less effective. Bear in mind also that the short sketch for use in church is not an easy option. It's a hard form to master. Like the short story, it has to be believable, punchy, direct and meaningful – and convey a message that will be of some use in worship.

Full-length plays

Writing plays is, of course, very different. Where a sketch can be simplistic, direct and include a certain amount of caricature, plays usually involve showing real-life people doing things that members of the audience might reasonably do in the same situation.

I believe the most important thing to consider when writing plays can be boiled down to one thing: *plot*. You may have a fantastic story to tell involving interesting characters, but if the audience can't work out where the story is going, they can easily become bored and restless. Map out your initial plot, with some kind of beginning (how are we going to be introduced to these characters?), a middle (what happens to those characters to make the essential conflict within the play: does someone die, get a new job or become pregnant?), and an ending (how does the situation begin to resolve itself?). Don't worry at this stage about subplots or extra characters. Just clarify in your own mind where you want the story to go and keep that piece of paper next to you as you write.

Realistic dialogue may be important in many sketches, but in plays it is vital. You want the world you are creating to be peopled not with cardboard cutouts but with flesh-and-blood characters with all sorts of different motivations, interests, reactions and emotions. Watch out for the way people talk to each other, look at each other, and use body language and gestures to convey meaning. Watch out for phrases and behaviour that help us to understand someone's character better. Is she always talking about how her father was better at DIY than her husband, and does that suggest she is trapped in a loveless marriage? Does he hurry past jewellery shops because he is scared of commitment? Those are the kind of things you need to work into your script to allow the audience to understand your characters better. Look at the opening sequence used in a film, then stop the video there. What do you understand about those characters from the brief glimpses you have had of their lives? How could the start of your play be like that?

The biggest danger for Christians, I believe, is presenting a play in which everything works out fine in the end. For most people, real life and working out your faith in the context of everything that the world throws at you is a difficult thing. We rarely see things completely resolved. Even when God seems to answer prayer or appears to heal someone, it may throw up a whole new set of problems. You risk leaving your audience feeling that somehow their faith isn't good enough if you present a pat, Christian answer to everything. So *leave some issues unresolved*. I wrote a play that was performed by Top Cat Theatre Company in 2001, entitled *Unforgivable Sin*. It dealt with the problem of whether to accept a convicted sex offender into a church congregation. There was a variety of reactions, from outraged hysteria to the belief that God could 'heal' that person, as indeed there might be in a similar situation in real life. The play ended with the sex offender being willing to change and accepting God's forgiveness for what he had done, but it left open the real possibility that he may strike again. If it hadn't done so, it could easily have been dismissed as a naïve, superficial examination of something that simply wasn't so simple in real life. To read more about it, look at www.topcattheatre.com.

Through the Church Year

ADVENT AND CHRISTMAS

1. Salty Towers: Bethlehem Branch

Aim: *This sketch is just an excuse to present the nativity story in a comic way, and serves as a good introduction to any Christmas theme. The characters may remind you and your audience of a certain Torquay hotel made famous in a 1970s sitcom. It needs to be performed at a hectic pace throughout.*

Cast: MR SALTY, *exasperated hotel owner;* MRS SALTY, *his battleaxe wife;* CARLOS, *their hapless Spanish waiter (all in 1970s-style costumes);* FELIX, *a Roman centurion;* MARY and JOSEPH, SHEPHERDS and WISE MEN *(all dressed in traditional Nativity costumes).*

Props: *Because there are so many entrances and exits, you will need to create some kind of 'set'. The most important feature is a front door that opens at the back of the stage and is large enough for several people to hide behind. You also need a counter on the left-hand side of the stage with a couple of phones and a sign saying 'Reception', and make sure there are several ways to exit (left behind the counter to the bar, right to the stairs, the kitchen and the shed). You also need: tape of the 'Hallelujah Chorus'; clipboard; census forms; doorbell; bowl of water; toy sheep; wise men's gifts.*

(MRS SALTY *is leaning against the counter engrossed on the phone*)

MRS SALTY: . . . Oh, I know . . . I know . . . it's terrible, isn't it? (MR SALTY *runs in with clipboard. She sees him and beckons him towards her. Into phone*) Hold on!

MR SALTY: (*through gritted teeth*) Yes, light of my life?

MRS SALTY: (*puts her hand over the receiver*) You have remembered to give out all those census forms to the guests, haven't you?

MR SALTY: No dear, I've just been up there assassinating them in cold blood. What do you think I've been doing?

MRS SALTY: And you have checked that we've not got too many staying tonight? We can't contravene fire regulations, tonight of all nights.

MR SALTY: Yes dear – we've got exactly 40.

MRS SALTY: Good, well that nice Roman centurion who's collecting the census forms will be here any minute. (*into phone*) Sorry about that. Where was I?

MR SALTY: Yes dear, and I must say how grateful I've been for your help. That's what I like about running this hotel as a family business. It means I do all the work and you run up a phone bill the size of the national debt. (*doorbell rings*)

MRS SALTY: (*into phone*) . . . Oh, I know. (*to* MR SALTY) That'll be him!

MR SALTY: Oh, well, I'll get it, shall I? No, no, don't feel you have to move an inch. I'll just paint the side of the hotel while I'm out there, shall I? Or shall I bring you another hundredweight of custard creams? (*he opens the door. It is* MARY *and* JOSEPH) Yes?

JOSEPH: Er . . . we'd like a bed for the night, please.

MR SALTY: Sorry. Full up. (*he shuts the door. The doorbell rings again.* MR SALTY *opens the door again*) Yes?

JOSEPH: Look, I wouldn't trouble you otherwise, but all the other hotels are full and Mary is just about to have a baby. Is there anywhere we can go?

MR SALTY: How about Beirut?

MRS SALTY: (*puts phone down and comes over*) Don't be so rude! (*to* MARY *and* JOSEPH) I am sorry about my husband. Do come in. Welcome to the Bethlehem branch of Salty Towers. I'm sure we can find somewhere for you.

MR SALTY: (*takes her aside*) But we're full up, dear!

MRS SALTY: We can't leave her on the streets in that condition!

MR SALTY: Oh, I *am* sorry. My mistake. (*to* MARY *and* JOSEPH) Please, do have my bed. I'll just go and sleep outside in a cardboard box. No, I insist! (*he walks out, then straight back in*) It's the census man! (*he starts running around frantically*) You shouldn't be here!

JOSEPH: We'll go anywhere – we don't mind!

MRS SALTY: Look, go out to the shed in the back. It's a bit dirty, but you can wait there until the census man has gone. (*doorbell rings.* JOSEPH *and* MARY *exit with* MRS SALTY)

MR SALTY: (*opens the door to reveal* FELIX) Good evening, sir . . .

FELIX: (*pushes past him*) The name's Felix. Is this Salty Towers?

MR SALTY: (*grovellingly*) Yes it is, and may I take the opportunity to say what a pleasure it is to see such a distinguished . . .

FELIX: You should have 40 people here. Is that right? (*moves off in the direction of the shed.* MR SALTY *gets in his way*)

MR SALTY:	Yes it is.
FELIX:	Well, I'll just check. (*moves off in the direction of the shed.* MR SALTY *gets in his way again*)
MR SALTY:	Er, no. You can't. Er . . . there are cows in that shed.
FELIX:	Of course there are! Aren't there usually? (*pushes past him*)
MR SALTY:	(*puts an arm across* FELIX'S *chest*) Er, yes. They are man-eating cows. Especially partial to Roman citizens. One ate a tax collector last week. Perhaps if you started upstairs I could . . . er . . . calm them down for you. (*shouts*) Carlos!
MRS SALTY:	(*emerges from the shed*) Ah, Mr Felix. How nice to see you. Shall we collect the census forms from the guests? (*she takes him off.* MR SALTY *smiles at them until they have gone, then goes into the shed.* CARLOS *runs on*)
CARLOS:	Qué? (*he looks around and starts to go off.* MR SALTY *reappears*)
MR SALTY:	Hot water! Hot water and towels! Carlos!
CARLOS:	Qué? Hot water?
MR SALTY:	Yes, go and get some! It's for the baby.
CARLOS:	Baby? You have baby, Mr Salty? (*he starts to laugh and point at him*)
MR SALTY:	Not my baby! Just go! (MRS SALTY *and* FELIX *appear with a pile of forms as* CARLOS *runs off the other way*)
FELIX:	Yes, it was good of you to have the forms ready, Mrs Salty. I make that 40 guests and four staff.
MR SALTY:	(*still looking the way* CARLOS *has gone and shouting after him*) Hot water and towels!
FELIX:	Hot water?
MR SALTY:	(*spins around and sees him*) Ah, yes. Ermintrude's just made a nasty mess in the

shed and . . . well, you can't be too careful as far as hygiene is concerned. Can I get you a drink from the bar? (*propels him towards the bar*)

FELIX: I think I'd better check that shed . . .

MR SALTY: It's not a pretty sight . . . (CARLOS *reappears with a bowl of hot water that he promptly tips over* MR SALTY) Aaaarrgghh! Carlos! (*he clips* CARLOS *around the ear*)

CARLOS: Ow! But Mr Salty! Is for baby!

FELIX: (*looking at his forms*) Baby? I don't have any details of a baby!

MR SALTY: Baby . . . er, yes, baby cow.

CARLOS: We no have baby cow. (MR SALTY *kicks his leg away.* CARLOS *falls over*)

MR SALTY: I am sorry – he's from Barcelona. We're just training him. (MARY *makes sound of a baby crying offstage.* MR SALTY *starts crying himself*) Er . . . yes, it's obviously been a very emotional day, what with a new cow in the family . . . (*aside*) apart from my wife, that is . . . (*to* FELIX) Would you like to have a drink with the old dragon while I get changed . . . ? (*a chorus of angels sing the 'Hallelujah Chorus' – either on tape, or using a real choir.* MR SALTY, MRS SALTY, CARLOS *and* FELIX *all look around them, mystified as to where the noise is coming from. When it finishes,* MR SALTY *smiles weakly at* FELIX) I do apologize. It's karaoke night next door again. (MRS SALTY *guides a bemused* FELIX *into the bar*)

CARLOS: I get you hot water, yes?

MR SALTY: No, that won't be necessary, thank you, Carlos. She could have had triplets by the time you come back. (*he goes off to get changed. The doorbell rings*)

CARLOS: Meester Salty? Meesis Salty? (*shrugs his shoulders and answers it himself. Three* SHEPHERDS *are at the door*) Welcome to our hotel. I from Barcelona.

SHEPHERD: Evening squire. Is this where the Saviour is?

CARLOS: Qué? Saviour? Is no Saviour?

SHEPHERD: (*pushes past him*) Well a whole host of angels told us it was, so it must be. They said there'd be a baby wrapped in swaddling clothes lying in a manger.

CARLOS: Baby! Ah, is baby, yes. In shed.

SHEPHERD: Yeah, this is it, lads. Come on. (SHEPHERDS *follow him in, complete with toy sheep. One of the sheep is left in the lobby.*)

MR SALTY: (*as he re-enters, wearing a different jacket*) Carlos! Who are these people? Why did you let them in?

CARLOS: Is come to see baby.

MR SALTY: (*clips him round the ear*) You stupid Spaniard! We've got the census officer in there checking up on how many people we've got staying here and you invite half the rural population of Judea in to have a look at a baby! (MR SALTY *picks up the remaining sheep just as* MRS SALTY *and* FELIX *re-enter.* CARLOS *goes into the shed.* MR SALTY *speaks to the sheep*) Come on now, get out!

MRS SALTY: Well, thank you very much for your time . . .

FELIX: Is that a baby sheep too?

MR SALTY: (*attempts to hide sheep behind his back, then realizes that won't work and holds it up*) Oh, this? Er . . . no, we've just got this in. It's tonight's dinner. (SHEPHERD *makes sound of sheep baa-ing plaintively off stage*) Well, we like to make sure our meat is fresh. (MR SALTY *throws the sheep towards the kitchen, then goes to the door and holds it open. As he opens it, we see three* WISE MEN *at the door. Nobody sees them for a while, as* MRS SALTY *helps* FELIX *put his Roman cloak on. One coughs to gain* MR SALTY'S *attention, and when* MR SALTY *realizes, he yelps and slams the door*) Er ... perhaps you'd like to come and look in our kitchen and see exactly how fresh our meat is, Mr Felix? (*he propels* FELIX *into the kitchen.* MRS SALTY *goes after him, still holding his cloak.* MR SALTY *opens the door again*) Yes?

WISE MAN: We've come to see the King of the Jews. We bear gifts. (*he holds one out*)

MR SALTY: (*taking them*) Well, that's very nice of you. I'll make sure he gets them. (*shuts door. Doorbell rings again, and* MR SALTY *opens the door again*) Did you want something else?

WISE MAN: We have travelled many miles. We would like to see your King.

MR SALTY: Just as I thought. Tourists! (*loudly, as if to an idiot*) Have you tried the palace?

WISE MAN: No, this King has just been born. We have seen the star! (*points upward*)

MR SALTY: (*takes a look above the hotel. He then thinks the* WISE MAN *is referring to the fact that his is a one-star hotel*) Ah, yes, I know. It *is* a shame they only gave us the one star, but I think you'll find the food's very good. (*sniffs*) What's that smell?

WISE MAN: It's frankincense.

MR SALTY: (*turning up his nose*) Well, perhaps Mr Incense could stand further away. Now, look, there is a baby in the shed here, but you can't ... (CARLOS *rushes in*)

CARLOS: Ah, Meester Salty! Is beautiful baby! You come see?

WISE MAN: He's in there, is he? Come on then, let's pay our respects. (*they troop through the hall to the shed*)

MR SALTY: What is it with this baby? Are you all relations or something? Look, I've got a hotel to run here! I can't have family reunions in my shed . . .

CARLOS: Meester Salty! He name baby after my brother!

MR SALTY: He did what?

CARLOS: He name baby after my brother who works in England! I ask his name and they say 'Immanuel!' (*pronounced as the Spanish name.* MRS SALTY *and* FELIX *re-enter as* MR SALTY *hits* CARLOS *again.* MRS SALTY *is still carrying* FELIX'S *cloak*)

FELIX: Well, thank you for the offer, Mrs Salty, but I haven't really got time for lunch . . .

MR SALTY: (*takes him and propels him towards the door*) Yes, well, perhaps you should go. It's been great meeting you. Give our regards to Caesar when you see him . . . (*throwing him out of the door and closing it*) I hope he enjoys spending the taxes I've worked my fingers to the bone for . . .

FELIX: (*re-entering*) But my cloak . . . ! (*he goes towards* MRS SALTY *as* MARY, JOSEPH, SHEPHERDS *and* WISE MEN *all emerge from the shed*) Wha . . . ? Who are these people, Mr Salty?

MARY: Mr Salty! Thank you so much for letting us use your shed. We thought we'd let you see the baby too. He's the Saviour of the World. The King of the Jews.

MR SALTY: (*looks open-mouthed from* MARY *to* FELIX *and back again, puts his hands over his face and sinks down to the floor. He shouts from behind his hands*) Oh my God!

JOSEPH: Yeah, he's that too! (*all freeze*)

2. The Birthday Party

Aim: *To remind us that Christmas is the time when we should be celebrating the fact that God gave us the ultimate present – and that there's only one way to repay him.*

Cast: JESUS, *who should be played as both sensitive and authoritative; and party guests – middle-aged* PETE *and* FRANK, *youngster* NICKY *and pensioner* ETHEL.

Props: *Several colourfully wrapped presents; birthday cake; party hats; party poppers; sack of 'presents'; one present wrapped in brown paper and string; glasses and bottles.*

(PETE, FRANK, NICKY *and* ETHEL *come on quietly, wearing party hats and holding party poppers, but trying not to be seen*)

PETE: OK, shh everyone. He's due any minute now . . . (*they find places to hide*)

FRANK: (*pops his head up and sees* JESUS *approaching*) He's here! Quiet now! (*they all crouch down out of sight until* JESUS *walks on stage. They all then jump out at him, popping party poppers and cheering*)

NICKY: Surprise, surprise!

JESUS: (*genially*) What's all this, then?

ETHEL: We're having a party for your birthday, dear!

JESUS: Oh – you shouldn't have!

FRANK: (*getting out cake with candles on*) Right everyone
          . . .

ALL: (*singing*)   Happy birthday to you!
                        Happy birthday to you!
                        Happy birthday dear Jesus,
                        Happy birthday to you!

          (*all pop more party poppers and cheer. They give*
          JESUS *a party hat, which he puts on*)

PETE: We couldn't fit all the candles on, but happy
          2,002nd [*insert correct year*] birthday!

ETHEL: I'll tell you what, young man! You don't look a day
          over 35! (JESUS *blows out the candles, to more cheer-
          ing*)

JESUS: So, what are we going to do to celebrate, then?

FRANK: Well, we've got presents to give, and we're going to
          have a big meal . . . the usual sort of thing.

ETHEL: Ooh, Frank! You'll just get sozzled and fall asleep
          in front of the Queen's Speech, like you do every
          year!

FRANK: Er . . . well, yeah! I've got some presents here, espe-
          cially for your birthday, Jesus! (*he gets out a
          present*)

JESUS: Oh, you're too kind, Frank!

FRANK: Yep, it's a big one, this . . . (*he goes past* JESUS *and
          gives it to* ETHEL) . . . and it's for you, Ethel.

ETHEL: Thanks so much, Frank!

FRANK: It's nothing, really. I just thought you could do
          with a new toaster. Your old one was something
          chronic, wasn't it . . . ? (*he carries on explaining
          about it as* ETHEL *unwraps it and* PETE *gets his
          present out*)

PETE: I've got one here, too! Here, Jesus, come and have
          a look at this one. It's one of these brand-new port-
          able CD players – I tell you, the reproduction on

this is amazing. It's like you've got one of those orchestras in your front room!

JESUS: (*slightly embarrassed*) Oh yes? Well, I don't know quite where I'd put it . . .

PETE: Oh, it's . . . er . . . it's not for you. It's for our Nicky! Here, love – there you go! (*gives it to her*)

NICKY: Oh, Dad – that's exactly what I wanted! Thanks! (*they all start to exchange other presents, and chat about them, laughing and drinking*)

JESUS: Right, well, thanks everyone for coming to my party, anyway. I've . . . er . . . brought some presents for you, as it happens. (*no one responds*) They're not for anyone in particular. You can all have all of them if you like. (*he starts to get them out of his bag and put them on a table. They are all labelled*) There's . . . erm . . . 'Complete and Everlasting Forgiveness' here. (*he looks around hopefully*) Anyone fancy that? It means everything you've done wrong will be forgotten about. It's worth having! No? How about 'Knowing that God Is with You All the Time'? That's anybody's. Or 'An Answer to Your Prayers'? No? A lot of people would love that one. What's this? 'Knowing that You're Going to Heaven when You Die'. Well, I'll just leave them here, in case you ever want them. (*he puts them back into the bag and starts to walk down the aisle or round the audience, looking back at the party in full swing. Everyone is still engrossed*) Well, thanks for thinking of me, anyway. Enjoy your party. I'll . . . er . . . see you next year. (JESUS *turns and walks slowly away. Party guests start to exit until only* ETHEL *is left. She looks at the bag of presents and calls Jesus back*)

ETHEL: Jesus! Jesus! (JESUS *returns*) I . . . er . . . I just wanted to say thank you for letting us have such a good

JESUS: party, and I'd like to have some of those presents you were talking about.

JESUS: (*gives her the whole bag*) They're all yours, and they come with all my love.

ETHEL: Thank you so much! I know you've really been through a lot to be able to give these to everyone for free. And I . . . er . . . I have got something from me to you as well.

JESUS: Oh, Ethel, thank you!

ETHEL: (*gives him tiny present wrapped in brown paper and string*) There's not much of it, and it's not really anything special, but I know you can do something with it.

JESUS: What is it?

ETHEL: It's the rest of my life. (*they freeze*)

3. Christmas Presence

Aim: *It aims to show how Jesus was God's greatest gift to the world, but tries not to downplay the importance of the actual presents children receive at Christmas.*

Cast: NARRATOR; KATE, *a slightly spoilt small girl, dressed in pyjamas and dressing gown, perhaps with plaited hair and freckles (can be played by a child);* DOLL, *an adult or child dressed as a baby and wrapped in Christmas paper;* MUM *and* DAD; GRANNY *and* GRANDAD *(optional parts).*

Props: *Wrapping paper for two presents; piece of jewellery; doll wrapped in a blanket; Christmas labels; nappy, dummy, bib and baby's bottle containing milk for person playing* DOLL; *Christmas tree.*

(Three presents are already on stage, under the Christmas tree. If you are able to have them, MUM *and* DAD, *and* GRANNY *and* GRANDAD *stand next to their respective presents.)*

NARRATOR: It was Christmas Day and Kate was really excited! (KATE *runs on and gasps at the presents under the tree*) She had been looking forward to Christmas all through December, and now it was here! She ran down the stairs to open all her presents. (KATE *goes to the first present – the* DOLL *– and looks at the label*) The first present she found was really exciting. The label said: 'To Kate, with love from Mum and Dad.' It was wrapped in very bright paper, and looked very expensive. (KATE *starts tearing the paper off*) It took a long time to get all the paper off, but when she opened it, inside there was the latest doll that had been advertised on the TV. It was very clever. It said her name . . .

DOLL: Hello, Kate! I'm your dolly!

NARRATOR: It drank milk from a bottle . . . (KATE *picks up bottle of milk and puts it in* DOLL's *mouth.* DOLL *takes a couple of gulps*) And the dolly wet itself . . . (DOLL *crosses legs and looks in need of the toilet*) It was very expensive, and Kate's mum and dad had spent a lot of money on it. (KATE *hugs* MUM *and* DAD, *if they are there*) Then Kate saw her second present. (KATE *goes to the second present, which is wrapped not quite so brightly, and looks at the label*) The second present she found was exciting as well. The label said: 'To Kate, with love from Granny and Grandad.' (KATE *starts tearing the paper off*) It was a smaller present, but when she opened it, inside was something very precious. (KATE *lifts a piece of jewellery out of the box*) It was a piece of jewellery that her granny had worn when she got married, and Kate's granny wanted her to wear it now. It was very precious, and it meant a lot to Kate and her granny. (KATE *puts on the piece of jewellery and hugs* GRANNY *and* GRANDAD) Then Kate saw her third present. (KATE *picks up a small, baby-shaped parcel, wrapped in a blanket, and looks at the label*) It didn't look quite as exciting as the others. The label said: 'To Kate, and the rest of the world, with love from God.' It wasn't wrapped in Christmas paper, but it was wrapped in a blanket. She opened it and saw what was inside. (KATE *opens it up*) Inside there was a little baby. (KATE *discovers a doll inside the blanket and holds it out as if she doesn't like the look of it*)

KATE: (*goes to* DOLL *and stamps her feet as she speaks*) But I wanted an expensive present, like the one from Mum and Dad!

NARRATOR: This is an expensive present, Kate. It cost God everything he had to give this gift to the world!

KATE: (*holding out her piece of jewellery*) And I wanted a precious present, like the one from Granny and Grandad!

NARRATOR: This is a precious present, Kate. This baby was God's only Son.

KATE: (*holding the baby by one of its legs as if she is about to drop it*) But it's just an ordinary baby! What's so special about that?

4. Bad Hair Day

 Aim: *To show how the real meaning of Christmas is often hidden behind the gaudy nature of other things we think of as 'Christmassy'.*

Cast: *Gloom-laden* SNOWMAN, *jolly* FATHER CHRISTMAS, *military-style* CHOCOLATE SOLDIER *with silver paper on legs, the camp* FAIRY *(played either by a woman or by a man in drag) and the bouncy* EASTER BUNNY *are all dressed in proper costumes – the more extravagant the better. The* VIRGIN MARY *is in an old, blue robe.*

Props: *The sketch was devised for use in churches with large Christmas trees at the front. When the decorations pretend to hang themselves on the branches, they can stand on chairs (make sure these are safe). It also works best with actors playing* JOSEPH, SHEPHERDS, *etc. standing to one side in a life-size Nativity scene, but a small crib can also be used. Also needed: book with 'The Christmas Story' on the cover; baby Jesus doll; Easter eggs.*

(*Enter* SNOWMAN *and* FATHER CHRISTMAS, *dusting themselves down*)

SNOWMAN: I can't believe how dusty that loft gets. Every year I wake up covered in layers of the stuff.

CHRISTMAS: Ho, ho, ho! You should be pleased,

snowman! I love this time of year – hanging on that tree and watching all the children tear open their presents.

SNOWMAN: Hmph. It doesn't make up for the eleven months we spend stuffed into a plastic bag and forgotten about, does it?

CHRISTMAS: Ooh, look. We've got some new recruits! It's another chocolate soldier! (CHOCOLATE SOLDIER *marches in and salutes*)

SOLDIER: (*militarily*) Cadbury's milk chocolate soldier, reporting for tour of duty on Christmas tree, sir!

CHRISTMAS: Ho, ho! There's no need to salute me, soldier! I'm not in charge here. It's the fairy that sits at the top!

SNOWMAN: (*inspecting* CHOCOLATE SOLDIER) They never last long, those chocolate decorations, do they? Usually eaten by Boxing Day.

CHRISTMAS: Ah yes, not like us – taken out and used every year! (*enter* VIRGIN MARY) Do you know, I've been on the tree every year since 1974!

SNOWMAN: (*glumly indicating* MARY) Oh, look. Here's some new decoration. She'll probably get a better branch than me this year . . .

VIRGIN MARY: I don't think I'm new. I've just come out of an old box.

SNOWMAN: Hmph. Well, you don't look very Christmassy. Where's your tinsel and your snow?

VIRGIN MARY: I don't know. I've just got this old dress. It's so long since I've been used, I'm not even quite sure what I'm supposed to be.

CHRISTMAS: (*shakes his head*) Oh dearie me. Well, I'm not sure you'll make it onto the tree, young lady.

We all have to be inspected by the fairy to make sure we look Christmassy enough before we're given a branch, you know.

SNOWMAN: Watch out! Here she comes . . . (*enter* FAIRY *flamboyantly*)

FAIRY: Ooh, what a day I've had! I've had no end of trouble with my frock! And I can't do a thing with my hair!

CHRISTMAS: Ho, ho, ho! But you look lovely and Christmassy!

FAIRY: (*flirtatiously*) Oh, Father Christmas, you big saucepot! But just look at the state of my wings! There's no glitter anywhere! (EASTER BUNNY *runs on throwing Easter eggs. The others all stare at him*)

BUNNY: Happy Easter! Happy Easter!

FAIRY: Easter Bunny! Will you get back into that loft! There's another three months before you come out of the box!

BUNNY: (*crushed*) Oh. Sorry . . . (*exits dejectedly with head down*)

FAIRY: Are we all ready, then? Once we're on the tree, they can switch on the lights and it will really feel like Christmas! (*looks at tree*) Oh, just look at those needles. Every time I move, I'll ladder my stockings! (FATHER CHRISTMAS *starts to laugh*) Do you think it's funny having six inches of cold pine stuck up your skirt for the twelve days of Christmas? Well, it's not, I can tell you! Now, come on – I want to see what you look like before we all go on the tree. (FATHER CHRISTMAS, CHOCOLATE SOLDIER, SNOWMAN *and* VIRGIN MARY *line up*) Father Christmas! Have you been polished this year?

CHRISTMAS:	No.
FAIRY:	Well, I can hardly see your jolly smile for dust. Chocolate soldier!
SOLDIER:	Yessir!
FAIRY:	Has someone been nibbling at your leg?
SOLDIER:	Yessir. One small boy couldn't keep his hands to himself before I was put on the tree, sir!
FAIRY:	Well stop making an exhibition of yourself and put your silver paper back on again! Do you want the whole world to see your soft centre? (SOLDIER *tries to put silver paper back properly on his leg*) And look at you, snowman! Your cotton wool is starting to unravel!
SNOWMAN:	I'm not as young as I was, you know!
FAIRY:	Well get yourself sorted out! (*comes to* MARY *and looks her up and down*) What's all this, then? You're not one of our normal decorations.
VIRGIN MARY:	No.
FAIRY:	You don't look remotely Christmassy! Where's your glitter? Or your red coat? At least you could have worn your best clothes to hang on the Christmas tree!
VIRGIN MARY:	(*downcast*) I'm sorry. I think I'm in the wrong place.
FAIRY:	And where's the wire to hang you from the branch? Right – I'm going to find out what's gone wrong. The rest of you – positions please! Quick, quick! (FATHER CHRISTMAS, CHOCOLATE SOLDIER *and* SNOWMAN *get into position within the branches of the tree, standing on ladders and chairs*) Come on, the tinsel and the lights are already up there. (*they start*

to suspend themselves from branches, holding out their arms and spinning slowly to the left and to the right. To MARY) And I'll find out where *you're* supposed to be! (*exits*)

SOLDIER: Er . . . I'm being spun around by this small boy, sir. Aarrrgghh! (*he starts spinning round much faster*) Leave me alone!

CHRISTMAS: Oh dear! You know what happens when they twist up your wire like that, don't you? (SOLDIER *comes to a stop, then spins round even faster in the other direction*)

SOLDIER: Aaarrghh! Just you wait! I'll give you indigestion on Christmas Day!

SNOWMAN: (*to* MARY) So – I didn't think you looked like a Christmas decoration. You don't have enough glamour to hang on the tree with us. You're probably something to do with the harvest festival or something!

VIRGIN MARY: Maybe. I don't feel very Christmassy. (*enter* FAIRY *with baby Jesus doll*)

FAIRY: (*very embarrassed*) Ah! Sweetie! I am sorry! There seems to have been a terrible mistake!

VIRGIN MARY: What's that?

FAIRY: I've just been reading the instruction manual. (*holds up book entitled 'The Christmas Story'*) It seems that you're actually more Christmassy than we are! (*hands her the book*) Have you read the story?

CHRISTMAS: *More* Christmassy? How can you get more Christmassy than Father Christmas?

VIRGIN MARY: (*reading the book*) Oh my goodness! They expect me to have a baby! In the middle of a haystack! Without even an epidural! And then I've got three kings coming to visit – with me in this tatty old thing!

FAIRY:	There you go. (*gives her baby Jesus doll*) Apparently, you belong over there. (*points to crib*)
VIRGIN MARY:	(*holds up the doll*) You mean this is . . .
FAIRY:	Yes. If it wasn't for you, none of us would be here!
VIRGIN MARY:	People are going to look at me and think about how a Saviour was born! What a privilege! (*she goes over to the crib*)
SNOWMAN:	What do you mean, none of us would be here? What's more important at Christmas than proper decorations?
FAIRY:	(*looking at crib*) What's more important, snowman, is what each of us decorations reminds people about. (*all freeze*)

5. A Very PC Christmas

 Aim: *To show that attempts to appear up to date or politically correct don't always work – and that the real hope for the future came from a newborn baby rather than a philosophy.*

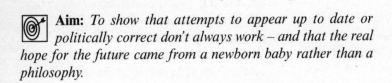 **Cast:** *The actors playing* MARY, JOSEPH *and the* SHEPHERD, *and the director* TOBY, *are all real luvvies. It works best if an actual child plays the part of the* BOY (*or* GIRL).

 Props: *Traditional Nativity costumes; scripts.*

(*Enter* MARY, JOSEPH *and* SHEPHERD *to form a typical Nativity frozen picture. They are holding scripts.*)

SHEPHERD: So my line is: 'It is as the angels said. A babe, wrapped in swaddling clothes, in a manger.' And then I worship him. It's hardly Shakespeare, is it?

MARY: Oh, Tarquin. Give it a chance. We haven't had our first run-through yet.

JOSEPH: I find that so annoying. They expect us to perform this piece with barely a rehearsal worth the name.

MARY: Well, the costumes are nothing special, are they, sweetie? I was promised sequins, and I look like I'm wearing someone's curtains.

SHEPHERD: And the script, darling! Some of these lines
            sound so antiquated. (*enter* TOBY, *the director*)

TOBY: Morning, team! Are we full of the joys of
            Christmas yet?

JOSEPH: Not really, Toby . . .

TOBY: Super! Well, shall we get started, then? (*he
            perches pretentiously on a chair*) Now, as you
            were told at your auditions, we're here to re-
            enact the birth of an obscure strand of religious
            belief. The title of our little tableau is 'Hope for
            a New Millennium'.

SHEPHERD: Well, Toby, if you don't mind, I was wondering
            if this really was the kind of thing you were
            after to illustrate that kind of thing . . .

TOBY: Ah! Well, this was the traditional script I was
            given, but – hey! – I'm open to any ideas from
            anyone on this. Why don't we have a little
            improvisation around the theme and see what
            we come up with?

MARY: OK, Toby. Well, first of all, I think it's going to
            be more relevant for some of the audience if
            we aren't dressed in these ridiculous robes. I
            mean – how are people supposed to relate to
            that?

TOBY: Great! OK, let's go for a more contemporary
            feel. (*they start to take Nativity outfits off*) Hey
            – you look more real already!

JOSEPH: I was just wondering about my motivation,
            Toby.

TOBY: OK, Randolph. You were playing the part of
            . . . (*looking at his script*)

JOSEPH: Joseph. The father. Or rather, he's not the
            father. And that's my big problem with this.

TOBY: Right. Well, I quite liked that. I think the fact
            that Mary is pregnant by someone who isn't her

husband is a real strength of the piece. There are plenty of people who can relate to that.

JOSEPH: Yes, but I wondered if we could tinker with the script a smidgeon and call him her birthing partner. And I think if he was gay, I'd understand his motivation a bit better. He would just be a supportive friend helping out at a time of crisis.

MARY: And I'm not sure about this location. I'd much rather be having this baby in a birthing pool.

TOBY: OK, love. Let's run with that. I like what I'm hearing. (*to* SHEPHERD) Perhaps, Tarquin, you could be their astral therapist, and come to visit them?

SHEPHERD: OK. Now, this bit where this angel is supposed to appear to me and tell me to go and look for the child. It's a bit sci-fi, isn't it? We don't just want to attract the anorak brigade. Can we make him a humanist messenger – and perhaps he could tell me something about what he's seen on my astrological chart?

TOBY: Humanist messenger. Yes, we don't want to restrict the appeal of this piece purely to religious fundamentalists, do we? Quite right, Tarquin.

MARY: Perhaps we could persuade one of those soap opera stars to play that part? Or a page three girl? We could do with a bit of celebrity.

SHEPHERD: I don't want anyone stealing my thunder, darling.

TOBY: No, no, that's good. Perhaps we could get some coverage in the papers. I was wondering about sponsorship. And maybe if we endorse some products during the show, it would help with our funding problems.

JOSEPH: This giving birth idea, Toby. Well, I don't really think people want to see an actual baby being born. It is all a bit (*searches for the right word*) gynaecological, isn't it? Hardly family viewing.

MARY: I'm not putting my legs in stirrups for the world to see. Is that what's in the script? (*she checks*)

TOBY: Well, I had wondered precisely how we might portray that, Portia.

JOSEPH: But you said this was about the birth of an idea. A philosophy. It's a symbol, isn't it, of a 'hope for the new millennium'?

TOBY: Yes . . .

JOSEPH: So, all that we need to show is that we are giving birth to that new idea. There's no mess involved with that, is there?

TOBY: And the idea being . . . ?

JOSEPH: Well, you know . . . it's all about tolerance towards other people, their feelings, their sexualities, helping everyone to get along together – that's what it's all about, isn't it?

SHEPHERD: Well, it doesn't say that in the original script, but I think that's what it really means.

TOBY: Great! Well, that was a very valuable session. Shall we just go through that? It's the year [*insert current year*], Mary is a homeless, single mother, with her gay birthing partner Joseph. You're in a birthing pool – though that's only symbolic – with a celebrity wearing sponsored swimming costumes. You think up this new philosophy for the millennium, and your astral therapist visits and affirms you in your chosen spiritual path. Let's just see that in action now. I'll have to be the page three model for now.

(*they strike up their various poses. Enter* BOY)

MARY: Gosh! Our first visitor already!

BOY: What are you doing?

JOSEPH: We're illustrating Christmas!

BOY: (*laughs*) No you're not!

TOBY: Oh my goodness! I am such a silly! Of course, this is going to mean *nothing* to the children who visit us. We've forgotten to include anything to do with the real meaning of Christmas!

MARY: What do you mean?

TOBY: We've left out Santa Claus! (*they freeze*)

6. Father of the Bride

 Aim: *In the Christmas story, Mary gets much attention as the mother of Jesus, but Joseph's role was just as important – even though he wasn't Jesus' 'real' dad. Imagine what might have happened if Joseph had decided not to stand by Mary, opening her to public humiliation and ridicule in a society where it was a scandal to be an unmarried mother. This sketch aims to tease out some of the tensions that might have derailed the birth of the Saviour.*

Cast: MARY, *who can be as young as 16;* ELIACHIM, *Mary's dad, who is a hot-tempered but principled Jewish man;* ANNA, *Mary's mum, who is a mildly stereotyped Jewish mother;* JOSEPH, *who is solid and sensible. All should be in some approximation of first-century Palestinian costume.*

Props: *Table; chair; duster.*

(ELIACHIM *enters at pace with* ANNA *and* MARY *following behind. They are in the middle of an argument*)

MARY:	Please, Father, don't be angry!
ELIACHIM:	How can you do this to your poor mother and father? We shall be the laughing stock of Nazareth!
ANNA:	(*with trembling lips*) We'll never be able to show our faces in the synagogue again!

MARY: But I'm trying to explain . . .

ELIACHIM: You're engaged to a good man, Mary. And now
              you're having someone else's baby? What's
              wrong? Is a carpenter not good enough for you,
              hmm? A good honest craftsman who will look
              after you and your children in your old age?

MARY: (*sinks into a chair*) Of course Joseph is good
              enough for me.

ELIACHIM: So why take up with another man, Mary? You'll
              bring shame on our family.

MARY: That's what I've been trying to tell you. There
              wasn't another man!

ANNA: (*looks her up and down, then turns away in aston-
              ishment*) We may not know much, Mary, but we
              know how you get pregnant. And there usually
              has to be a man involved somewhere!

MARY: I haven't had any relations with another man.
              (*looks up at* ANNA *and speaks quietly*) I believe
              this child is 'Messiah'.

ELIACHIM: (*stares incredulously*) Messiah?

MARY: Yes, Father. Don't you remember the Scriptures?
              The Messiah will be born of a virgin.

ELIACHIM: (*stares at her*) You think that your baby will be
              the Messiah?

MARY: (*stands, frustrated that he doesn't understand*)
              Yes I do! An angel of the Lord visited me and
              told me so.

ANNA: An angel visited you? Here?

MARY: Yes.

ANNA: (*panic stricken*) But . . . but look at the state of
              the place! I mean, I haven't dusted for weeks!
              (*picks up duster and starts cleaning furiously*) I
              can't believe you didn't introduce us!

MARY: Well, it was the middle of the night!

ELIACHIM: Mary, you've had twelve weeks to come up with

a decent explanation for this! Is that the best you can manage? (*pause*) What does Joseph think of your little story?

MARY: (*hangs her head*) He doesn't believe me. He wants to call the wedding off.

ANNA: (*as if that proved it*) And this is a surprise to you?

MARY: I needed to tell you because he is coming to talk to you about it.

ELIACHIM: Fine. I shall tell him that we'll send you into the mountains for a few months to have the baby. He will be free of his pledge to you. (*he turns as if to go*)

MARY: (*close to tears*) But, Father, I'm just trying to do the Lord's will! (*she grabs hold of him*) What about Aunt Elizabeth? She became pregnant even though she and Zechariah are in their sixties. Zechariah was struck dumb when he found out!

ANNA: Well, I was pretty speechless myself!

MARY: He said the angel Gabriel visited him too.

ELIACHIM: (*lifts his palms to the heavens in despair*) So now I'm supposed to be happy because I have two crazy people in my family? (*enter* JOSEPH)

JOSEPH: Mary? What's wrong? (*he goes to her*)

ELIACHIM: Ah, Joseph! You're the only sensible one among us! You've come to break off the engagement.

JOSEPH: Well . . . erm . . . no, I haven't.

MARY: (*astonished*) Really?

ELIACHIM: You want to go through with this?

JOSEPH: Yes, I do, Eliachim. I believe Mary needs me to be with her.

MARY: Oh, thank you, Joseph! (*she hugs him*)

ELIACHIM: Now, let's just see if I've got this straight, Joseph. You say that this baby isn't yours? But you still want to go through with this wedding?

JOSEPH: That's right!

ANNA: Ah, Joseph. Such a good boy! I remember when you were growing up. I said to your mother: 'He'll make Mary a fine husband . . .' (*she goes to hug him with both arms outstretched*)

ELIACHIM: Why have you changed your mind?

JOSEPH: Well, this angel appeared to me last night . . .

ANNA: (*stops herself just before she hugs him and walks away*) Oh heavens, another one!

JOSEPH: . . . and the angel said I should not be afraid to take Mary as my wife, because her baby is from the Holy Spirit.

ANNA: (*looking upwards*) Is this angel ever going to visit the poor mother of the bride? Or do I just get to hear about all of this second hand?

MARY: Oh, Joseph! I'm so glad! (*she hugs him*)

ELIACHIM: (*pacing around*) OK, OK. So you want to get married! Great! You want to have this baby and let everybody know that you think he is something special! Fine! Just promise me one thing. (*he stops pacing and faces* MARY *and* JOSEPH) When you have this baby, make sure you're here in Nazareth with your own father and mother to look after you, hmm?

MARY: I'm not going anywhere, Father. (*she puts her arm around* JOSEPH *and looks at* ANNA *and* ELIA-CHIM) I think people will be talking about the birth of this baby for years to come. Just imagine: it could really put Nazareth on the map! (*they freeze*)

7. Unto Us a Child Is Born

Aim: *First performed as part of a one-act play festival by Bench Theatre Company in Havant, this aims to get away from the traditional Christmas elements of pantomime and Nativity to present a contemporary story about the real family tensions that surround all of us at Christmas. If it has a message, it is that people sometimes matter more than principles. It is the ideal length for a group that has mastered the sketch format and would like to try something a little more challenging. In some ways, a church building is the ideal place to perform it, as some of the action is supposed to happen there. We used a real baby to play the part of Sarah's baby, which certainly added to the mood of the play.*

Cast: DONALD, *an evangelical vicar in his late forties (dressed in clerical shirt, dog collar and sensible jacket);* MARJORIE, *his long-suffering wife, who is around the same age (blouse, long skirt and cardigan);* SARAH, *their teenage daughter who is now eight months pregnant (relatively trendy maternity outfit – with lots of padding);* GARY, *the baby's father from the local council estate (ripped jeans, a scruffy jumper and an army jacket);* TONY, *Donald's curate, who is in his thirties (clerical shirt, dog collar, thin jumper, slightly trendier trousers than* DONALD*);* DARREN, ABI, *and* GAVIN, *children in this year's Nativity play (normal children's clothes, over which they put tea towels, curtains, sheets and*

other pieces of material to represent Nativity outfits); MRS
ARKWRIGHT, *well-meaning church busybody in her fifties
(smart hat and coat, tweed skirt and jacket); other children
can play other* SHEPHERDS *or* WISE MEN *in the final scene.*

Set: *The stage is divided into two distinct areas. On one side is*
DONALD's *study, which is denoted by a desk and a swivel chair.
There is a word processor and phone on the desk, and books
and papers are scattered liberally all over it. On one side there
is a bookshelf heaving with voluminous theological commen-
taries and newer paperbacks. Above it are several dozen
Christmas cards hung up on a piece of string from the front to
the back of the stage. There is also a more comfortable chair
towards the front of the stage. The other side is the front of the
actual church, which is denoted by an altar and a lectern.*

Props: *'Christmas' file; telephone; cups, saucers, tea
tray and plate of biscuits; tea towels, sheets and bits of
string as Nativity costumes; Nativity scripts; bus stop; baby
doll; tape of pub noise; pub stools; pub glasses; clerical robes;
tape of organ music; Bible; piece of corrugated iron; £5 and
£10 notes, tape of Christmas carols.*

Scene One – the study

(Lights up on the study. DONALD *strides in looking tight-lipped
and carrying a file marked 'Christmas'. He sits at the desk,
picks up the phone and starts to dial)*

DONALD: Hello? Fiona? Sorry to bother you – it's Donald
            Mortimer here. It's just about . . . *(listens for a
            moment)* Um, yes, well I think that prayer was
            really helpful . . . yes, I sensed we were getting to
            the root of the problem when you said you
            thought she had problems seeing God as her
            father . . . well it is quite a common thing among

those who have been treated badly by their own fathers . . . um, terrible, that's right . . . well, if you ever need anyone else to help with counselling, do feel free . . . no, my pleasure . . . Ah yes, well, it was the readings for the Christmas carol service I was phoning about, as a matter of fact. I was just wondering – do you think someone in the youth group would like to do an extra one? . . . No, well, someone has just had to drop out unexpectedly and . . . oh yes, Felicity – she'd be perfect, I think, yes . . . OK, I'll drop the details around to her later in the week . . . OK, bye then. (*he puts the phone down and starts making a note on a piece of paper in his file. Enter* MARJORIE *with two cups of tea*)

MARJORIE: Look, I'll do it if you want me to, Donald.

DONALD: No, no – it's all sorted out now.

MARJORIE: (*putting one cup down on the desk and standing holding the other one*) It's just that I might be at the hospital that night, that's all. It'd be worse if you had to find someone to fill in for me at the last minute.

DONALD: (*still not looking up*) Well, Felicity O'Connor's doing it now.

MARJORIE: Oh, that'll be nice. I always thought she had a good speaking voice. Her mother will be pleased.

DONALD: (*matter-of-factly*) Yes, she's the kind of daughter you really can be proud of.

MARJORIE: Oh, Donald! Don't be like that! Why can't we be proud of Sarah after all she's achieved? Those ten GCSEs . . .

DONALD: (*snorts*) The only thing she'll achieve is driving me to an early grave. (*he sips his tea*) Is there sugar in this? (MARJORIE *rolls her eyes* – DONALD *always asks the same question. He takes another uncertain sip)*

MARJORIE: Look, we've got to make a real effort for Christmas. I don't think my mother wants to hear you two bickering like you did last year.

DONALD: (*stands and starts walking around the room*) Bickering? I was telling her to watch out for . . . for that layabout from the estate. And look what happened. (*he stares glumly at the wall*)

MARJORIE: Let's not start that again, dear. Who knows – if you hadn't gone off at the deep end, they might have stayed around . . .

DONALD: It wasn't just my fault, dear!

MARJORIE: No dear. (*she stands and starts to massage his shoulders*) But now they're back – let's try and make a go of it. Please? For Christmas?

DONALD: (*muttering*) Yes, yes, I'm sure we can pretend everything's all right for a few days . . .

MARJORIE: (*decisively*) Good (*picks up her tea again and goes to leave*) Right – I'll leave you to it. Got much to do?

DONALD: Well, I still haven't done the sermon rotas for the new year, and Tony needs his before he goes away. It's difficult because I want to do this series on Romans.

MARJORIE: What? And you think he can't do it?

DONALD: No, I think he'd do it very well – but I don't think it would fit in with what I want to say. As far as he's concerned, the wages of sin are a light slap on the wrist when you meet your maker.

MARJORIE: (*pauses at the door*) He's not that bad!

DONALD: Isn't he? Don't you remember the sermon he did about the Ten Commandments? I think by the end he'd whittled it down to about seven polite suggestions . . . (MARJORIE *smiles and starts to*

	go and then stops as DONALD *turns back to his work*)
MARJORIE:	Er, Donald . . . (SARAH *comes in, very heavily pregnant, as* MARJORIE *holds the door open*)
DONALD:	Umm . . . ?
MARJORIE:	Someone to see you! (*she smiles brightly at* DONALD *and exits*)
SARAH:	(*covering her uncertainty behind a brave front*) Yeah, Dad, I was just wondering if I could . . . erm . . . borrow the car tonight?
DONALD:	You what?
SARAH:	Borrow the car. I'm supposed to be going uptown to see a few mates, you know . . .
DONALD:	What makes you think I'm going to lend you the car when you're in that condition?
SARAH:	Aw, go on, Dad, please . . .
DONALD:	Don't be ridiculous! Sarah, do you really think I'm going to let any daughter of mine ride off to some pub with a few of her girlfriends when she's eight and a half months pregnant? You must think I was born yesterday!
SARAH:	(*defiant*) So that's no, then . . .
DONALD:	First you embarrass me in front of the whole church. Then you disappear for weeks on end. Now you want to make it worse by parading yourself around the whole town.
SARAH:	Oh, right, I get it. This is just 'cos you don't want people to start gossiping, right?
DONALD:	Sarah! I am concerned about you as well! Shouldn't you be taking things easy?
SARAH:	It's only because everyone in your church thinks you shouldn't have sex until you've been married 20 years. You make me sick sometimes! I'm going out! (*she starts to stomp off*)
DONALD:	Sarah! Where are you going?

SARAH:	(*with her hand on the door*) Out of here would be a start! Anyway – isn't it time for *Coronation Street*?
DONALD:	(*looks at his watch*) Is it?
SARAH:	That's right. You go and enjoy your own fantasy world for half an hour. Don't let anything from the real world bother you, eh? (*she slams the door behind her and exits*)
DONALD:	You cheeky young . . . (*stops himself and sits, feeling frustrated. He checks his watch again*) Oh . . . Tony! (*he gathers together his bits of paper and dashes out of the door. Lights fade*)

Scene Two – the church

(*Lights up on the church, where* TONY *is rehearsing with* DARREN, ABI *and* GAVIN. *The boys are dressed in traditional children's Nativity costume – tea towels on their heads and sheets held in place with bits of string.* TONY *is sitting directing*)

TONY:	Now, I'm not sure about this part.
ABI:	What part?
TONY:	The angel saying: 'Unto you is born this day a Saviour who is Christ the Lord.'
ABI:	Eh?
TONY:	Well, it just seems a bit . . . twee. A bit infant school. What do you think, Abi?
ABI:	(*shrugs her shoulders*) Dunno.
TONY:	The whole bit with the angels, it just seems so . . . unnecessary. I mean, who's to say what those shepherds really saw? Assuming there were actually shepherds, of course . . .
GAVIN:	(*puts his hand up*) Erm . . . please, sir . . .
TONY:	Put your hand down, Gavin. You're not at school now.

GAVIN: Yeah, I was just going to say you've got to have the shepherds, right, because it's me and Rachel, and we haven't got any other parts.

TONY: No, Gavin, that wasn't . . .

GAVIN: Only, like, Abi here is like the Virgin Mary and before that she's the archangel (*he pronounces 'arch' as if it were an architectural feature*) Gabriel, and it's not really fair . . . (*enter* DONALD. GAVIN *self-consciously tails off*)

DONALD: Tony! Sorry I'm late! How's it going?

TONY: Well, er . . . we don't actually seem to have everyone quite here at the moment.

DONALD: Perhaps they've been scared off by your radical interpretation, Tony, who knows? I trust we're still keeping Jesus in the Nativity this year?

TONY: (*grimaces*) Oh, come on, Donald! There's not much even I could do to the Nativity story.

DONALD: Indeed, no.

TONY: But you did want to see it before we did it.

DONALD: (*fears* TONY *thinks the worst*) Yes, but not to check up on you, old son. Just to . . . well, have a look at it.

TONY: (*tentatively*) Well, as it happens, I have changed one or two bits.

DONALD: Ah.

TONY: You don't mind?

DONALD: Well . . .

TONY: I just wanted to make the thing more relevant. I mean, the parents who come and see this have heard it so many times before. We want to make it really live for them. Shepherds watching their flocks and hosts of angels don't make much sense to Fred the electrician down the road.

DONALD: So . . . ?

TONY: Jesus is champion of the underclass, right? He's born into a draughty old barn. Not in a sanitized manger with a halo, but a dirty old rusty feeding trough. There's real muck and smelly animals.

DONALD: You're not suggesting a cow in the chancel, surely? (*children snigger*)

TONY: It'd be interesting . . . (*sees* DONALD's *face*) Yes, well, perhaps not. But we want to show the Hylton Park estate people he's one of them. A craftsman – a carpenter . . .

DONALD: But he wasn't one of them. I mean, he isn't . . .

TONY: Look, we'll show you. Erm . . . can you read for us, Donald? (DONALD *takes the script reluctantly*) OK – if you could be the narrator. We'll take it from the top.

DARREN: The top?

TONY: The beginning. (DARREN *takes his position as Joseph, with* ABI *as Mary. They stand self-consciously in the middle of the stage.* DONALD *stands to one side, trying to scan the words quickly*)

DONALD: Right. Erm . . . let's see now. 'It was 2,000 years ago when Joseph and Mary had to go to Bethlehem for a census . . . (*incredulously*) It was a bit like signing on.' You can't say that!

TONY: People understand the dole.

DONALD: Yes, but it's nothing to do with . . .

TONY: (*waving away his protestations*) OK, OK – I'll cut that bit out.

DONALD: 'Everyone had to go to the place where they were born, so Joseph and his (*with disdain*) girlfriend Mary went to Bethlehem . . .' I guess we don't refer to her as a virgin, do we?

TONY: You know my theological problems with the virgin birth. (GAVIN *and* DARREN *have got out a bus stop*)

GAVIN: Are we still using this?

DONALD: (*incredulously*) What's that for?

TONY: Well, we're assuming they're doing the equivalent of getting on the number 53 bus.

DONALD: (*resignedly*) Right, fine. If you say so . . .

TONY: OK, Abi – off you go.

ABI: (*self-consciously*) 'Flippin' 'eck, Joseph – I'm knackered. Can't we stop somewhere?'

DARREN: 'What about this Travelodge, here, Mary?' (*he knocks at imaginary door as* DONALD *mouths the words 'Travelodge' in despair*)

GAVIN: (*as the innkeeper, wearing an apron*) 'Clear off, yer scroungers. You can't afford it in here.'

DARREN: 'We're not scroungers. It's just that the Roman government doesn't give income support to low-paid carpenters.' (ABI *drops the baby doll she had tucked up her dress.* DARREN *and* ABI *burst out laughing as they see it*)

TONY: OK, let's do that bit again.

DONALD: Listen, Tony, I'm going to have to leave you to it. I'm supposed to be doing a marriage preparation course at quarter past.

TONY: Fine.

DONALD: Listen, about the script. I appreciate what you're trying to do, but . . .

TONY: Don't worry. It'll be fine.

DONALD: You seem to have cut out the three kings.

TONY: Well, come on now, Donald – you don't seriously believe the Magi were anywhere near Jesus at his birth, do you? The research shows that if they did come it was two or three years later.

DONALD: But you've replaced them with three winos.

TONY: Yes, well, you're more likely to see tramps in this dump than kings, aren't you?

DONALD: (*slightly exasperated*) That's not the point. (*controls himself*) Look, don't you think you're losing something of the magic of Christmas here?

TONY: No, I don't. I think we've produced something that will make people sit up and take notice – rather than something that makes their eyes glass over because they've heard it so many times before.

DONALD: (*pauses, then drops his eyes and raises his hands in defeat*) OK, Tony. We'll do it like this. But don't be surprised if their mums and dads complain at their precious ones having to spout some pseudo-political mumbo-jumbo. (*realizes he has gone too far*) Sorry, Tony. I'm just under a lot of pressure at the moment. I'll see you tomorrow. (*exits*)

TONY: (*nods at* DONALD *as he leaves*) Fine. (*turns to the kids*) OK – shall we go from the bit where Mary gets turned down for a council house because she hasn't been on the waiting list long enough? (*lights fade*)

Scene Three – the pub

(*Later the same night. General pub noise in the background.* SARAH *brings two pub stools to the front of the stage and sits on one. As the lights come up, she is drinking on her own. Enter* GARY, *who stops and thinks about whether to speak to her*)

GARY: Sarah?

SARAH: (*turns and sees him. Her face falls*) What do you want?

GARY: Dunno, really. Just saw yer and thought I'd say hello. What yer doing here?

SARAH: Just waiting for Janice, actually.

GARY: Oh. Right. (*he hovers indecisively*)

SARAH: Go on, then. Sit down.

GARY: (*he does so*) Shouldn't you be taking it easy, like?

SARAH: Oh, get a grip, Gary! You sound just like my dad! Anyway, what's it to you? I didn't think you wanted anything to do with me.

GARY: Aw, come off it, Sarah. It wasn't just me. You were sick of that bedsit too.

SARAH: Yeah, but I didn't walk out and leave you six months pregnant. What did you expect me to do – get a job to pay the rent?

GARY: No, 'course not. (*pause*) So, er . . . you back with yer old man, like?

SARAH: Yeah.

GARY: Everything all right?

SARAH: What do you think?

GARY: I mean with the baby, like?

SARAH: (*icily*) Yes, everything's fine. You feel better now?

GARY: Eh?

SARAH: Now you've got that off your conscience. You don't need to feel so guilty now, eh? Now you know mummy and daddy are taking care of me you can go back to your smackhead mates.

GARY: (*mutters*) Haven't got any smackhead mates.

SARAH: They're pretty spaced out most of the time.

GARY: Listen, I gotta go, right?

SARAH: Don't let me stop you.

GARY: Gotta see a man about a . . .

SARAH: I don't want to know.

GARY: I'll see the baby, yeah?

SARAH: Depends.

GARY: Oh. Right. Yeah – see yer around then.

SARAH: Maybe.

GARY: (*makes as if to go, then turns back*) Oh, and, like,
            happy Christmas and that. Hope the baby's
            OK.
SARAH: (*sighs*) Just go, Gary. Save your breath.
(*lights fade.* SARAH *takes the two stools away*)

Scene Four – the church

(*Lights up on church as* DONALD *is just finishing off a service.
He is robed and wears the beatific smile he uses for church.*
MARJORIE *is sitting in the congregation with her back to the
audience.* MRS ARKWRIGHT *is on the other side at the front*)

DONALD: (*making a sign of the cross as the lights fade up*)
            . . . and the blessing of the Father, the Son and
            the Holy Spirit be with you all, now and always.
            Amen. (*organ music plays.* DONALD *starts
            shaking hands with imaginary people at the back
            of the stage.* MARJORIE *and* MRS ARKWRIGHT *both
            get up at the same time and turn towards the audi-
            ence. They smile weakly at each other*)
MRS ARK: Not long now, then, Mrs Mortimer.
MARJORIE: I'm sorry?
MRS ARK: Your Sarah. Not long now, I'll wager.
MARJORIE: Oh. No, that's right. Any day now, really.
MRS ARK: I just thought I'd better warn you. (*she looks
            around furtively*) Mothers' Union. (*pats her nose
            secretively, as if that is all she needs to say*)
MARJORIE: What about it?
MRS ARK: Well, I wouldn't rightly like to say, but there's
            been . . . well, you know . . . not that I would
            dream of ever saying this myself, you under-
            stand, but . . . well, rumblings.
MARJORIE: Rumblings?
MRS ARK: I mean, it's not for me to tell a vicar and his wife
            how to run their family . . . who's perfect, after

all? But . . . well, I'll say no more about it. (*she folds her arms and looks away*)

MARJORIE: Oh. Right.

MRS ARK: . . . Except to say that they've . . . well, I heard that the committee thought it inappropriate for your husband to come along on the 14th of next month, that's all.

MARJORIE: The 14th? (DONALD *has started to approach them*)

MRS ARK: Well, I'll wish you all the best, Mrs Mortimer. See you next Sunday. (*she starts to bustle away.* DONALD *takes her hand and shakes it*)

DONALD: Morning, Mrs Arkwright. How are you?

MRS ARK: Um, well, fair to middling, thank you. (*she avoids his eyes*)

DONALD: Good, good. I'll see you at the Monday Afternoon Fellowship next week, then?

MRS ARK: Maybe, vicar. Bye for now. (*exits*)

MARJORIE: (*sidles up to* DONALD *and says quietly*) What are you doing for the Mothers' Union on the 14th, dear?

DONALD: Erm . . . 'The Christian Family', I think. Why?

MARJORIE: Nothing, dear. (*lights fade*)

Scene Five – the study

(*Enter* DONALD *in a half-light. He switches on his desk lamp, takes out his Bible and starts to read. He doesn't get very far before he starts looking up at the wall*)

DONALD: (*praying quietly with his eyes open*) Oh Lord, what can I do? Sometimes I just feel so useless. You try and do the best you can, hold the parish together, help people with their faith . . . And then I get Tony doing his thing . . . And Sarah . . . Lord, you know I want to do the right thing

... it's right to provide some kind of moral guidance for people these days, but what do you do when it's your own little girl? ... It's tearing me apart ... Soften her heart, Lord – and mine ... (*he continues praying silently.* MARJORIE *pops her head around the door*)

MARJORIE: (*quietly*) Donald? Tony's here.

DONALD: (*sits up and gets out his file*) Yeah, OK. Send him in. (MARJORIE *goes.* TONY *enters. He and* DONALD *shake hands*)

TONY: Morning, Donald. How's things?

DONALD: Well, you know ...

TONY: You're looking tired.

DONALD: We waited up for Sarah last night. It was about two-ish when she got in.

TONY: Oh. (*shakes his head*) It's such a shame. She is a really nice girl. At least she's still speaking to you.

DONALD: Barely.

TONY: (*with real concern*) I don't quite know why you let it get to you so much, you know. It's not as if you've failed with her or anything.

DONALD: Haven't we?

TONY: What? Because she got pregnant?

DONALD: It might not matter to you, Tony ... (*enter* MAR-JORIE *with tray with two cups of coffee and biscuits*)

TONY: No, no. It's OK. I do understand. I ... I guess I just have different priorities.

DONALD: Hm, thanks dear. (MARJORIE *lays down the tray on the coffee table*) Biscuit, Tony?

TONY: No thanks. (*smiles as* MARJORIE *passes him coffee*) Thanks, Marjorie.

DONALD: (*sips his coffee*) Is there sugar in this?

MARJORIE: No dear, cyanide as usual ... (*she shakes her head at* TONY, *who appreciates the joke*)

SARAH: (*from offstage*) Mum! Mum!

MARJORIE: Is that Sarah?

SARAH: (*gets to the door and puts an anguished face around it*) Mum! It's starting! (*she is breathing deeply and sweating slightly. She comes further in, still holding onto the door. She is still in her nightdress*)

MARJORIE: Goodness! Quick, get into the car. (DONALD *has stood up, but seems uncertain what to do*)

SARAH: I can feel it coming, Mum!

MARJORIE: (*supports her as she tries to step gingerly out of the study again*) Are you coming, Donald?

DONALD: I . . . erm, I really don't know whether I . . . I've just got . . . er, a fair bit on today, that's all.

TONY: (*stands*) I could come back . . .

DONALD: No, no, Tony. Don't worry.

MARJORIE: (*as she takes* SARAH *out, looking meaningfully at* DONALD) Are you sure? (*he nods, but doesn't look at her*) Bye, then, dear.

TONY: I really could leave you to it, you know.

DONALD: No, no. You're OK. (*pause, then he sits and starts looking for the right piece of paper*) We need to sort out this sermon series.

TONY: (*sits*) I know you feel disappointed with her, but you wouldn't want to miss the birth completely, would you?

DONALD: (*gazing into the middle distance*) Some bastard offspring of a jobless layabout from the estate . . . No thanks. (*he comes to*) I'm sorry, Tony, I didn't . . .

TONY: (*slightly disconcerted*) Yeah. No, that's OK.

DONALD: I just . . . (*he is close to tears*) Oh, I don't know what to think any more. I might have to tell her I can't baptize my own grandchild . . .

TONY: It's hard, I know.

DONALD: (*trying to recover his composure*) Now – about these sermons.

TONY: Erm, yes. You mean the series on Practical Caring?

DONALD: Ah, no. I think you'll find we decided to postpone that one.

TONY: Did we?

DONALD: Yes. Evening services over the summer, we decided, didn't we?

TONY: What? When no one's going to be there?

DONALD: (*uneasy*) Well, not exactly no one . . .

TONY: Oh yes, we've got your Alpha courses for new Christians first, haven't we?

DONALD: And Romans.

TONY: And Romans? (*meaningfully*) So we're doing all the heavy theological bits explaining how people can come to faith now – and postponing the sermons about caring for people until later? (DONALD *averts his eyes*) So, which bit of Romans do you want me to do?

DONALD: Well, I thought you could do chapter 13.

TONY: What? 'All those in authority have been put there by God?' (*sarcastically*) Thanks very much! Well, I know what I'll be saying about that!

DONALD: Oh, let's not turn it into a socialist rally this time, eh, Tony?

TONY: It's got to be from the heart, Donald. There's absolutely no point pretending to believe something you don't.

DONALD: (*wistfully*) No, you're right. There's no point at all. (*lights fade*)

Scene Six – the church

(*Lights up on* TONY, GAVIN *and* DARREN *carrying a piece of corrugated iron. They take it onto the stage and lean it against the altar or something similar*)

TONY:	Thanks, lads. That's great.
GAVIN:	Where did you get this? The tip, was it?
TONY:	Yeah. Good, eh?
GAVIN:	(*unimpressed*) It's a bit mucky.
TONY:	(*adjusts it slightly*) Yeah, well, it's supposed to be.
DARREN:	So is this really like where Jesus was born?
TONY:	(*delighted* DARREN *is beginning to understand*) Yeah. It was pretty much like this.
DARREN:	(*pause*) I told my dad about the new script you wrote.
TONY:	Oh yeah? What did he say?
DARREN:	(*embarrassed to have brought the subject up*) Well, you know . . . I told him what I had to say . . .
TONY:	(*puzzled*) Yes? And?
DARREN:	Well, he didn't like it. Said it was a bit odd.
TONY:	Oh.
DARREN:	All that stuff about council houses and stuff – he said they never 'ad that when Jesus was born.
TONY:	Well, yes, strictly speaking . . .
DARREN:	'E said 'e didn't wanna come and see it.
TONY:	(*taken aback*) Oh. But – all I wanted to do was show how Jesus is like . . . well, like part of the Hylton Park estate. He was a working-class lad, like you.
DARREN:	Jesus isn't nuffink like me. Even I know that.
TONY:	But he's on your side!
DARREN:	Yeah? Well if he is, why can't he do something

	about people getting jobs and having no money? (*he stalks off*)
TONY:	Well, he does sometimes . . . Darren! Darren? What's wrong with him?
GAVIN:	Dunno. (*pause*) My mum doesn't wanna come either.
TONY:	Why?
GAVIN:	She said sumfink about not wanting to be . . . (*struggles to remember*) pasteurized . . . I think.
TONY:	Pasteurized . . . ? Oh, you mean patronized.
GAVIN:	That's it.
TONY:	Great! Just great! And after all I've tried to do . . .
GAVIN:	She said she just preferred it with the shepherds and the wise men.
TONY:	(*head in hands*) OK. Fine. Great.
GAVIN:	(*pause*) So do you still want this, then? (*pointing to the corrugated iron*)
TONY:	No, Gavin. I don't think so. (*lights fade as they start to carry it off*)

Scene Seven – the study and the church

(*The church is in darkness as the lights go up on the study.* DONALD *is writing. He gets up and is about to stride out of the door when* MARJORIE *enters*)

MARJORIE:	Donald. She's waiting in the car outside.
DONALD:	(*pause*) So?
MARJORIE:	So you still haven't seen her since the baby was born.
DONALD:	I can't, Marjorie.
MARJORIE:	Why not? It's your own grandson.
DONALD:	Marjorie, I've been preaching about people not having sex outside marriage for 20-odd years.

How can I condone it in my family if I say it's wrong for others?

MARJORIE: If you don't see her now, you may never see her again.

DONALD: (*looks away for a moment, then, as if coming to his senses*) Look, I'm late for the carol service . . .

MARJORIE: (*putting her foot down*) Hang the carol service, Donald! This is important!

DONALD: But I need to . . .

MARJORIE: Haven't you delegated the whole service to Tony and the others?

DONALD: (*opens his mouth as if to say something else, then closes it*) Yes.

MARJORIE: Well, then . . . ?

(DONALD *sits and they continue mouthing silently to each other*)

(*Lights up on the church.* TONY, *who is in his dog collar and clerical shirt, but is not wearing robes, is coming to the end of his introduction*)

TONY: . . . And so it is with great pleasure that I introduce some of the children from the Hylton Park youth club with their version of 'The Nativity'. (GAVIN, DARREN *and* ABI *mount the stage.* ABI *as the Virgin Mary looks heavily pregnant, and is wearing traditional blue and white.* DARREN *is Joseph,* GAVIN *the innkeeper, and* TONY *narrates silently as they start to mime the story* . . .)

(*Lights switch back to the study*)

DONALD: . . . And where's Gary? Has that bumbling oaf thought to come and be with her? I mean, it is his fault . . .

MARJORIE: (*gently*) I don't think even he could make Sarah pregnant by himself, Donald . . .

DONALD: But he's not offered to help her out, has he?

MARJORIE: He's only got his income support, dear. Don't
              you think that means she needs us even more?
              (*they continue talking silently*)

(*Lights switch back to the church.* DARREN *and* ABI *are
approaching* GAVIN)

TONY: . . . Joseph went up from the town of Galilee to
              Bethlehem, the town of David. He went to reg-
              ister with Mary, who was pledged to be married
              to him and who was expecting a child.

DARREN: 'Excuse me, but we are very tired and we need
              somewhere to stay. Do you have a room?'

GAVIN: 'All I have, sir, is an old stable.'

DARREN: 'That's fine. We'll take that, please.'

(*Lights switch back to the study.* MARJORIE *has got up and gone
to the door. During this exchange,* DARREN *and* ABI *move to the
'stable' and* ABI *starts to cradle a doll to represent Jesus*)

MARJORIE: I'm going to get her now, Donald.

DONALD: Marjorie, I've . . .

MARJORIE: Please don't try and stop me. (*exits*)

(*Lights switch back to the church.* ABI *is cradling the doll*)

TONY: The time came for the baby to be born, and she
              gave birth to her firstborn, a son. She wrapped
              him in swaddling clothes and laid him in a
              manger. (ABI *does so*)

(*Lights switch back to the study.* DONALD *is pacing nervously
around*)

DONALD: Lord, please – I don't know what to think or say
              . . . Whatever happens with Sarah, I still need
              your help . . . .Lord, please give our family the
              strength to pull itself back together . . . (*the door
              opens.* SARAH *enters nervously with her baby, with*

MARJORIE *urging her on.* DONALD *has his back turned. As* TONY *starts to speak,* DONALD *turns and sees the baby*)

TONY: 'The people walking in darkness have seen a great light;

On those living in the land of the shadow of death, a light has dawned.

You have enlarged the nation and increased their joy;

They rejoice before you as people rejoice at the harvest . . . (DONALD *takes the baby from* SARAH. *As he does so, a smile creases across his face and his eyes start to well up with tears*)

. . . For unto us a child is born.

Unto us a Son is given,

And the government will be on his shoulders.

And he will be called Wonderful Counsellor, Mighty God,

Everlasting Father, Prince of Peace.'

SARAH: Dad . . . I'm sorry . . .

DONALD: (*reaches out with his other arm to embrace her at the same time as the baby*) I know . . . I know. So am I. This is just . . . well, it's wonderful.

(*Lights switch back to the church. Enter* GAVIN *and a couple of others as shepherds*)

TONY: The shepherds said to one another: 'Let us go to Bethlehem and see this thing that has happened, which the Lord has told us about.' So they hurried off and found Mary and Joseph and the baby, who was lying in the manger.

(*Lights come up in the study, but the church also remains lit. Enter* GARY, *cautiously, into the study.* DONALD *is still rocking the baby, but his mood changes when he sees* GARY)

DONALD: What do you want?

GARY: Er, yeah. Sorry, like. I just saw the door open and thought . . . (*sees the baby*) Sarah, is that . . . ?

SARAH: Yes. What are you doing here?

GARY: Look – I'm not going to stop or anything. I've just brought this . . . (*he rifles in his pockets and pulls out some grimy notes as* WISE MEN *come into the Nativity scene in the church*)

TONY: They saw the child with his mother, Mary, and they bowed down and worshipped him. Then they opened their treasures and presented him with gifts of gold, frankincense and myrrh. (*Wise men kneel in front of* ABI *and* DARREN)

GARY: (*handing the money to* SARAH) I wanna be, like, well, more of a father, you know. (*he makes as if to go*)

SARAH: Gary . . . (*she smiles at him weakly*) Thanks. I don't really need this, but . . . well, I'm glad you've given it to me – to us.

GARY: Yeah, well, I'd better be off . . .

MARJORIE: Are you sure you won't stop for a cup of tea?

DONALD: Marjorie!

MARJORIE: (*thinks she's spoken out of turn*) I'm sorry, I wasn't . . .

DONALD: Gary – would you like a brandy? It is Christmas, after all!

GARY: (*breaks out into a grin*) Erm . . . yeah. Yeah, all right! (*all freeze. Christmas carols can play as they exit*)

8. Half-Baked Resolutions

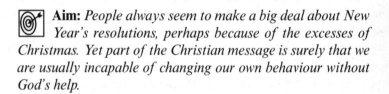

Aim: *People always seem to make a big deal about New Year's resolutions, perhaps because of the excesses of Christmas. Yet part of the Christian message is surely that we are usually incapable of changing our own behaviour without God's help.*

Cast: COOK, *dressed in traditional cook's hat and apron*; MUM; DAD; BOY; GIRL

Props: *Pieces of turkey; bottles of wine; armchairs; Christmas presents; piece of cake.*

(*Enter* COOK, *who takes up a position near the front of the stage from which he/she can see what is happening to the family*)

COOK: Hello, and welcome to 'Cooking on a Shoestring'. Today's recipe is something for the New Year. We're going to be looking at how you can cobble together a few half-baked resolutions. Here's the ingredients you'll need. (*enter* MUM *and* DAD, *wearing Christmas party hats and carrying bottles of wine and some left-over turkey*) Take a couple of plump specimens, (MUM *and* DAD *look at each other's girths*) and give them a really good stuffing over Christmas. (*they both cram turkey into their mouths*) That's right.

Make sure you fill every crevice with the richest food you can find. Add wine . . . (*they both drink from the bottles*) and more wine . . . (*they continue drinking*) and any other alcohol you can find lying about the house . . . (*they finish their bottles.* DAD *hiccups slightly. They are both now unsteady on their feet*) and leave to marinade for several hours in front of a warm TV. (MUM *and* DAD *flop into chairs and fall asleep*) Now spice up your dish with some excited children. (BOY *and* GIRL *run on, holding presents*) Sprinkle on some expensive presents, (*they open their presents*) and carefully break them into pieces over the next few days. (BOY *accidentally breaks his present, and looks at the two pieces he now has*) Now, heat up the whole family carefully, (BOY *tries to grab* GIRL's *present. They end up fighting*) and keep stirring constantly. (MUM *and* DAD *wake up and try to pull them apart*) Bring it all nicely to boiling point. (MUM *and* DAD *start arguing with each other about who bought which present.* BOY *and* GIRL *are still fighting*) Now add some well-seasoned guilt, (MUM *and* DAD *stop arguing*) melt a couple of consciences, (BOY *and* GIRL *stop fighting and shake hands*) and shovel on a thick layer of sentiment. (MUM, DAD, BOY *and* GIRL *join hands to sing 'Auld Lang Syne'*) You now have the traditional mixture for a fairly unappetizing set of resolutions. (BOY, DAD, MUM *and* GIRL *loose hands and all speak very unenthusiastically*)

BOY: I won't fight as much this year.
DAD: I won't eat as much this year.
MUM: I won't drink as much this year.
GIRL: I won't argue as much this year.
COOK: Leave to simmer at room temperature for . . . oh, about a couple of hours. (MUM *takes a quick swig of*

wine, which she tries to drink surreptitiously. DAD *sees her and produces a huge slice of cake, which he starts to eat deliberately in front of her.* BOY *starts pushing* GIRL *around again, and they soon descend into another fight*) And repeat every year until you realize how difficult they are to keep down. Thank you, and goodnight from us. (*Exit* COOK. *Family exit, still arguing among themselves*)

9. Love Is . . .

Aim: *To show that the biblical notion of love and the popular conception of romantic love do not always go hand in hand. The aim of setting the sketch immediately after a couple get married is not to be cynical about marriage, but to illustrate that sometimes we can be at our most selfish when we think we are at our most 'romantic'.*

Cast: NARRATOR; *sickly romantic couple* MR *and* MRS LOVELY, *who quickly turn into a bickering married couple. As many* WEDDING GUESTS *as you like can be used at the start of the sketch. Alternatively, we can imagine they are there.*

Props: *Two chairs, confetti; steering wheel; map; 'Just Married' sign.*

(*Two chairs are laid out on stage with a 'Just Married' sign hanging from one of them.* WEDDING GUESTS *appear, throwing confetti on* MR *and* MRS LOVELY *and hugging them as they appear onstage. They can ad-lib the usual comments about 'Enjoy your honeymoon!', 'We're so happy for you!' and 'It's been a lovely wedding!'* MR *and* MRS LOVELY *mime getting into the car and waving goodbye to their* WEDDING GUESTS *as they drive away*)

MRS LOVELY: (*cuddles up to* MR LOVELY'S *left arm as he drives*

	away) Ooh, wasn't that nice? It was such a lovely reception!
MR LOVELY:	(*pats her hand affectionately with his right hand*) Yeah. Everyone went to so much trouble!
MRS LOVELY:	And now we're married. You're a lovely husband! (*she plants a kiss on his cheek*) I love you so much!
MR LOVELY:	(*glances at her and smiles before looking back at the road*) I love you too, sweetheart!
MRS LOVELY:	(*in a sickly, romantic way as she snuggles up to him even more*) Love you more, sugarplum!
MR LOVELY:	(*in an even more sickly romantic way as he extracts his left arm from her embrace and puts it round her shoulders*) Love you even more, you little snuggle-pops! (MRS LOVELY *smiles contentedly and closes her eyes*)
MRS LOVELY:	So – where are we going for this honeymoon, then?
MR LOVELY:	Well, you'll just have to wait and see, won't you?
MRS LOVELY:	(*playfully*) Oh, tell me! I've been dying to know!
MR LOVELY:	(*firmly*) No! I've kept it secret for six months. I'm not going to say now!
MRS LOVELY:	(*getting annoyed*) I can't wait any longer! Go on!
MR LOVELY:	(*more firmly*) No! It's a secret!
MRS LOVELY:	(*moves away from him and folds her arms*) I want to know now!
NARRATOR:	Love is patient . . .
MR LOVELY:	(*angrily*) Well, I'm not telling you! OK? Now shut up, I've got to concentrate on the road. (*pause.* MRS LOVELY *starts to cry*)
MRS LOVELY:	Don't you care about my feelings?

MR LOVELY:	(*glances at her*) Oh, don't start crying! You're so touchy these days!
NARRATOR:	. . . love is kind . . .
MRS LOVELY:	(*sulkily*) Hmph. Well, Sheena's husband took her to the Seychelles!
MR LOVELY:	We've been through this before. I don't like flying!
MRS LOVELY:	(*studying her nails*) Sheena's husband doesn't like flying either . . . but he still took her abroad . . . (*no response from* MR LOVELY) And he lets her drive the car once in a while!
NARRATOR:	. . . it does not envy . . .
MR LOVELY:	Yes, but Sheena's husband can't afford the honeymoon I'm taking you on! He's only on about £30,000 a year, isn't he? That's about the size of my Christmas bonus!
NARRATOR:	. . . it does not boast . . .
MRS LOVELY:	Don't start on that again!
MR LOVELY:	Well, you brought him up. I mean, it's not as if I'm not generous. Remember how much I gave to charity last year! More than you, anyway!
NARRATOR:	. . . it is not proud . . .
MRS LOVELY:	(*tearful*) You always try to make me look small. As if I'm worthless or no good at anything.
MR LOVELY:	Well, come on, love. (*he glances at her, looking her up and down*) It wasn't your brains I married you for, was it?
NARRATOR:	. . . it is not rude . . .
MRS LOVELY:	(*dissolving into sobs*) That's it! You can sleep on the floor tonight!
MR LOVELY:	(*in a more conciliatory tone, as he realizes he has gone too far*) Oh, I'm sorry, love. That was

a bit uncalled for. (*he tries to touch her on the shoulder, but she recoils from him*) I didn't mean that. You're not stupid or worthless. You do have brains. Just because you've not been to university, that doesn't mean you aren't clever . . . (MRS LOVELY *looks at him, feeling unsure*) Come here. (*he holds out his left arm to her, continuing to look between her and the road.* MRS LOVELY *tentatively cuddles up to him again*) I'm really sorry, sweetheart. I shouldn't be so insensitive.

MRS LOVELY: (*reluctantly*) OK. I forgive you.

MR LOVELY: Great! Does that mean we can still have sex tonight?! (MRS LOVELY *hits him hard*)

NARRATOR: . . . it is not self-seeking . . .

MRS LOVELY: You pig! You only ever think of one thing!

MR LOVELY: (*innocently*) What? What did I do?

MRS LOVELY: (*hitting him again*) Sometimes I really hate you! Why did I ever marry you?

NARRATOR: . . . it is not easily angered . . .

MR LOVELY: (*trying to defend himself as blows rain down on him*) What's wrong with you? What's all this about?

MRS LOVELY: You're so insensitive! That's the seventeenth time today that you've hurt my feelings!

NARRATOR: . . . it keeps no record of wrongs.

MR LOVELY: The seventeenth? Are you keeping count?

MRS LOVELY: Right, husband-of-mine! I'm going to make you pay for this! I'll find a way of getting you back for every time you've hurt me!

MR LOVELY: (*nervously*) Erm . . . what do you mean?

MRS LOVELY: (*enjoying the thought*) Oh, I don't know . . . ripping up all your suits? Recording over the football matches you videoed? Flirting with your mates?

NARRATOR: Love does not delight in evil, but rejoices with
                the truth . . .

MR LOVELY: (*makes as if to stop the car*) Right. That's it!
                Get out!

MRS LOVELY: What?

MR LOVELY: No honeymoon for you. I'm going by myself!

MRS LOVELY: But you can't make me get out here. We're in
                the middle of the city. And it's dark! What if I
                get mugged? Who'll defend me?

MR LOVELY: Well, it won't be me . . .

NARRATOR: . . . it always protects . . .

MR LOVELY: . . . because I'll be halfway to Cleethorpes! (*he
                suddenly realizes he's told her the honeymoon
                destination, and clamps his hand over his
                mouth*)

MRS LOVELY: What? Is that where we're going?

MR LOVELY: Erm . . . well, yes. But it's a really nice hotel
                near Cleethorpes!

MRS LOVELY: Yeah, right!

MR LOVELY: It is, honestly! Trust me!

MRS LOVELY: Why should I?

NARRATOR: . . . always trusts . . .

MR LOVELY: It'll be fine! Really!

MRS LOVELY: No chance! I'm not going there with you. I'd
                rather take my chances finding a taxi!

NARRATOR: . . . always hopes . . .

MR LOVELY: (*with mock nonchalance*) Fine! See if I care.
                You try to get home from here!

MRS LOVELY: OK! I will! (*she mimes getting out of the car
                and storms off*)

NARRATOR: . . . and always perseveres. (*pause.* MR LOVELY
                *deliberately looks the other way from the direc-
                tion in which she has gone. Gradually, he starts
                to soften and looks around. She is nowhere to be
                seen. He waits a little longer, then realizes that*

she's not coming back. He mimes adjusting the mirror and undoing the handbrake. MRS LOVELY *suddenly runs back, flings open the door and throws her arms round his neck*)

MRS LOVELY: I'm sorry! I still love you really!

MR LOVELY: I know, snuggle-kins. I love you as well!

MRS LOVELY: I'm sorry we had a fight.

MR LOVELY: So am I!

MRS LOVELY: It doesn't mean that we don't care for each other, does it?

MR LOVELY: Of course not! I don't think *anyone* could love you more than I do! (*they freeze*)

10. And God Created Woman

Aim: *A simple sketch about parents for Mothering Sunday. The* NARRATOR *should start off the sketch very seriously, as if reading the start of the Bible – perhaps from a lectern.*

Cast: NARRATOR; *stressed-out* MAN; *hassled-looking* WOMAN; *scruffy-looking* BOY, *who has greasy hair and wears dirty clothes; pretty-looking* GIRL, *who wears a summer dress and has her hair in plaits.*

Props: *Bottles of milk; screwdriver; tape of dance music.*

NARRATOR: In the beginning, God created the heavens and the earth. Then God said: 'Let us make man in our own image.' So he did. (*enter* MAN, *who stands, legs astride and arms by his sides, looking pleased with himself*) And God said: 'Well, that's OK, but I could do better . . . ' (MAN *looks crestfallen*) And so God created woman. (*enter* WOMAN, *who pushes* MAN *out of the way and takes up the same pose herself*) And so God created them, male and female. And they became married couples. There were down-to-earth couples

... (MAN *grabs woman by the hand and yanks her offstage*)

MAN: (*in broad northern accent*) 'Ere, get your coat, love. You've pulled.

NARRATOR: ... middle-class couples ... (MAN *and* WOMAN *reappear, and mime holding some wine glasses*)

WOMAN: (*in middle-class accent*) ... so she came over for dinner with the most delightful bottle of Saint Emillion 97 and told us about back-packing in Outer Mongolia ... which was nice.

NARRATOR: ... Christian couples ... (MAN *and* WOMAN *assume the same poses as above*)

WOMAN: (*in exactly the same accent*) ... so she came over for dinner with the most delightful bottle of non-alcoholic grape juice and told us about being a missionary in Outer Mongolia ... which was nice.

NARRATOR: ... and complicated couples ... (MAN *and* WOMAN *become a soon-to-be bride and groom pouring over a list of people*)

MAN: So who's going to be on the top table?

WOMAN: OK. Bride's father next to me, bride's step-mother next to you. Bride's father's second wife opposite you.

MAN: Your mum's third husband?

WOMAN: (*winces*) Doesn't want to come if second husband is there.

MAN: My mum's new boyfriend?

WOMAN: Between the bridesmaids.

MAN: And Dad's new boyfriend?

WOMAN: (*pause as she thinks*) Erm ... next to the vicar?

NARRATOR: And God saw that couples were good. And

God said: 'Let us make children in our own image, (*enter* BOY *and* GIRL, *who lie on the floor like babies*) and let them disturb the sleep of their parents every single night for weeks. (BOY *and* GIRL *cry uncontrollably.* MAN *and* WOMAN *rush over to try and help*) And let them do nothing but eat and sleep and dirty their nappies for months. (MAN *and* WOMAN *try to feed* BOY *and* GIRL *with bottles of milk*) But let them have some wind and let Mum and Dad mistake it for a smile and say . . .'

MAN/WOMAN: (*scrunch up their faces at* BOY/GIRL, *look at each other and say together*) Aw! But they *are* worth it!

NARRATOR: And so there were children . . . Pretty children. (GIRL *stands up and poses, fluttering her eyelashes*)

MAN: (*cuddles her*) Aw! Aren't you Daddy's little girl?

NARRATOR: . . . ugly children . . . (BOY *stands up pulling a face*)

WOMAN: (*pushes him away*) Ugh! Aren't you someone else's little boy?

NARRATOR: . . . happy children . . . (BOY *and* GIRL *join hands and skip along together.* MAN *and* WOMAN *look on blissfully*)

NARRATOR: . . . and quarrelsome children.

BOY: (*starts hitting* GIRL) That was your fault!

GIRL: No, it wasn't! It was yours! (BOY *and* GIRL *start fighting on the floor.* MAN *and* WOMAN *drag them away from each other*)

NARRATOR: And God saw that children were good. And by creating children, God had also created parents. There were dads. Strict dads . . .

MAN: (*shouts at* BOY *and* GIRL) You two can stay in your bedroom until you learn how to behave yourselves!

BOY: But, Dad! I'm 34 years old. I need to go to work.

NARRATOR: . . . trendy dads . . . (*cue up-to-date music on tape.* MAN *starts dancing ineptly as* BOY *and* GIRL *point and laugh*)

MAN: Hey, what's this groovy sound? Is it some of that hippity-hop music you're always playing?

GIRL: Dad! You're *so* sad!

NARRATOR: . . . and dads who know how to have fun.

BOY: (*as young boy*) Horsey! Horsey! (MAN *gets onto all fours,* BOY *climbs on and* MAN *goes galloping around the room. He collapses in a heap, exhausted*) Again! Again!

NARRATOR: And God saw that dads were good. God also created mums. Sexy mums . . . (BOY *and* GIRL *exit.* WOMAN *pulls* MAN *towards her and runs her fingers through his hair*)

WOMAN: So, how do you fancy an early night, then?

MAN: Mmm, well, that sounds great . . . (BOY *and* GIRL *come running in, both talking at the same time*)

BOY: Dad! Can you help me with my model aeroplane . . .

GIRL: Mum! Can I have my pocket money, please . . . (MAN *and* WOMAN *disentangle themselves quickly*)

NARRATOR: . . . career-minded mums . . .

WOMAN: (*rushes in and talks to others quickly*) OK, love. You make the packed lunches and take the kids to school, I'll put the washing on and pick them up at four. I'll be late home,

	but don't worry – I'll pick up a sandwich later. (*she starts to hurry out*)
BOY:	Mum! (WOMAN *turns back*)
WOMAN:	What?
BOY:	It's Saturday.
NARRATOR:	. . . single mums.
GIRL:	Mum, why haven't we got a daddy, like the others in our class?
WOMAN:	Well, you have got a daddy, but he doesn't live with us any more.
BOY:	Doesn't he love us, then, Mummy?
WOMAN:	(*patiently*) Of course he loves *you*. He just doesn't love Mummy any more.
NARRATOR:	. . . and tired mums.
MAN:	(*from one side of stage*) Sweetheart! Do you know where my clean shirt is? (WOMAN *runs towards him, but before she gets there . . .*)
BOY:	(*from the other side*) Mum! Can you help me with my homework? (WOMAN *runs back towards him, but before she gets there . . .*)
GIRL:	(*from the other side*) Mum! Can you give me a lift to my dance class, please? (WOMAN *runs back towards her, but ends up collapsed in a heap on the stage*)
NARRATOR:	By the seventh day, God had finished the work he had been doing, so he rested. But on the seventh day, Mum was still cleaning, and ironing, and cooking, and being a taxi service for her kids. (WOMAN *gets up and mimes to each of those tasks very quickly until she falls over*) And so God created Mothering Sunday, when the rest of the family could say thank you and take a bit of the strain off Mum. (MAN, BOY *and* GIRL *lift her to her feet. She puts her arms round them*

and they freeze in family picture-type pose)
And Mum saw that it was very good. And
she wished it happened more than once a
year . . .

11. Marriage Guidance Counsellor

Aim: *This sketch is about our prayer lives. It asks us to examine how we often choose to communicate with God by comparing what happens in our own spiritual lives with what might happen if we acted the same way in a marriage relationship.*

Cast: *Sympathetic counsellor* FIONA, *dressed professionally; and bewildered wife* PHYLLIS, *dressed like an old woman. Either or both parts could be played by men.*

Props: *Traditional office set-up with desk and chairs – or perhaps two comfy chairs as you might find in a counselling room; file of papers.*

(FIONA *leads* PHYLLIS *confidently into the room.* FIONA *is carrying a file of papers and has the soothing manner of a professional counsellor*)

FIONA: (*indicates one of the chairs as she sits in the other one*) Please, do take a seat, Mrs . . . um . . .

PHYLLIS: (*nervously as she sits*) It's Brown. Phyllis Brown.

FIONA: (*smiles broadly*) Thank you, Mrs Brown. Well, welcome to Gerrem-Together Marriage Guidance Bureau. 'Together in a flash or you don't pay the cash!' Now, what can we do to help you today?

PHYLLIS: Well, it's our marriage, you see . . .

FIONA: (*nodding sympathetically*) Mmm, yes . . .

PHYLLIS: Well, it's just not working any more. And I don't understand why.

FIONA: OK. What makes you say that?

PHYLLIS: We don't seem to be communicating like we used to. I never really know how Harold feels any more.

FIONA: (*starts taking notes*) And how long has this been going on?

PHYLLIS: Since just after we got married. We were so much in love, and we used to spend so much time together. But it just seemed to go off the boil. (*her eyes start to well up with tears*)

FIONA: And have you talked to your husband about it?

PHYLLIS: Oh yes. We have a little quiet time together for about 15 minutes before breakfast.

FIONA: A quiet time?

PHYLLIS: Yes, that's right. I read something that he's written, and then we have a little chat about it.

FIONA: (*confused*) So . . . you only actually speak to each other for those 15 minutes a day?

PHYLLIS: (*looks embarrassed*) Well, to be honest with you . . . sometimes I'm in such a hurry, I don't actually get to talk to Harold at all. Once or twice a week, I just forget completely.

FIONA: You forget? Even though he's there with you?

PHYLLIS: Well, it's easily done, you know. When you've got to put your teeth in and get dressed and watch a bit of breakfast telly . . .

FIONA: (*uncertainly*) And what do you say to each other when you do talk?

PHYLLIS: Oh, you know . . . I ask him to take care of the family. It's the same kind of thing every day. But I feel better for it.

FIONA: And what does he say to you?

PHYLLIS: (*looks slightly ashamed*) Well, I don't always have
            time to listen to what he has to say. Sometimes I
            just skip that bit . . .

FIONA: Right. And you never speak to him during the
            rest of the day?

PHYLLIS: I sometimes think about him if I see a picture of
            him. Or if I spot something that he's created – you
            know, in the garden or something.

FIONA: Do you cook for each other? Do housework
            together?

PHYLLIS: Oh yes, I'm always working away for him in my
            own little way. And he helps me out as well.

FIONA: But how do you know what to do?

PHYLLIS: Well, it's obvious, isn't it? Things that will help
            people. I don't need to consult him about that!

FIONA: Right . . .

PHYLLIS: I do go along to a meeting every week with other
            married people, and the person in charge tells us
            what he thinks our spouses might be saying. But
            it's all very general. Nothing specific.

FIONA: OK. And you have no idea what your problem
            with Harold might be?

PHYLLIS: (*looks bewildered again*) Well, no. I'm only doing
            what they said I should do when I got married.
            They said that if I was committing the rest of my
            life to Harold, I should be prepared to spend 15
            minutes a day talking to him. That's how I could
            have a proper relationship.

FIONA: Ah, well, maybe that's your problem. (*she takes a
            deep breath*) Perhaps you should spend more time
            talking to him.

PHYLLIS: (*looks uncomfortable*) But I wouldn't know what
            to say!

FIONA: Talk to him just like you'd talk to anyone. Just like you're talking to me! And why not do it all the way through the day?

PHYLLIS: But I couldn't do that. He's my *husband*, you know!

FIONA: And why don't you put aside some time to listen? So you know what he wants and how he feels?

PHYLLIS: Well . . . he might say something that I don't want to hear!

FIONA: Maybe he will, Mrs Brown. But you'll never know until you start, will you? (*they freeze*)

12. Blameless

Aim: *We seem to be creating a 'victim culture' in Britain in which personal responsibility gets forgotten about in the rush to ascribe blame to someone else for any perceived ills that befall us. What's the point of talking about 'sin' if people can't even accept that they've done anything wrong? First we need to show how ridiculous it can be always to look for scapegoats elsewhere. This sketch is a deliberate send-up of the increasing number of adverts encouraging us to make money by finding someone to blame.*

Cast: *Confident* CELEBRITY; *hapless victims* JEREMY, CYNTHIA, MELANIE, BRIAN *and* GRAHAM. *Others can be* CAMERAMEN *and* WOMEN *or* CALL CENTRE WORKERS.

Props: *Lots of desks, chairs and telephones; pile of books; bathing costume and sunglasses; tape of sad music; cigarettes and cigarette packet.*

(*Enter* CELEBRITY, *in newly pressed suit, walking through rows of desks at which* CALL CENTRE WORKERS *are silently answering the telephones. He walks along, talking to an imaginary camera, or to* CAMERAMAN)

CELEBRITY: Hi, I'm a celebrity has-been who you may recognize from 1970s public information videos about crossing the road. I'm now reduced to starring in adverts such as these . . . (*turns to face another camera and puts on more serious face*) Have you been the victim of an accident in the home or at work in the last two years? You could make stacks of money in compensation by calling us – Blame Someone Else Ltd. Here's Jeremy. (*enter* JEREMY, *carrying a huge pile of books*) He was injured at work when he tripped and fell. (JEREMY *trips, falls and rolls around on the floor, seemingly in agony*) We made a claim against his firm for using dangerously deep-pile carpet.

JEREMY: (*stands and delivers his lines to a different camera in totally wooden voice*) Those nice people at Blame Someone Else won me £2,000 in compensation. They could do the same for you. (*gives camera unconvincing thumbs-up*)

CELEBRITY: Or what about Cynthia? (*exit* JEREMY, *enter* CYNTHIA, *in bathing costume and sunglasses*) She booked a holiday in the Arctic Circle, (CYNTHIA *shivers*) then sued her travel agent for compensation after she developed a mild chill. She won £5,000 in an out-of-court settlement.

CYNTHIA: (*only slightly more animatedly than* JEREMY) They should have told me that it was cold in Greenland. It was their fault!

CELEBRITY: Then there's the tragic case of Melanie Smith. (*exit* CYNTHIA, *enter* MELANIE, *smoking, with* BRIAN, *her husband. Cue sad music*) She smoked 60 cigarettes every day from the age of 8 to 38. (*affecting some emotion*) Her life was tragically cut short by lung cancer. She died before she'd even reached 40 years old, leaving two children and a heartbroken husband, Brian. (MELANIE *keels over and dies. Music ends*) With our help,

Brian sued the cigarette company for not warning Melanie that smoking could kill. He won £1.2 million.

BRIAN: How was Melanie to know that smoking could be bad for her? Those tobacco companies deliberately misled her by printing on their packets: 'Smoking kills.' It should have said: 'Smoking kills you when you are just 38 years old.' I mean, she was addicted to fags. It wasn't *her* fault people kept selling them to her!

CELEBRITY: Or perhaps you're like Graham . . . (*exit* MELANIE *and* BRIAN. *Enter* GRAHAM) Graham is completely normal. He has a normal IQ, a normal job, a normal wife and an average number of normal children. He's just ordinary. So we helped Graham by finding him someone to blame for that. We sued his parents for passing on their DNA, and so not allowing him to be extraordinary in any way.

GRAHAM: I won £5 million. You can too if you use Blame Someone Else Ltd.

CELEBRITY: Call us now on our freephone number: 0800 55115511. Remember – if we don't make you any money, you don't pay a penny. All your legal costs will be met and any stirrings of your conscience will be dealt with. (*winds himself up for the pay-off line*) Blame Someone Else Ltd – because it's never your fault! (*all freeze*)

13. Man-eater

Aim: *We sometimes forget how shocking some parts of the Bible are. The example of the prophet Hosea, who was asked by God to marry an adulterous wife as a picture of God's relationship with his unfaithful people, is a case in point. As with* 'Marriage Guidance Counsellor', *this sketch aims to show just how ill-equipped the church is to be called the Bride of Christ. And it reminds us of God's faithfulness to us.*

Cast: GOMER, *a prostitute. She wears a low-cut top, feather boa, leather skirt, high heels and stockings – or as much of that as she can get away with. The more forward she can be, the better the point is made. And the more responses she gets out of her 'victim' (who needs to be a plant in the audience), the better.*

Props: *If it is possible to do so, put a red light bulb in one of your lights and turn it on as* GOMER *enters; a chair.*

(GOMER *enters seductively and immediately approaches any men in the front row*)

GOMER: Well, hello, you . . . what brings you to this part of town? (*she drapes her feather boa around the man's neck*) Are you looking for a good time? Well, you've come to the right place! (*she spies another man looking at her*) Oh, you as well, sir! You are a

naughty boy. I hope you weren't looking at me
lustfully . . . (*she plays with the second man's hair*)
You know that people would pay good money to
look at me like that . . . would you like to pay me
some good money, sir? (*she ad-libs in this fashion
for as long as she dares*) So, would anyone like to
come up here and chat with me? (*audience plant
raises a hand immediately.* GOMER *points him out*)
You're keen, aren't you, sir? Come here, then. (*the
plant comes to the front*) You are a naughty boy.
But then, I'm a *very* naughty girl. (*she sits him
down in a chair, and puts one of her feet between his
legs*) How much do you think I'm worth, sir? Go
on, how much . . . ? (*she encourages him to reveal a
figure*) You see, my husband thinks I'm only worth
15 shekels. (*she affects sadness*) Can you believe
that, sir? I'm worth more than that, aren't I? (*she
moves around behind him and holds his head close to
her stomach while she plays with his hair*) Oh, does
it surprise you that I'm married, sir? Yes . . . to a
man called Hosea. (*to man*) Do you know him?
No, well, he's a prophet. Not much of a job if you
ask me. That's why I'm the breadwinner. He makes
people miserable with his prophecies. I make them
happy with my . . . (*she smirks*) well, let's just say I
just make them happy! Are you enjoying yourself,
sir? (*she fiddles with his shirt collar, or starts easing
his tie off*) I hope you've got a few pounds on you,
sir, because I'm not cheap . . . Well, I'm a mother
of two now . . . I know, sir, you can't believe it, not
with my figure . . . (*she goes and sits on his knee*)
Anyway, as I was saying, my husband decided that
he wanted to marry someone who would definitely
be unfaithful . . . so he chose little old me! And
guess, what . . . I was. (*she places his hand on her*

back) Well, this is the only thing I know how to do. I'm no good sitting at home just looking after the children. And someone had to earn some money . . . Well, you'll never guess what . . . I was with someone just like you – a punter who couldn't keep his hands to himself. (*she slaps the hand on her back*) And do you know what Hosea did? He came looking for me, and gave my . . . .well, let's say my 'representative' on the street . . . he paid him off. He bought his own wife back . . . can you believe it? Just so that he could hang onto me for good. (*she starts tracing a line along his face with her finger*) But it hasn't worked, has it, sir? Not now you've got your hands on me . . . If he asks, I'll say it was all your fault . . . You seduced me . . . (*considers*) Do you feel sorry for him, sir? Do you think I treat him badly? Well, maybe there's someone who *you* treat even worse. (*she freezes or flounces out*)

14. Real Sacrifice

 Aim: *We often talk about giving things up for Lent as if it was a really big sacrifice. It's good to remind ourselves of what sacrifice really means, and what kinds of things others were prepared to sacrifice as they obeyed God's commands.*

Cast: ABRAHAM, *who should be dressed as an old Israelite man, with a walking stick;* ISAAC, *his youthful son, who can be played by a child; voice of* GOD *(can be someone offstage using a microphone);* TRAMP, *who should be dressed in old clothes;* CHRISTIAN, *in normal clothes.*

Props: *Walking stick and big knife; bundle of wood; coffee cups.*

(ABRAHAM *and* ISAAC *are walking on the spot.* ABRAHAM *is carrying a bundle of wood and has a big, dangerous-looking knife strapped to his side*)

ISAAC:	Oh, Father, this is really exciting! I'm really glad you said I could come with you to do this sacrifice!
ABRAHAM:	Well, Isaac, God said I should take you with me this time.
ISAAC:	Brilliant! What happens when you do the sacrifice, then?
ABRAHAM:	(*stops and thinks*) Well, I burn the sacrifice as

116

an offering to God and ask him to accept it as a worthy substitute for all that I have done that is sinful. And in that one moment, when he cleanses me of all that separates me from him, I can see right into his heart. (*he looks away as if remembering*) You're struck dumb by the awesomeness of his power, your breath is taken away by his holiness and your spirit shudders at his ultimate goodness.

ISAAC: Fantastic! I can't wait to see it for myself! I want to be right in the middle of it all!

ABRAHAM: (*looks away in regret*) Hmm. Well, you will be, don't worry. (*he turns and they walk on in silence for a while*) Isaac – you know your place in history, don't you?

ISAAC: Yes, Father. You've told me many times. You said about how God promised you would have many descendants, but you weren't sure how that could happen because Mother was without child. And then I was born, and God said it would be through me that you would be the father of a great nation.

ABRAHAM: That's right, son. That's what he said.

ISAAC: Why do you ask?

ABRAHAM: Oh . . . no reason. Just that, well, if anything was to happen to you, I trust that God would still keep his promise.

ISAAC: What – you mean if I was attacked by wild bears and killed, you think God would bring me back to life?

ABRAHAM: Yes. Something like that. (*they walk on in silence again for a while*)

ISAAC: Dad?

ABRAHAM: Yes, son.

ISAAC: There is just one thing that bothers me.

ABRAHAM: What's that?

ISAAC: Well, usually when you go to sacrifice some-
             thing, you take an animal with you to kill. A
             lamb or a calf or something. You don't seem to
             have any sacrifice with you today.

ABRAHAM: Oh, I have, son.

ISAAC: Oh. What – is it under your tunic? Is it a very
             small sacrifice today, then?

ABRAHAM: No, Isaac. Today's sacrifice is about the biggest
             I could ever make. (ISAAC *looks confused. They
             stop.* ABRAHAM *puts down the bundle of wood
             and grabs* ISAAC) Today, Isaac, God has asked
             me to sacrifice you.

ISAAC: (*terrified*) Dad! Sacrifice me! What do you
             mean?

ABRAHAM: Lie down, son.

ISAAC: Dad! This can't be what God told you! You
             must have it wrong!

ABRAHAM: (*forces* ISAAC *to lie down*) Remember what we
             said – if anything happens to you, God will
             make sure he keeps his promise.

ISAAC: How can he keep his promise if I'm burnt to
             death, Dad?

ABRAHAM: (*gets out a big knife*) Believe me, son. This is
             going to break my heart. (ISAAC *is terrified.*
             ABRAHAM *holds him down with one hand and is
             just about to plunge the knife into him when a
             voice is heard offstage*)

GOD: Abraham! Abraham!

ABRAHAM: (*straightens up*) Yes, Lord?

GOD: Abraham! Don't lay a finger on the boy. Now I
             know that you fear God, because you weren't
             afraid to keep from me your only son. Now I
             know you have real faith.

ABRAHAM: Thank you, Lord.

GOD: See, there is a ram caught in the thicket over there by its horns. That can be your sacrifice today.

ABRAHAM: Thank you, Lord.

ISAAC: (*stands up*) Dad! Oh, you had me really frightened there. You knew that was going to happen, didn't you? It was just your little joke!

ABRAHAM: (*looks directly at him*) It was no joke, Isaac. Having faith in God means being prepared to do what he wants, however much he asks of you. And nothing I have, however precious, comes before God. (*they freeze. Enter* CHRISTIAN *and* TRAMP. CHRISTIAN *can be drinking coffee, as if at the end of a church service*)

CHRISTIAN: Well, praise the Lord! Didn't you think that was a great service!

TRAMP: Erm . . . well, I've just got here, love.

CHRISTIAN: That superb worship with the really evocative guitar work, the crescendo of voices in harmony, the real sense of the Spirit resting on each and every individual. Marvellous!

TRAMP: Erm . . . yeah, right.

CHRISTIAN: And that challenging, radical message to each one of us to go out and evangelize the world – not by what we say, but by what we do. That vicar is *such* a good preacher.

TRAMP: He don't do nothing for me. I just come here for somewhere to keep warm.

CHRISTIAN: I don't know about you, but I'm going to commit myself to praying every single day for the needs of this parish. Because there are so many needy people around.

TRAMP: Too right.

CHRISTIAN: (*looking at* TRAMP *for the first time*) Shall I

	include a word of prayer for you in my daily meditations?
TRAMP:	Erm, no. No, I just need somewhere to sleep tonight. And a bite to eat.
CHRISTIAN:	Ah! Right. Well, what an opportunity! Here's a real chance for someone in the congregation to put into practice some of the things we've learnt in this service. (*looks around*) Now, we do have a catering co-ordinator and a casual accommodation committee chairman at this church. I wonder where they are.
TRAMP:	I was just wondering if you had a few pounds so I could pay my way in the hostel tonight.
CHRISTIAN:	(*looks aghast*) Well, yes, but it would leave me a bit short for tomorrow . . .
ABRAHAM:	(*unfreezes and speaks to* ISAAC *as before*) Today's sacrifice is about the biggest I could ever make . . .
TRAMP:	What about a few pence for a sandwich, then?
CHRISTIAN:	Well, strictly speaking, I'm not the person to ask about that. (*trying to catch someone's eye*) Erm . . . Gladys! I think someone here would like a quick word!
ABRAHAM:	Having faith in God means being prepared to do what he wants.
CHRISTIAN:	I really hope you manage to keep warm and get something to eat. Now, listen, I don't want to appear rude, but I really must catch that person over there to talk about next Sunday's family service. You know how precious time can be.
ABRAHAM:	Nothing I have, however precious, comes before God. (*they all freeze*)

15. By Royal Appointment

 Aim: *An ordinary donkey is asked to serve the King on a very important day: what a privilege! Yet we are also asked to serve the King every day of our lives. We could learn something from the humility of this donkey and its realization that this King is different from all others.*

Cast: DONKEY. *The actor can wear a rudimentary costume of large ears and a tail, but a full-scale panto-mime horse costume should be avoided. This is a young donkey, so the part can be played like an excited child.*

Props: *None.*

(*Enter* DONKEY)

DONKEY: (*enthusiastically*) Hey – have you heard what happened to me? I had to carry the king on my back the other day! (*he laughs*) That's right, me! I'm only tiny, and I live in this really small village, but they wanted me! Can you believe it? I'd never been ridden by anyone before. I couldn't even stand up properly. There I was, just playing in the field with my mum, and two of the king's men came. They wanted to borrow me for a special ride! Well, I'd never been anywhere without my mum, and there they were – untying me and taking me to meet the king! On my own! Well, my mouth went dry, and my head was spinning round. I'd never met anyone important before. I didn't know whether to bow or curtsey or just bray politely. I mean, having a king on your back – that's what those posh horses do. You know, the thoroughbreds. You see them, don't you? They grow up in palaces and they get taught how to do one of those military trots, (*he demonstrates*) and they get brushed every day so they look really beautiful. They seem to know how to walk with their head up and their back straight. (*he demonstrates that, then looks disconsolate*) Me – I was all over the place! I'm only a tiny colt, and he was a fully grown man. He felt really heavy! And the path we were on – well, it was full of stones. I could hardly put one leg in front of the other without falling over. My knees were wobbling and my heart was pounding! The king had to lift his legs in the air so that they didn't drag along the floor. He didn't even have a saddle, so I thought he might slip off at any minute! I felt so ashamed. I mean, it would have been quicker for him to walk! (*pause as he gazes unhappily into the distance, then he starts to smile and looks happier*). But he didn't complain. In fact, he started to whisper in my ear. He was saying: 'Good boy!' and 'Keep going!' and 'You're doing well!' That nice voice – he didn't sound like the kind of king who would order people around. And I took some big breaths, and went a bit more slowly. (*he demonstrates*) 'Just take it one step at a time,' I thought. And then I heard some cheering. I looked up, and there were people there, waving and shouting. They must have seen that I was struggling, because they started to put their coats on the ground for me to walk on. And they cut down these branches to make the path smoother. (*his smile grows broader*) Imagine that for a tiny colt like me! People making a fuss of me as I went past, holding out their hands for the king to touch. It was great! And I lifted my head up and brayed loudly, and they all laughed – and the king smiled and patted me on the head. And then they started cheering and singing 'Hosanna to the Son of David.' I remembered a story my mum had told me. It was about this king who was also a son of David. She said he was born in a stable and put into the trough where we eat our food. My mum said one of her cousins was there when that baby was born. I thought it was one of those stories that mums tell – you know, just to get you to sleep. But it made me think – was this the same king? The king who wants to use stables and donkeys when he could have palaces and golden chariots? I said that to my mum when I got back to the village. She was really proud of me. She said people would be talking about what I'd done for years. I said: 'Don't be silly!' but then she told me another story. About a prophet who said that the real king would choose to enter Jerusalem on the foal of a donkey. The real king! The king who chooses the smallest and the weakest for the really big things. The king who whispers gently in your ear. That's the kind of king I wanted to carry. That's the kind of king I was happy to serve. (*he freezes, then trots off*)

16. Lifetime Guarantee

Aim: *Jesus' life and death are often thought of as God's rescue plan for the entire human race. But did God have any other options? It's useful on Good Friday to look at why Jesus had to die. This sketch also picks up some of the understandable anger that many people feel about the extent of suffering within the world, though it doesn't seek to answer all those questions. It could, therefore, be used at an evangelistic event.*

Cast: *Calm, unruffled* CREATOR *(ideally played by an older man with a mischievous twinkle in his eye); person of either sex to represent* MANKIND.

Props: *Desk; chair; sign saying 'The World: Customer Service'; notepad; pen; globe.*

(CREATOR *is sitting behind a desk busily doing some work. The sign reading 'The World: Customer Service' is on his desk. Enter* MANKIND, *angrily. He is carrying a globe*)

CREATOR: Can I help you, sir?

MANKIND: Yes. You can do something about this! (*he slams the globe down on the desk*)

CREATOR: What seems to be the problem, sir?

MANKIND: (*indicates the globe*) *This* is the problem. The world. I'd like it changed, please.

CREATOR: (*furrows his brow*) I'm sorry?

MANKIND: I'd like it changed. For a better one.

CREATOR: And why is that, sir?

MANKIND: Well, just look at it! It's faulty. It's broken. You're the one who made it. So I'm bringing it back for you to change it for a new one.

CREATOR: (*peering at the globe*) What exactly is wrong with it, sir?

MANKIND: (*incredulous that such a question could even be asked*) What's wrong with it? Where do I start? Earthquakes, famines, wars, volcanoes, natural disasters all over the place! There's starving children here, (*points to Africa*) fanatical terrorists there (*points to the Middle East*) and not much left of the ozone layer here (*points to the Arctic Circle*). Quite frankly, this was a shoddy piece of workmanship, and as the manufacturer, you should be ashamed of yourself!

CREATOR: Indeed, sir. I do see what you mean. (*he picks up a notepad and starts writing*)

MANKIND: Now I'm sure there must be some kind of lifetime guarantee on this, and as I can't see it getting better, I'd like to get a new one and start again. I mean, I don't know how you think people can live in these conditions.

CREATOR: (*humouring him*) OK, sir. Assuming that I was to honour this 'guarantee', what kind of new world would you like?

MANKIND: Right, well, for starters, let's have all our natural resources back – all the oil, all the coal, all the rainforests that we had to start with. (CREATOR *makes a note*) Let's eradicate all of these natural disasters and let's go back to before global warming started.

CREATOR: Would that be back to the Ice Age, sir?

MANKIND: (*he hasn't thought of this*) Erm . . . no, no. Just restore the ozone layer to what it was like before. Right, we want no more famines, no more wars, no more hungry people. Decent housing for everyone, no more AIDS or other diseases, no more extinct animal species . . .

CREATOR: So you'd like some dinosaurs, then?

MANKIND: Um. Well, no. But perhaps a few more of the endangered animals. Tigers and whales, that kind of thing.

CREATOR: (*arching an eyebrow*) More whales!

MANKIND: No more intolerance. We want people to live together in harmony, so there should be no more wars.

CREATOR: So we don't want people who will start wars any more?

MANKIND: That's right.

CREATOR: Which other people don't you want to be there?

MANKIND: Well . . . no paedophiles, no murderers, no rapists – in fact no criminals of any kind. People should be free to go about their business in safety.

CREATOR: (*making a note*) So . . . no people who could become criminals. What about people who get angry with one another?

MANKIND: No, we don't want that! No arguments! (*as if an idea has hit him*) Ah! So no politicians – then we'd be free to rule ourselves!

CREATOR: So no governments. And no laws, presumably.

MANKIND: (*excitedly*) Well, that's right. If there's no criminals, we don't need any laws. We'll just be free to get on and live our lives.

CREATOR: OK. Let me see if I've got this right. (*he flicks back a few pages*) We don't want people who cause environmental problems, people who have arguments, people who don't tolerate others' opinions. We don't want greedy people who eat more than others or take more money than they need – because that would leave some people hungry. We don't want people who use the world's natural resources, or who hunt animals. Is that about right?

MANKIND: (*less certain now*) Ye-e-s. I think so.

CREATOR: So that would be a world without human beings, then? That's the kind of new world you'd like me to create for you?

MANKIND: (*realizes what he has asked for*) Well . . . no, not with *no* human beings. Just the ones who are nice to everyone all the time . . . . (*his voice trails away*)

CREATOR: Have you met any humans like that?

MANKIND: Um. Not really. (*pause*) Sorry, that's not really what I wanted.

CREATOR: No, it wasn't.

MANKIND: Isn't there any way that you can put things right? I mean, you created this place. You should be able to sort out everything that's wrong with it!

CREATOR: (*solemnly*) There is one thing I can do.

MANKIND: Is there? Really! And you'll do it?

CREATOR: (*looks straight at* MANKIND) Absolutely. I guarantee it. (*they freeze*)

17. His Blood Shed for Me

 Aim: *One of the hardest things to understand is the concept that Jesus had to die because of the things we all do wrong. The idea of this sketch is to link in Jesus' death more directly with something one named person did or didn't do. It may be slightly unfair on Nicodemus, but it ends with the hint that perhaps we're all somehow to blame.*

 Cast: NICODEMUS, *dressed in an approximation of first-century Palestine costume.*

Props: *A cloth.*

(*Enter* NICODEMUS, *perhaps wiping his hands on a cloth*)

NICODEMUS: (*speaks directly to the audience*) I've just come from burying him. He's at peace now. (*pause*) I don't know if you know what it's like. To cradle the head of a loved one in your arms, to hold the dead weight of a lifeless body, to feel the congealed blood between your fingers. (*he looks away, as if holding back strong emotions*) It's bad enough when it's someone you care deeply about. When it's someone you think might be even more special . . . (*he shakes his head, then turns back to the audience*) My name's Nicodemus, and I'm one of the

128

Pharisees. We live and breathe the Jewish law, so if I tell you about this, you mustn't breathe a word to anyone. (*he looks furtively around to see if anyone is listening*) You see, I was intrigued by this Jesus. His attitude towards our laws, our Scriptures – it was fascinating. For us Pharisees it's vitally important to keep the Sabbath holy, not to do anything that anyone might think of as work. It's one of the ten great commandments that God gave us. Yet I saw this man perform what I can only describe as a miracle on the Sabbath in front of everyone in the synagogue. It was so blatant – I think he did it deliberately to make us think about how we interpreted this law. (*he holds out his arm and demonstrates what happened*) This man had a shrivelled hand, and Jesus got him to stand up and stretch it out. Jesus looked at us directly and said, 'What is lawful on the Sabbath: to do good or to do evil, to save life or to kill?' (*shrugs his shoulders*) We couldn't answer. We were so keen on the details of whether this or that was allowed that we'd forgotten . . . well, some of us had just forgotten about the kind of God we were supposed to be serving. This man's hand . . . well, I saw the tendons of his arm strengthen and the blood flow into his fingers. I swear to you – I'd never seen anything like it! Some of my colleagues started talking about getting rid of him. They thought he was dangerous. There were too many people who liked him and wanted to challenge our authority. I said . . . (*looks away, ashamed of himself*) I said nothing. I didn't want to disagree. (*pause.*

Looks back at the audience) I went to see this Jesus. I wanted to see what made him tick, where he thought his authority came from. But I went at night. I didn't want anyone to see me. He talked about being 'born again', which I didn't understand. He talked about God sending his Son into the world to save it, and he seemed to think he was that Son. That was blasphemous talk – normally I would have written him off as self-deluding . . . but every-thing else he said seemed to make sense. The next day, one of my Pharisee friends asked me what I thought of this Jesus. (*looks away, ashamed again*) I lied. I said I hadn't given it much thought. (*looks back at audience again, now speaking softly*) Then there was the trial. They arrested Jesus and brought him before the Jewish ruling council. Caiaphas, the High Priest, asked him directly whether he was the Christ, the Messiah that we Jews had been waiting for. I was thinking: 'Say yes! And perform some miracle that will convince them!' If he had, they would have had to believe him! (*as if trying to convince himself*) Wouldn't they? At one point Jesus looked straight at me. It was strange. He didn't look scared or panic stricken. It was a calm, cool gaze. I had to look away. Caiaphas followed his eyes and looked at me as well. I could have said something then, but I said nothing. I was terrified of being found out. They might have executed me as one of his followers. (*looks down. He speaks more slowly*) I survived. But he died the most terrible death, with the nails ripping through his flesh, flies crawling around his mouth and his lungs gasping for air. Afterwards, my friend Joseph offered to bury him, so I helped embalm the body and wrap it in strips of cloth. And as we placed it in the tomb, all I could think of was that he had been a special person, who I did nothing to help – even when he was staring death in the face. (*looks directly at the audience and speaks more deliberately*) Can you imagine how that feels – somehow feeling responsible for someone else's death? Feeling that this one man had to suffer because of the things you'd done . . . or not done? That's a feeling *I* can never forget. (*he pauses a moment, then walks off*)

18. Devil's Advocate

 Aim: *To show how powerful the message of Easter is.*

 Cast: *Head devil* SATAN, *who is dressed as a senior executive; junior devils* SPRITE, SPOOK *and* SCREWTAPE, *all in business suits.*

 Props: *Table and chairs set out as if for a business meeting in* SATAN'S *office; 'souls forecast' chart.*

(SPRITE, SPOOK *and* SCREWTAPE *are talking quietly as* SATAN *sweeps in*)

SATAN:	Morning, fellow demons. I have to say that Head Office wasn't too pleased with the results of your last assignment.
SPRITE:	No, sir. Sorry, sir.
SATAN:	It was a very responsible position to be in. Saul was one of our best projects. We had big plans for him.
SPOOK:	Yes, sir. We know. But we didn't think anything would happen on the back street to Damascus. Not much usually does.
SATAN:	(*angrily to* SPOOK) Demon, you were on a 24-hour vigil! You shouldn't have stopped tempting him for a second! Anyway, we've taken you off missionary prevention.

SPOOK: Thank Lucifer! We've had a devil of a job trying to keep him quiet.

SATAN: We'd like you to work on something else. (*he perches on the edge of the desk*) I hardly need remind you of the dire situation that the Hades Corporation has been placed in as a result of the 'Easter' debacle. There have been rumours to the effect that we might be going out of business. (*the devils express surprise*)

SPRITE: What?

SATAN: Yes, I'm afraid so. Unless we can keep this whole affair quiet, then we are in big trouble. We're already experiencing a fall in annual intake of 30 per cent in the last decade, (*he holds up a chart which shows 'souls' against 'time' with the graph plummeting*) and we have a very poor souls forecast for the rest of the century. All because of one embarrassing lapse of concentration in AD 33. Our research shows we can't change what happened, but if we can stop them celebrating it, business might improve. Any ideas? Sprite?

SPRITE: (*who is slightly dim, and caught off guard*) Er . . . persecution, sir?

SATAN: Persecution?

SPRITE: (*growing in confidence*) Yeah, sir. Slaughter a few of them. Get them torn to pieces by lions or crucified. Stick a few in prison and torture them. Like in Operation Nero. Then they'll soon forget about the Enemy.

SATAN: (*scathingly*) Really? You haven't been a senior demon very long, have you, Sprite? Operation Nero was hardly one of our more successful campaigns. Those who were killed went straight upstairs and those who weren't were inspired by the martyrs and became even bigger problems. It's hardly a very subtle technique, is it? It's old hat. We're looking for a new technique.

SPOOK: What about divisions, sir?

SATAN: (*interested*) Go on.

SPOOK: Denominationalism, sir. It's something new we're working on. We get a few of them to concentrate unduly on some fairly unimportant issue of doctrine and blow it out of all proportion. Then you leave the rest to those old faithfuls pride and self-righteousness.

SATAN: Sounds promising. Could we apply it to this particular problem, do you think?

SPOOK: It's been very successful in trials, sir. One approach that we could try is to get them debating about the essential nature of 'the resurrection' (*puts on quavering vicar's voice*) 'Was it physical or would it be more constructive to see it as a purely spiritual phenomenon?' You know the sort of thing. That way they forget completely about the actual consequences of it. Gives us bags of room for manoeuvre.

SATAN: I like it. What about the ones on our side? We don't want them to even *think* about the resurrection.

SCREWTAPE: (*supremely smooth*) Very easy, sir. We distract them. Get them to think about anything else apart from the facts.

SATAN: How would you do that, Screwtape?

SCREWTAPE: Well, this ritual they go through every year to celebrate the Enemy's supposed 'victory'. We could twist it, just ever so slightly. We could get them to celebrate 'new life' as a concept, not anybody's new life in particular. Turn it into something for everyone, for people of all religions, by getting them to celebrate the beginning of spring instead.

SATAN: (*stands*) Worshipping creation instead of the creator!

SCREWTAPE: Got it in one, sir. We could make it a celebration with flowers and rabbits, fluffy yellow chicks. Give them an excuse to drink a lot, and give them a bank holiday to recover.

SATAN: (*getting excited*) Easter rabbit . . . no, Easter hares. Easter bunnies – that's got a certain ring to it! And, yes, you're right – it doesn't change anything, but it completely disguises the true meaning of the festival!

SPOOK: (*slightly peeved at being outdone*) Do you really think people would fall for that, sir? Rebirth as a concept? Newborn chicks and cuddly bunnies?

SATAN: I can see it doing very well. All we need is something that people can market, something that people can make a profit out of, and then this whole idea could take off . . .

SCREWTAPE: Like a lovely, cuddly, newborn baby, sir?

SATAN: Nice idea. Unfortunately we've already pencilled that one in for Christmas.

SPRITE: Eggs, sir!

SATAN: I'm sorry?

SPRITE: Eggs. People could give them to each other.

SATAN: (*stands behind* SPRITE *and leans on the back of his chair*) Not quite what we're looking for, demon. Something a little more marketable, perhaps?

SPRITE: (*thinks hard, then it comes to him*) Eggs made out of chocolate!

SATAN: (*pause, then looks at* SPOOK) Perhaps you're right. Not even human beings are *that* stupid! (*all freeze*)

19. Emmaus Road

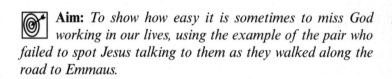 **Aim:** *To show how easy it is sometimes to miss God working in our lives, using the example of the pair who failed to spot Jesus talking to them as they walked along the road to Emmaus.*

Cast: NARRATOR, CHORUS, *who work as one, making the noise of various sound effects as indicated.* CLEOPAS, SIMON *and* JESUS *come out of the chorus to say their lines. The rhythm of the walking and talking should give an overall rhythm to the sketch.*

 Props: *Bread.*

(CHORUS *line up in the middle of the stage.* NARRATOR *is somewhere to the side*)

NARRATOR:	Sunday. The third day after Jesus had died. Two men went for a walk.
CHORUS:	(*they walk on the spot, stamping their feet rhythmically on the floor*)
NARRATOR:	One was called Cleopas. He was an intelligent man. (*one of the* CHORUS *steps forward*) He knew his Old Testament backwards.
CLEOPAS:	(*in time with the continuing rhythm*) Malachi, Zechariah, Haggai, Zephaniah, Habakkuk . . . (*he counts off the books on his fingers*)

137

NARRATOR: (*interrupting*) He could debate with the Pharisees ... (CLEOPAS *turns to look at members of the* CHORUS *on his right and waggles a finger at them.* CHORUS *stop walking.*)

CHORUS: (*erupting into a noisy debate, like the House of Commons*)

CLEOPAS: (*as House of Commons Speaker*) Order! Order!

NARRATOR: . . . settle scores with the Sadducees . . . (CLEOPAS *turns to look at members of* CHORUS *on his left and waggles a finger at them*)

CHORUS: (*even noisier debate*)

CLEOPAS: (*even louder*) ORDER! ORDER!

NARRATOR: . . . and his synagogue had even voted him Most Likely to Become a Rabbi. (CLEOPAS *looks proud*)

CHORUS: (*raising an imaginary glass*) Mazel Tov! [*Hebrew for 'Congratulations!'*]

NARRATOR: The other was called Simon. (*another of the* CHORUS *steps forward*) He was a dangerous revolutionary, who thought Jesus was coming to take over as Israel's king.

SIMON: (*punching the air with his fist and shouting*) Power to the people!

NARRATOR: Both of them had no idea why Jesus had died. So they went for a walk.

CHORUS: (*walking on the spot*)

NARRATOR: They tiptoed past the Roman centurions . . .

CHORUS: (*they tiptoe to the same rhythm, putting their fingers to their mouths*) Shhh!

NARRATOR: . . . sneaked out of the city gates . . .

CHORUS: (*they each pretend to open a creaking gate by putting one arm horizontally in front of their chests, pushing it with the other hand and making a 'creaking' noise*)

NARRATOR: . . . and set off for Emmaus.

CHORUS: (*walking on the spot*)

NARRATOR: And as they walked, they talked.

CHORUS: (*in time with the rhythm*) Blah-blah-blah-blah, blah-blah-blah-blah . . .

NARRATOR: (*as* CHORUS *continue*) They talked about everything that had happened in Jerusalem in the past few days. Just then a stranger joined them. (CHORUS *halts rhythm, mid-blah. One of* CHORUS *steps forward as* JESUS) He asked:

JESUS: What are you talking about?

NARRATOR: So they told him.

CHORUS: (*walking on the spot and speaking in time with rhythm*) Jesus-blah-blah-blah, prophet-blah-blah-blah, died-blah-blah-blah . . .

NARRATOR: They told him they had hoped that Jesus would restore Israel to its former glory.

CHORUS: (*punching the air with their fists and shouting*) Power to the people!

NARRATOR: They told him that Jesus had died. And they told him that some women said they'd seen Jesus alive.

CHORUS: (*walking on the spot and speaking in time with rhythm*) Women-blah-blah-blah, emotional-blah-blah-blah, hysterical-blah, blah, blah . . .

NARRATOR: And the stranger said: (CHORUS *halts rhythm*)

JESUS: How foolish you are! Don't you understand what had to happen?

NARRATOR: And, as they walked . . .

CHORUS: (*walking on the spot*)

NARRATOR: . . . the stranger began to explain everything that was said in the Scriptures about Jesus.

JESUS: Moses-blah-blah-blah, Isaiah-blah-blah-blah . . .

NARRATOR: (*building up to a climax*) Now Cleopas had debated with the Pharisees and settled scores with the Sadducees. He was very intelligent. He had a ready answer for every intellectual challenge. So when the stranger explained the Scriptures, he said:

CLEOPAS: (*jaw drops in shock*) Blimey!

NARRATOR: And Simon was a fearsome warrior, a subversive zealot. So when the stranger explained the Scriptures, he said:

SIMON: (*scratching his head*) Crikey!

NARRATOR: And both of them said:

CHORUS: (*together*) If only *Jesus* was here!

NARRATOR: And when they got to Emmaus, the stranger looked as though he was going further, so they said:

CHORUS: (*posh voices*) Do stay for tea.

NARRATOR: So he went into the house with them, and started to eat a meal.

CHORUS: (*sound of eating.* JESUS *goes behind the altar and picks up bread*)

NARRATOR: But when the stranger took the bread and broke it, (JESUS *breaks the bread*) Simon and Cleopas realized who the stranger was.

CHORUS: (*jaws drop in shock*) Blimey!

NARRATOR: It was Jesus. And they hadn't realized.

CHORUS: (*in Homer Simpson style as they each hit their head with the palm of one hand*) D'oh!

NARRATOR: But just then he disappeared from their sight. (JESUS *crouches down behind the altar*) So Simon and Cleopas ran back to the disciples . . .

CHORUS: (*running on the spot*)

NARRATOR: . . . and told them:

CHORUS: (*out of breath, pointing frantically back the way they came and leaning on each other for support*) It's . . . .Jees . . . .Jesus. H-he's . . . he's . . .

NARRATOR: Now just take your time. Deep breaths, now.

CHORUS: (*take deep breaths together*)

NARRATOR: Now, what was it you wanted to say?

CHORUS: (*illustrating each word with dramatic gestures*)
            Jesus! Walking! Talking! Alive!

NARRATOR: How often are we walking . . .

CHORUS: (*walking on the spot*)

NARRATOR: . . . and talking . . .

CHORUS: (*in time with rhythm*) Blah-blah-blah-blah,
            blah-blah-blah-blah . . . (JESUS *stands up and
            reappears in the line-up*)

NARRATOR: . . . and have no idea that Jesus is walking along
            beside us, helping us to understand what is
            going on?

CHORUS: (*freeze in pose with their hands scratching their
            heads*) Blimey!

20. Playstation

 Aim: *It's unusual to combine the Christmas and Easter message in one sketch or one service, but this sketch could be performed at either festival. It uses the imagery of computers to show why it was necessary to send Jesus into the world as a baby, and how he emerged victorious after his resurrection. It is a condensed and updated version of a twelve-episode children's serial written for the Scripture Union beach mission in Abersoch, North Wales.*

 Cast: GAMESMASTER *(perhaps an older man), dressed in white or something that marks him out as being in charge; his son* GAMEBOY, *dressed similarly, but perhaps in white shorts and T-shirt to mark him out as being younger;* LARA CROFT, *dressed in shorts, with her hair in a ponytail like the computer character;* MICHAEL OWEN *in full England kit (if possible) with football;* JAMES BOND *in full tuxedo (if possible), with a wristwatch. (Substitute for three more up-to-date computer characters if necessary.)*

Props: *Computer 'console' with buttons and dials that the* GAMESMASTER *can stand behind; each computer character should come on stage with some kind of recognizable 'virus' attached to their backs – perhaps a black splodge of paint, cut out and attached with Velcro so that it can be ripped off; football; small toy gun.*

(*Enter* GAMESMASTER. *It may be helpful for him to be placed slightly higher up than the computer characters – perhaps in the pulpit*)

GAMESMASTER: Welcome to the Playstation! I am the Gamesmaster, and this is the computer-generated world I have created. I made all the hardware you can see around you, and all the software that makes it work. Let me introduce you to some of our computer characters. Here's Lara Croft, the feisty female heroine of our best-selling game. (*enter* CROFT, *kicking the air and practising her punches*) Here's Michael Owen, star of the football game in which you pretend to be the England manager. (*enter* OWEN, *dribbling a football in front of him*) Here's James Bond, star of our 007 game based on his films. (*enter* BOND, *coolly and suavely, holding a small gun, which he fires to one side.* GAMEBOY *runs on to talk to* GAMESMASTER)

GAMEBOY: Dad! Dad!

GAMESMASTER: And this is my son, the Gameboy!

GAMEBOY: Dad! Something's gone wrong with the Playstation!

GAMESMASTER: What do you mean? It looks fine to me!

GAMEBOY: There's a computer virus on the loose. I'm afraid it might attack our characters!

GAMESMASTER: Well, we've built in some pretty solid anti-virus protection to these games, son. (CROFT *suddenly spasms, clutches her back and falls over, gyrating on the floor. She rips the 'virus' off her back and throws it towards* GAMESMASTER. *He picks it up*) Gameboy! I think you're right! Look at the size of this! I think this could be (*dramatically to the audience*) the 'Sintendo' virus. It's certainly the worst I've ever seen! (CROFT *starts pushing* OWEN *and* BOND *around*) Look! It's making our computer characters do the opposite of what we want!

GAMEBOY: I'm afraid it might spread, Dad! Remember, they only have one life before Game Over comes up! (OWEN *has a similar spasm and falls to the floor, infected by the virus*)

GAMESMASTER: This is really serious, Gameboy! I need someone whom I can trust to go in and deal with it face to face. I don't want it getting into my hard drive! (BOND *has his spasm and becomes infected by the virus*)

GAMEBOY: Do you want me to do it for you, Dad?

GAMESMASTER: OK, but you need to know that you could be infected with this virus as well.

GAMEBOY: That's OK, Dad. As long as you're still in control of the game! (*he gets ready to leap into the game*) I'll see you soon, Dad!

GAMESMASTER: Bye, son. (GAMEBOY *leaps over to where the computer characters are. They are behaving very oddly, with* BOND *and* OWEN *virtually fighting.* GAMESMASTER *watches*)

GAMEBOY: OK, everyone. Cool it! (*he tries to separate them*)

OWEN: (*aggressively*) What are you doing inside our computer game?

CROFT: We were doing fine until you came along!

GAMEBOY: But you've been infected with the Sintendo computer virus. It's making you do the opposite of what the Gamesmaster wants!

BOND: The name's Bond. James Bond. And I take orders from nobody.

GAMEBOY: You do! You're supposed to follow the rules laid down by the Gamesmaster for playing the game!

OWEN: (*laughs*) Ha! You don't believe all that Gamesmaster rubbish, do you? Everyone knows that computer games were just created in an accidental explosion of circuit boards and wires!

CROFT: Yeah – there's no computer virus here! Get lost, will you? (*they advance on* GAMEBOY *menacingly*)

GAMEBOY: Look, you need to know that you'll never get onto the next level of your computer games unless you get rid of the virus!

BOND: Really! What an intriguing concept. And how would one do that?

GAMEBOY: (*takes a deep breath*) By transferring your viruses onto me.

CROFT: But then your file would be so corrupted that it would have to be deleted.

GAMEBOY: I know. But it's the only way to get rid of this virus once and for all. (CROFT, BOND *and* OWEN *whisper briefly to each other*)

OWEN: OK. We'll give you our Sintendo viruses and then we'll see what happens.

GAMEBOY: Thank you. (*he holds out his hands.* OWEN, BOND *and* CROFT *look at each other, then hand over the 'viruses' from their backs.* GAMEBOY *spasms each time he grabs hold of one, briefly assumes the shape of a cross, then falls to the floor. He is dead*)

BOND: He's been deleted!

CROFT: (*can feel something happening to her*) Wow! Suddenly I feel . . . so much more powerful. Like I could defeat anyone up to level nine on my game! (*she does some high kicks and punches as she exits*)

OWEN: (*also feels something*) Yeah! I feel like I could score the winning goal in the World Cup Final! (*he gets the football, dribbles it and kicks it powerfully offstage. He exits celebrating the 'goal'*)

BOND: (*also feels something*) Why, yes, now you mention it. I do feel as though I could defeat all of my enemies combined. (*talks into his wristwatch*) M? Q? I'm coming in for my next assignment. Get out all the gadgets and . . . (*he rubs his hands in anticipation*) watch out, all you ladies! (*he exits, leaving* GAMEBOY *still on the floor*)

GAMESMASTER: (*fiddling with the controls he has in front of him*) Gameboy! I'm trying to reboot you! (*finally presses a big button*) There. That should do it! (GAMEBOY *stands up*) Are you OK, Gameboy? That virus hasn't erased your memory, has it?

GAMEBOY: No, Dad, it hasn't. Has the virus gone?

GAMESMASTER: It's not gone completely, son. Some of the characters will still have it. But at least now we know how to get rid of it. (*smiles at* GAMEBOY) Thanks, son.

GAMEBOY: Now all I've got to do is convince those computer characters that I've been rebooted.

GAMESMASTER: Some of them will believe you, son. But some of them won't . . . (*they freeze*)

21. The Z-Files: Resurrection

 Aim: *To remind us that both Jesus' resurrection and the coming of the Holy Spirit were supernatural events which had an extraordinary impact at the time.*

Cast: PILATE, *who is in charge of the investigation;* CAIAPHAS, *his somewhat nervous sidekick; dim-witted* SOLDIER; *down-to-earth* MARY; PETER *the apostle – all dressed in period costume;* VOICE. MOULDY *and* SKULKER *are in smart, modern dress – as in the TV programme. They speak with American accents.*

Props: *Pilate's desk; 'tomb' (which can be simply behind a convenient pillar or pulpit); shroud; mobile phones; papers; ID for Skulker; Dr Luke's manuscript; sound effects of wind, fire and babble of different languages; bright light (shining from offstage); taped X-Files theme tune.*

(PILATE *is sitting at his desk when* CAIAPHAS *walks in*)

PILATE: Ah, Caiaphas. Thanks for coming. Been having a few problems, I hear.

CAIAPHAS: (*nervously*) Nothing we can't handle, Pilate.

PILATE: (*stands and begins to sound threatening*) That's not what I've heard. Crucify him, you said. It'll cause no fuss, you said. He's only got about a dozen followers, you said.

CAIAPHAS: Erm, yes . . .

PILATE: I let you kill this innocent man because *you* told me there'd be no problems. Now, let me get this straight. These (*holds sheaf of papers*) are all from people saying they've seen this two-bit preacher alive. That sounds dangerous to me.

CAIAPHAS: Your Excellency, I had no idea that putting him to death would cause you so many problems . . .

PILATE: (*puts his face very close to* CAIAPHAS' *face*) Oh no, Caiaphas. This isn't my problem. The Jews are your people, not mine. If you remember, I washed my hands of the whole thing.

CAIAPHAS: Yes, sir.

PILATE: So, what are you going to do about it?

CAIAPHAS: We're going to stop this rumour spreading, sir. We're going to discredit their supernatural rubbish.

PILATE: And how will you do that?

CAIAPHAS: Don't worry, sir. I've hired some experts . . .

('X-Files' *theme tune.* MOULDY *and* SKULKER *walk on from the back in modern dress.* SOLDIER *comes on in front of the tomb.* MOULDY *and* SKULKER *stop and look into the tomb.* MOULDY *pulls out the shroud. Music stops*)

SKULKER: (*shows her ID*) I'm Agent Dana Skulker from the FBI. This is my partner, Agent Fox Mouldy. (*leafs through sheafs of paper*) Soldier, you say in your statement that Jesus' followers stole the body while you were asleep?

SOLDIER: (*looks shifty*) Erm, yeah. That's right.

SKULKER: All of you were asleep? All twelve of you? Handpicked soldiers from the elite Roman force on guard duty?

SOLDIER: Yeah. It had been a very tiring day . . .

SKULKER: And none of you was woken by the sound of this huge boulder being moved away from the entrance to the tomb?

SOLDIER: Yeah. Erm . . . I mean, no. I mean, what was the question?

MOULDY: Soldier – we're here with the full authority of Pontius Pilate and the chief priests. We need to know what actually happened.

SOLDIER: (*reluctantly*) An earthquake moved the stone away. We looked and the body had gone.

MOULDY: (*holds up shroud*) Skulker – have you seen this? This is the shroud the body was wrapped in.

SKULKER: So?

MOULDY: So it was still lying in there as if it was round a body. Almost as if it had been spirited away.

SKULKER: Don't jump to conclusions, Mouldy. I'll send it for analysis. At the laboratory in Turin. (*to* SOLDIER) One thing, soldier. Why were you guarding a dead man?

SOLDIER: He'd threatened that after three days he might rise from the dead.

MOULDY: So it was a possibility?

SKULKER: Mouldy – all these do-it-yourself Jewish Messiahs claimed they would rise from the dead.

MOULDY: Yeah. But how many of them worried the authorities so much they guarded the place with a crack legion of Roman troops?

(SKULKER *goes to see* MARY, *while* MOULDY *sits down at the desk and starts looking through some files*)

SKULKER: Miss Magdalene? Can I have a few words? About this Jesus?

MARY: Yes. He's come back from the dead. Isn't it wonderful?

SKULKER: Yeah, right. He was some kinda hero for you, right?

MARY: He saved me from being stoned to death. He forgave me. He accepted me.

SKULKER: You were a hooker?

MARY: Yes, but that's all forgotten about now. Oh, I thought he was dead, but when he appeared to me in the garden I realized he really was who he said he was. My Lord.

SKULKER: You think he was some kind of god?

MARY: The God. My master.

SKULKER: Right. You know, after something like the bereavement of a close friend, some people experience a condition known as post-traumatic stress disorder. Sometimes that involves flashbacks or delusions . . .

MARY: Oh, it wasn't just me! All the disciples have seen him. He cooked fish for us and ate it. He got Thomas to feel his wounds. It wasn't a fantasy. It was him! (SKULKER's *mobile phone rings. It is* MOULDY)

MOULDY: Skulker – you've got to see this. I've just seen this doctor called Luke who's collected evidence from people all over the country about this Jesus. He was seen healing people, casting out evil spirits and even one time raising someone from the dead. I've got sworn witness statements here.

SKULKER: What? From his followers?

MOULDY: No, all sorts of people. One is a Roman centurion. Another is one of the Pharisees.

SKULKER: So what did he do wrong, Mouldy? Why did they kill him?

MOULDY: I don't know, Skulker. The trial documents have been removed from the files. But he claimed he

was the Son of God – whatever that means. I'm
going to see these disciples. (*hangs up*)

SKULKER: So, Mary. How many other people have seen
him alive?

MARY: Well, he appeared to 500 of us at one time. They
can't all have been imagining it, can they?

(MOULDY *knocks on a door.* PETER *answers furtively*)

MOULDY: Simon Peter the fisherman?

PETER: Who wants to know?

MOULDY: Mouldy. FBI. We want to talk to you about
Jesus. I've seen your friend, Dr Luke.

PETER: Come in. All the believers are gathered here. We
know the truth about Jesus. He's appeared to all
of us.

MOULDY: So why are you locked away in here?

PETER: We're scared. The authorities killed Jesus, didn't
they? What would they do to us? Look – we've
been studying these Jewish Scriptures. It's all
here about the Messiah coming, about the
wonders he will perform . . . and about his
death.

MOULDY: (*takes the documents*) You think it was meant to
be? (PETER *nods*) And rising from the dead?

PETER: That's the final proof.

VOICE: Peter! Come quick!

PETER: (*as he runs off*) What is it? (*sound of wind
blowing, fire burning and the babble of different
languages*)

MOULDY: (*as effects start, he rings* SKULKER) Skulker! Get
round here, quick. (*he looks into a dazzling light
that is being shone from offstage*) It's some kind
of supernatural phenomenon. It sounds like a
hurricane blowing through the room. But every
door and window is shut. Now there's . . .

Skulker, I don't believe this . . . it looks like each of these disciples is on fire, but they're not burning. And the looks on their faces – it's like they're in ecstasy . . . and now they're talking in all kinds of different languages . . . (*he listens for a while as voices reach their crescendo.* SKULKER *races on and pulls* MOULDY *clear. Effects die away*)

(PILATE *and* CAIAPHAS *return to the desk.* SKULKER *and* MOULDY *march in and place a file on the desk*)

PILATE: So, what's going on? Why have 3,000 people suddenly announced they want to change their religion?

SKULKER: Sir, there have been some unexplainable spiritual phenomena over the last few days in Jerusalem. It may have been the result of some kind of mass hallucination . . .

MOULDY: What I saw yesterday was no hallucination. There was a frightened bunch of fishermen and prostitutes who were transformed into preachers and theologians.

SKULKER: There were some unexplainable behavioural changes . . .

MOULDY: Sir, everything I have heard seems to suggest this man Jesus had the ability to transcend the usual rules of physics and nature. I have evidence here (*waves Luke's manuscript*) from a prominent doctor who has sworn statements from witnesses about miraculous happenings over the past three years. All I suggest is that he has become some kind of spiritual being.

CAIAPHAS: Impossible!

MOULDY: We would like permission to investigate further, sir. We already have reports that these disciples are now exhibiting some of the same supernatural gifts as their leader.

PILATE: No. There will be no more investigation. We will say the disciples stole the body and then managed to convince themselves their leader was alive again.

SKULKER: But you know that isn't true.

MOULDY: (*bangs fist on desk*) You've got to let us carry on with this investigation. What about our evidence?

PILATE: Once we've rounded up these disciples, everyone will forget about this 'evidence'. This Z-File is now closed. (*picks up the file and exits with* CAIAPHAS)

SKULKER: I can't explain any of this, Mouldy. I don't understand it – but I'm sure the truth is out there.

MOULDY: No it's not, Skulker. (*holds up Luke's Gospel*) The truth is in here. (*they freeze*)

22. The Pentecost Technique

 Aim: *Our understanding of God is so limited that we often try to put him in a box, trying to replicate the way he has worked in the past to encourage him to do so again in the future. We end up with books, pamphlets and sermons about evangelistic techniques, methods of worship or ways of summoning God's Spirit to work in power – but you can't boil down evangelism to a particular technique. Imagine what might have happened if one of the early churches had decided that you could . . .*

Cast: PETER, *the apostle, who can be represented as a bluff, plain-speaking northern fisherman;* BARTHOLO-MEW, *a more diffident, intellectual type;* OTHER DISCIPLES *can be supporting* BARTHOLOMEW. *All are dressed in clothes giving the impression of first-century Palestine.*

Props: *A big roll of parchment (or modern-day file of papers); notebook.*

(BARTHOLOMEW *is putting the finishing touches to a roll of parchment entitled 'Evangelism Strategy'. He lifts it up and flicks through it, looking pleased with himself. He can be smiling and nodding happily at* OTHER DISCIPLES *if they are there. Enter* PETER, *who is obviously on his way somewhere else)*

PETER: (*looks at him quizzically*) All right,
                  Bartholomew?

BARTHOLOMEW: (*turns and sees* PETER. *Smiles beatifically*)
                  I'm just so pleased, Simon Peter! I mean,
                  seeing so many people added to the
                  number of believers in Jerusalem. Well . . .
                  it's fantastic. And I'm sure our Lord Jesus
                  would have been very proud of you.

PETER: (*embarrassed*) It's not me, Bartholomew.
                  It's God who's doing the work.

BARTHOLOMEW: But it has been great, hasn't it? I mean,
                  since that amazing day on Pentecost, so
                  many people have started following him.

PETER: Well, we're just following instructions,
                  Bartholomew. To make disciples of all
                  nations, as he said. (*makes as if to move on*)

BARTHOLOMEW: Ah, well, that's what me and some of the
                  lads wanted to talk to you about, actually,
                  Peter.

PETER: Oh?

BARTHOLOMEW: Yes. (*looks around at* OTHER DISCIPLES *for
                  support if they are there. They signal that he
                  should say what's on his mind*) You see,
                  we're just a little concerned about this
                  business of reaching right the way to the
                  ends of earth with this gospel message.
                  We've been doing some calculations.
                  (*someone passes him a notebook*) Now, on
                  Pentecost itself, there were 3,000 people
                  baptized. Now that was a good start. But
                  since then . . . well, we haven't been quite
                  as productive, have we?

PETER: (*puzzled*) Every day the Lord adds to our
                  number!

BARTHOLOMEW: Yes, but not as many as there were to start with. Some of the disciples thought that . . . well, it was about time we had some sort of outreach strategy. Otherwise, we might not hit the target our Lord set us. You know, his four-point plan for evangelism: 'Jerusalem, Judea, Samaria, and the ends of the earth . . .'

PETER: Strategy . . . ?

BARTHOLOMEW: Yes, well, a small sub-committee of us have been working on it. (*he passes* PETER *a huge roll of parchment*) We've thrown around a few ideas and managed to put together a mission statement. And we've worked out a programme of speaking engagements for you, Peter . . .

PETER: Speaking engagements?

BARTHOLOMEW: Well, yes. (*showing* PETER *what is written on the parchment*) We realized that our most successful strategy to date was to have the Holy Spirit come in power, tongues on fire land on people's heads, and for us all to start speaking in different languages. Now, that draws a crowd of people who are amazed and can't believe what's going on. That's your chance to stand up and preach about Jesus in the town square. We thought that if we could repeat that in other significant cities around the Mediterranean over the next six months or so, then train others to do the same thing . . . well, this new religion could spread like wildfire.

PETER: But I don't want to go to other cities. I'm happy speaking to my own people.

BARTHOLOMEW: Ah. Now, we may need to tinker slightly

with the text of your speech before you start delivering it to the Gentiles.

PETER: The text of my speech? I don't even remember what I said!

BARTHOLOMEW: (*points out a section*) It's Appendix 4 of our working group's draft report, actually . . .

PETER: (*angrily*) But what I said was spontaneous! It just came out like that because we'd been touched by the Holy Spirit of God!

BARTHOLOMEW: Absolutely! And we'd like you to replicate that spontaneity throughout the Roman Empire over the next few years! Peter – you're our biggest asset! And your evangelistic method has been the most successful one we've used so far! We're thinking of publishing it under the title 'The Pentecost Technique' . . .

PETER: (*losing his patience*) It wasn't my method, Bartholomew! Haven't you remembered anything that our Lord said? He said that it was the Spirit of God that would show people that they were sinful. All we have to do is be faithful and tell others about what happened to Jesus, and live our lives in the way that he commanded us to. God will look after the rest. (*he flings the roll of parchment back at* BARTHOLOMEW)

BARTHOLOMEW: OK, OK, I get the message. (*with a hint of burning martyr*) Maybe I should try Philip. Apparently he has an outreach programme that's worked wonders among the Ethiopian eunuch community. (*they freeze*)

23. Highway Code

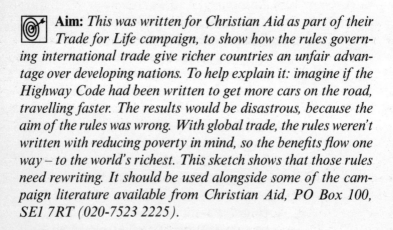

Aim: *This was written for Christian Aid as part of their Trade for Life campaign, to show how the rules governing international trade give richer countries an unfair advantage over developing nations. To help explain it: imagine if the Highway Code had been written to get more cars on the road, travelling faster. The results would be disastrous, because the aim of the rules was wrong. With global trade, the rules weren't written with reducing poverty in mind, so the benefits flow one way – to the world's richest. This sketch shows that those rules need rewriting. It should be used alongside some of the campaign literature available from Christian Aid, PO Box 100, SE1 7RT (020-7523 2225).*

Cast: ONE *and* TWO *narrate on either side of the stage. They can use scripts if necessary.* THREE *and* FOUR *(and others, if desired) act out the mime between them.*

Props: *Chair on raised platform; large sign saying 'Brand New Highway Code' or Highway Code booklet with new cover; steering wheel (optional); traffic warden's ticket/policeman's helmet; OAP's stick; cash; wine bottle/beer can; goods for poor country to sell; book of 'trade rules'.*

(ONE *and* TWO *enter and stand either side of the stage.* THREE *and* FOUR *stand between them*)

158

ONE: Welcome to our training day:

TWO: 'The Brand New Highway Code'. (THREE *and* FOUR *hold up a sign saying 'Brand New Highway Code' or a Highway Code book with a new cover*)

ONE: Now updated to help you all

TWO: Speed up and hog the road. (THREE *sits and gets out steering wheel*)

ONE: Lesson one: put your foot down. (THREE *puts his foot down hard and throws his body back in the chair as if accelerating*)

TWO: Drive as fast as you can go. (FOUR *moves his head to show a car passing quickly, and makes the noise of tyres screeching*)

ONE: Your minimum is seventy. (THREE *leans forward to show the car grinding to a halt*)

TWO: It's wrong to go too slow. (FOUR *becomes a traffic warden and gives* THREE *a ticket, or puts on policeman's helmet and wags finger at* THREE)

ONE: Lesson two: you never stop

TWO: For those that cross the street. (FOUR *becomes an OAP with a stick walking slowly in front of the car*)

ONE: Kids and OAPs should move

TWO: Or they'll become dead meat. (THREE *makes the sound of a car horn.* FOUR *leaps into the air and gets out of his way*)

ONE: Lesson three: don't stick to roads,

TWO: The pavement's yours as well. (THREE *turns the steering wheel towards* FOUR *and aims directly for him*)

ONE: Who cares if someone's in your way?

TWO: They'll never live to tell. (FOUR *pretends to have been hit and falls over dramatically*)

ONE: Lesson four: no charge for fuel!

TWO: Your petrol will be free. (THREE *gets out cash.* FOUR *springs up and shakes his head*)

ONE: You can drive across the world, (THREE *puts foot down again*)

TWO: Polluting all you see. (FOUR *is left coughing at the exhaust fumes*)

ONE: Lesson five: build bigger roads. (FOUR *pretends to be building a new road in front of the car*)

TWO: There'll be no traffic queues.

ONE: Lesson six: please drink and drive! (THREE *drinks from a bottle/beer can as he drives*)

TWO: We'll have no ban on booze!

ONE: If you think this all sounds odd,

TWO: Pedestrians aren't protected. (THREE *runs over* FOUR *again*)

ONE: Remember our aim: more fast cars,

TWO: Whoever it affected.

ONE: If you think our rules aren't right,

TWO: And that our aim is wrong,

ONE: (*contemptuously*) You should see the rules on trade, (THREE *stands up as rich country.* FOUR *crouches on the floor as poor country*)

TWO: That keep rich countries strong. (THREE *flexes muscles*)

ONE: They were made to increase trade,

TWO: Not tackle poverty. (FOUR *offers* THREE *some goods*)

ONE: *They* have got their aims all wrong,

TWO: Not my friends here and me. (THREE *shakes head and produces book of trade rules, which he brandishes at* FOUR)

ONE: If we can change the Highway Code,

TWO: Perhaps it's time to try

ONE: To change the rules of trade, because

TWO: Bad rules mean . . . people die. (FOUR *slumps to the floor.* THREE *stands on him as he exits, looking satisfied*)

24. Distracted of Tunbridge Wells

 Aim: *For many people, church can be something of a routine during which our thoughts may not be entirely focused on the God we claim to be worshipping. All of us no doubt get distracted by other things that go on around us, and the times of genuine encounter with God can be rare. Liturgy, songs, sermons and times of silence can all help to bring us closer to God, but if we recited some of the things we were really thinking during parts of the service, it might sound something like this.*

 Cast: *As many as you like!*

Props: *All the cast should have the same service book from which they are reciting.*

(ALL *stand. They recite in a flat monotone*)

ALL: I believe in God, the Father almighty,
        creator of heaven and earth . . .
        At least I think I do.
        I mean, I come to church every week and recite this
           kind of thing,
          so I must do, I suppose. (*all look to one side of the church*)
        Oh look, that nice young couple are here again this
          week.

I really must ask them later if they are interested in helping to lead Sunday School . . . his only Son, our Lord.

He was conceived by the power of the Holy Spirit, and born of the . . . (*simultaneous puzzled expression*) did I remember to turn the oven down before I came out?

Because otherwise the roast will be burnt to a cinder . . .

Crucified, died and was buried.

He descended to the . . . . (*simultaneously noticing something ahead of them*) oh look, the curate's preaching again today.

That'll be good, because the vicar does go on a bit, and I haven't read the Sunday papers yet . . .

. . . and is seated at the right hand of the Father. (*all simultaneously turn the page*)

He will come again to judge the living and the dead . . .

I don't really know what that means.

I like Jesus in the New Testament. He seems so real and human, but he also knows the right thing to say in every situation, and I wish I could have been around at the time.

I believe that I don't really deserve what Jesus did for me, because I'm so hopeless at being a Christian that I can't even concentrate on what I'm saying in church . . .

I believe in the Holy Spirit . . . though I get a bit uncomfortable with all that clapping and arm-waving . . .

The holy catholic church . . . though sometimes it drives me mad . . .

The communion of saints . . . though if people knew more about me, they wouldn't call me a saint . . .

The forgiveness of sins . . . and my only hope is that
those things that I know I do wrong all the time
have been obliterated thanks to Jesus . . .
The resurrection of the body,
And the life everlasting. Amen.

25. Beanz Meanz Thanx

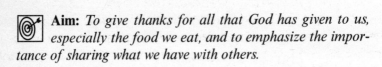

Aim: *To give thanks for all that God has given to us, especially the food we eat, and to emphasize the importance of sharing what we have with others.*

Cast: CAN OF BEANS, *who can be dressed in bright red inside some kind of cardboard tube with 'Heinz Baked Beans' written on the side, and speaks with a cultured accent;* SHEAF OF WHEAT, *who can be dressed in beige with a few bits of wheat stuck round his middle, and speaks with a rural accent;* SATSUMA, *who can be dressed in bright orange, ideally within some kind of spherical orange costume, and speaks with a Spanish accent;* VICAR, *whose voice can be spoken into a microphone offstage or recorded onto tape.*

 Props: *Other items of harvest produce; table.*

(BEANS, WHEAT *and* SATSUMA *are sitting on a table at the front of the church. If possible, they should be among all the other harvest gifts that others have brought to church*)

BEANS: (*yawns as if waking up*) I say, is it teatime yet? (*opens his eyes and looks around him and leaps up in shock*) Aargh! Where am I?

WHEAT: You're in church, mate.

BEANS: (*looking frantically around*) What am I doing here? I live in the kitchen cupboard.

WHEAT: Not any more, mate. You've been given away.

BEANS: (*amazed*) Given away! An expensive tin of beans like me!

WHEAT: Expensive? You're so cheap they're practically giving you away at Tesco's! First aisle, special offer, five tins for a pound.

BEANS: (*disgruntled*) How dare you! I wasn't bought under any special offer!

WHEAT: No, but you were at the back of the cupboard. 'For emergencies only', you were.

BEANS: Can you see this, young man? (*points out 'Heinz' label*) This means I'm a proper brand! I'm not some cheap supermarket own-label can, you know!

WHEAT: Oh yeah? Well, have you seen your 'best before' date?

BEANS: I . . . well . . . (*he strains his neck to try to read what is written on top of his head, but can't*) I can't see it from here!

WHEAT: No. Well, take it from me, mate – you're on the turn. (*he waves his hand in front of his face as if to get rid of the smell*)

BEANS: (*feeling very sorry for himself*) So what are you saying . . . ?

WHEAT: Well, just that it wasn't much of a sacrifice to bring you to the harvest festival today, that's all. Maybe you were all they could find five minutes before they came.

BEANS: (*indignant*) Well, what about you? Look at the state of you!

WHEAT: What's wrong with me?

BEANS: You're just a bit of stubble left over in the field after the farmer harvested his crops.

WHEAT: Ah, but you can make lots of things out of me! Flour, bread, biscuits, cake . . . you name it, mate,

I'm involved.

BEANS: But if we're here for the harvest festival, these church people must be giving us to some needy families and pensioners. What are they going to do with a bit of wheat . . . unless they happen to have a flour-mill in the garden? I mean, look at you – you haven't even been refined!

WHEAT: (*feeling very sorry for himself*) So what are you saying . . . ?

BEANS: Well, just that maybe you weren't so much of a sacrifice, either . . . mate! And at least I'm ready to eat!

WHEAT: Well . . . as long as they've got a tin opener . . . (*folds arms and turns away from* BEANS)

BEANS: Hmph! Well, at least I'm not covered in insects and soil . . . (*folds arms and turns away from* WHEAT)

WHEAT: (*looking over his shoulder back at* BEANS) Hmph! Well, at least I don't make people break wind . . .

SATSUMA: (*who has remained motionless until this point*) Look, will you two just shut up?

BEANS: (*turns to look at the rest of the harvest produce*) Who was that?

SATSUMA: It was me! I'm the little satsuma at the end of the table!

WHEAT: You're tiny!

BEANS: Yeah! And your skin's going a bit mouldy! (*comes over and grabs a piece of peel, which he drops on the floor in disgust*)

SATSUMA: Am I really? Oh dear, I didn't think I felt very well!

WHEAT: Yeah! (*also comes over and grabs some peel*) Look at the state of you! You're peeling already!

SATSUMA: Please stop that! (*pathetically*) I don't like it when people start taking the pith out of me!

BEANS: Whoever brought you didn't care very much about harvest!

SATSUMA: Do you really think so? I thought it was a real privilege to be laid on the table in God's house as part of the thanksgiving.

WHEAT: No, you were a real afterthought! Tell you what – if we sit with you, it will make us look really good! (WHEAT *and* BEANS *settle down next to* SATSUMA. *They look puffed up with pride, while* SATSUMA *is squashed between them feeling sorry for himself. They freeze*)

VICAR: (*as voiceover*) . . . And this, of course, is the satsuma that Susie brought. It was in her school packed lunch on Friday, but she decided to go hungry and give it to someone who needed it more than she did. Thank you, Susie. More than anyone else, you've really captured the spirit of the harvest festival.

HARVEST

26. We Plough the Fields

 Aim: *Harvest may be a good time to remind ourselves that modern intensive farming may not have done us any favours. Instead of giving thanks for the size of the harvest, perhaps we should start thinking about the quality of it.*

Cast: *The two farmers,* FARMER GILES *and* FARMER STILES, *can speak in rural accents, but should not be stereotypes. Their measured tone and the repetitions involved contrast with the seriousness of what they are saying. The* CHOIR *can be anything from two to 50 people, and should be dressed in cassocks and placed behind the farmers or to either side. In extremis, the farmers could sing the verses themselves.*

Props: *Bits of straw.*

(GILES *and* STILES *pretend to be leaning against a gate. They are chewing straw*)

STILES: How's your crop doing these days, then, Farmer Giles?

GILES: Well, it be very plentiful, Farmer Stiles, thank you for asking. Ever since I starting spraying it with pesticides to kill them weeds and them insects, I've been gathering more and more harvests every year.

STILES: That's very good, Farmer Giles. (*pause*) So you be spraying your crops with poison?

GILES: (*nods sagely*) That's right.

STILES: And that poison goes on the crops I eat?

GILES: That be right, Farmer Stiles.

STILES: Be that not a bit dangerous for my health, Farmer Giles?

GILES: That may be, Farmer Stiles. But look how plentiful the harvest is!

CHOIR: (*singing*) We plough the fields and scatter
      Pesticides on the land;
      Our crops are fed and watered
      By pharmaceutical hands.
      We spray the crops in springtime
      With drugs to swell the grain;
      And chemicals in our food
      Could make me ill again.

GILES: How are your animals doing these days, then, Farmer Stiles?

STILES: Well, they be very productive, Farmer Giles, thank you for asking. Ever since I starting feeding my dairy cows hormones and bits of other animals, they've been producing gallons and gallons of milk.

GILES: That's very good, Farmer Stiles. (*pause*) So you be feeding your cows with hormones to produce more milk, and bits of other dead animals because it's cheaper?

STILES: (*nods sagely*) That's right.

GILES: And that goes in the milk I drink and the beef I eat?

STILES: That be right, Farmer Giles.

GILES: Be that not a bit dangerous for my health, Farmer Stiles?

STILES: That may be, Farmer Giles. But look how productive those cows are!

CHOIR: (*singing*) All things bright and beautiful
      All creatures great and small –

> Our cows have eaten lots of them
> BSE has hit them all.

STILES: How are your animals doing these days, then, Farmer Giles?

GILES: Well, they be very productive, Farmer Stiles, thank you for asking. Ever since I started injecting my chickens with antibiotics to make them grow faster, they've got fatter and fatter.

STILES: That's very good, Farmer Giles. (*pause*) So your chickens are given antibiotics that kill some of the helpful bacteria inside them?

GILES: (*nods sagely*) That's right.

STILES: So that be good conditions for salmonella to spread, then?

GILES: That be right, Farmer Stiles.

STILES: Be that not a bit dangerous for my health, Farmer Giles?

GILES: That may be, Farmer Stiles. But look how fat the chickens get!

CHOIR: (*singing*) Each little egg that hatches
> Put the chick inside a crate,
> Pump it full of drugs and see –
> It's plump and on your plate.

GILES: D'you know, Farmer Stiles, they say that organic farm down the road had no BSE and no foot-and-mouth disease.

STILES: Is that right, Farmer Giles? But they don't use no pesticides or chemicals down there, do they?

GILES: That be right, Farmer Stiles. And they don't feed their cows hormones and their chickens antibiotics.

STILES: (*pause*) Seems a bit daft to me. I mean, look at the size of their harvest!

GILES: That's right. There's not much to give thanks for on their farm, is there? (*they laugh*)

CHOIR: (*singing*) We thank you, then, our Father

For all things bright and good
The seed-time and the harvest
Our life, our health, our food:
We've messed with your creation,
To get more crops and meat.
By playing God on our farms,
Who knows what's safe to eat?

All good gifts around us
Are sent from heaven itself:
Then thank the Lord,
   Oh thank the Lord
For preserving our good health!

27. Urgent Appeal

Aim: *In some ways this is a risky sketch to perform in that it uses the same kind of format as some of the organizations it is trying to help. It is not meant to satirize the aid agencies themselves, or their methods, but to make us think more carefully about our response. Many in the West have become so sanitized to these kinds of appeals that we almost need to hear what the reverse might sound like to draw our attention to the plight of the world's poorest people. To work best, it needs to be performed with absolute sincerity – and followed up well. One World Week is a good time to remind ourselves that if we all took our spending options as consumers more seriously, the injustices of poverty would be eradicated much more quickly.*

Cast: TV PRESENTER *(ideally non-white); possibly a* CAMERAMAN; *plus* SHOPPER, COMMUTER, BOY *and* BUSINESSMEN.

Props: *A mock camera (optional); designer shopping bags; mobile phone; non-designer trainers; flip chart.*

(PRESENTER *enters. He moves through the crowd of stationary British people in the same way as a TV reporter might move through a crowd of starving people in Africa. He speaks with the utmost sincerity as if to a camera just in front of him – or to a* CAMERAMAN *walking backwards with a camera)*

PRESENTER: I'm here on behalf of the Third World in the heart of leafy England to see for myself just some of the terrible conditions many of the population are living in, and why they desperately need our help. I've come here, to the high street of a typical town, to see some of the deprivation for myself. As you can see, I'm surrounded by shops that are selling only the most basic of designer clothes, luxury food and chart-topping CDs. (*kneels beside a* SHOPPER *who is clutching onto several designer shopping bags*) Some of these shoppers here have literally reached the end of their credit card limits. Can you help? Just £3.50 would buy this harassed shopper a cappuccino at her local coffee shop. Yes, that's right, just the price of a couple of blankets for a homeless Indian would get her back on her feet and feeling refreshed after a busy afternoon's shopping. So please do give generously. (*he stands again and walks on*) As you may know, economic recession hit many of the shareholders here quite hard. Some of them can barely scrape together a decent investment portfolio even now. (*stops next to* COMMUTER *in pinstriped suit who is talking silently into a mobile phone*) Could you help this man to invest a little more in companies that manufacture the landmines that cripple your family and friends? Just £200 would be enough for him to start a cash ISA so that he could benefit from not paying tax. Yes, that's right, just the price of keeping half an Afghan village fed through the winter would help him save up for the luxury yacht he needs when he retires. Ring us with your donation on the freephone number appearing on your TV screen now. (*he stands again and walks on*) Or could you sponsor a child here in England? Here's one boy who needs your help. (*kneels next to miserable-looking* BOY) He's been deprived for years of the brand-name trainers that his friends wear. I'm sure you can imagine the devastating effects of being bullied at school and taunted by his friends. Could you help? Just £70 of your money would pay for one pair of the latest trainers to hit the market. Yes, just the price of providing clean drinking water for one African village would put a smile back on his face and a logo back on his feet. (*he stands and walks on*) Or perhaps you feel that you'd like to do more. Perhaps you'd like to make a contribution to one of the global, transnational companies that desperately needs to make that last million dollars to beat last year's record profits. (*he stops near some* BUSINESSMEN *in suits scratching their heads as they examine an advertising concept on a flip chart*) If you don't act now, countless numbers of innocent advertising executives like these will lose their jobs because they haven't persuaded enough of us in the Third World to spend a year's wages on Big Macs and Nike trainers. So, go on, be generous, and pick up the phone now. We have thousands of poorly paid women and children in sweatshops around the world just waiting to take your call. Make sure that you call us – Third World Aid to England. (*he indicates all the people he has walked past*) We have literally years of experience of supporting these kinds of people. (*he smiles sincerely into the camera and walks off*)

28. Betty the Vampire Slayer

Aim: *Halloween is obviously not a Christian festival, but increasing numbers of churches are holding alternative events on Halloween to try to distract youngsters from a less-than-helpful emphasis on evil spirits and darker supernatural forces. Although such events are laudable, what seems to have been forgotten is that we have already backed the winner in any fight between supernatural forces. Rather than avoid talking about them with young people, perhaps we should emphasize that they hold no fear for us. This sketch is an attempt to show that Jesus has more power than the high-kicking heroine of any TV series.*

Cast: *The* VOICEOVER *can be read by someone offstage – using a microphone and speaking in the deep American growl of those who do film trailers;* FRED *and* VELMA *are the typically naïve victims of 'slasher' movies;* GHOST, WITCH, VAMPIRE *and* ZOMBIE *are supernatural stereotypes;* BETTY, *an older woman with a cheerful demeanour and matter-of-fact approach to spiritual warfare.*

Props: *There may be a temptation to go over the top with all sorts of special effects and make-up for the evil characters. In fact, a more light-hearted approach – with masks from a joke shop and a sheet with a hole in it – may be better for the purpose. Also needed: brown paper bag; trolley with tea cups and tea urn; tape of music.*

(*Dramatic music starts: perhaps the theme from* The Omen)

VOICEOVER: (*as melodramatically as possible*) It was just another Halloween night in Nowheresville . . . (*enter* FRED *and* VELMA, *carrying a brown paper bag of 'treats' and looking happy with their night's work*)

FRED: (*knocks on imaginary door, shouting*) Trick or treat!

VOICEOVER: . . . but when Fred and Velma knocked on the door at the end of the street, it turned into a night like no other . . . (ZOMBIE *opens door and smiles at* FRED *and* VELMA)

ZOMBIE: Come in. I think we might have something for you inside! (FRED *and* VELMA *look at each other, shrug their shoulders and enter.* ZOMBIE *slams door behind him and rubs his hands with glee. Lights are dimmed, leaving only* FRED *and* VELMA *in a spotlight surrounded by shadows*)

VOICEOVER: This Halloween night, Fred and Velma would be the treat . . . (*enter* GHOST, WITCH *and* VAMPIRE, *who move menacingly towards* FRED *and* VELMA. VELMA *holds her head in her hands and screams*)

VAMPIRE: How nice of you to pop in like this! Saves us going outside! (FRED *holds his head in his hands and starts screaming too*)

GHOST: (*hovering behind them*) Whoo! Whoo! (VELMA *turns and sees* GHOST *and starts screaming even louder*)

FRED: (*grabs her by the arm to calm her down, then shouts*) Velma! We've got to get out of here! (*all freeze*)

VOICEOVER: It was time for a new kind of hero. Someone who would laugh in the face of evil. Someone who would kick the spirits out of Halloween

House. It was time for . . . Betty, the Vampire Slayer! (*dramatic music stops suddenly. Lights go on full. Enter* BETTY, *an older woman, pushing a trolley with teacups and a tea urn. She is humming 'At the Name of Jesus', or another hymn*)

VAMPIRE: Aaarrgghh! Not Betty! (VAMPIRE, GHOST, WITCH *and* ZOMBIE *hold their heads in their hands and scream in the same way as* VELMA *and* FRED *did*)

BETTY: (*holding out a tea cup*) Cup of tea, anyone? (VAMPIRE, GHOST, WITCH *and* ZOMBIE *all run off, still screaming*)

FRED: (*takes cup of tea*) Thanks for saving us, Betty! But why did they run away?

BETTY: Ah well, young man. That's because at the name of Jesus, every knee must bow.

VELMA: Huh?

BETTY: (*as she leads them off*) Don't you go to church, young lady? You'll find out there what I'm talking about. Evil spirits don't stand a chance when you pray in Jesus' name . . .

VOICEOVER: Betty the tea lady stars in the new production of *Betty the Vampire Slayer*. Rated PG. See your local parish church for details.

29. No Greater Love

 Aim: *It might seem odd to perform drama on Remembrance Sunday. Indeed, something humorous would be entirely inappropriate. But if this sketch, about the true story of Father Maximilian Kolbe, is performed sensitively, it should add to the occasion. It draws together two strands – the remembrance of those who died to preserve freedom during wars, and the example of Jesus who died in our place. This sketch would also be appropriate for a Good Friday service or a service on the 14th August, Maximilian Kolbe's feast day.*

Cast: GAJOWNICEK *(pronounced Ga-jow-ni-check), who narrates most of the sketch, and can be dressed in modern-day costume;* KOLBE *(pronounced Col-bee),* PRISONER 1, PRISONER 2 *and others who are dressed in rags with enamel mugs hanging from their belts and need to look slightly undernourished;* KROTT, *an SS man, and other* GUARDS, *who need to have at least the impression of a soldier's uniform, if not the full Nazi regalia. Given the subject matter, they should avoid German accents and speak normally, but crisply.*

Props: *Planks; stones; soup in a tureen; bowls; bread; cutlery; tape recording of whipping noise (optional).*

(PRISONERS *enter carrying planks or stones on their backs.* GUARDS *watch them at work, cajoling them and hitting some of them so they fall over. They struggle to get up again until* GUARDS *force them to do so.* PRISONER 2 *remains on the ground*)

GAJOWNICEK: Auschwitz, 1941. The largest death camp built by the Nazis, where several million Jews and Catholics are put to death. Hitler's objective: in his hatred for Jesus Christ, he wants to remove all witnesses to the revelation of the God of Israel and those who believed he was born of the Virgin Mary. When they enter Auschwitz, prisoners are told that Jews will only live for two weeks, Catholic priests for one month. Into this hell steps a Polish priest, Father Maximilian Kolbe. (*enter* KOLBE, *running steadily with a plank on his back. Nazi guard* KROTT *is snarling behind him*)

KROTT: Faster, Kolbe! Run faster! You lazy, good-for-nothing piece of Polish scum. Do you believe in Christ?

KOLBE: I do. (KROTT *hits him and* KOLBE *falls to the ground.* KROTT *spits on him*)

KROTT: I said, 'Do you believe in Christ?'

KOLBE: I do. (KROTT *kicks him in the stomach.* KOLBE *doubles up in pain*)

KROTT: Get up! (*to one of the* GUARDS) Give him 50 lashes! (GUARDS *drag him off. The sound of whipping can be heard – either as a sound effect on tape, or created live by hitting a wall with a belt. We hear* KOLBE's *screams.* KROTT *stalks off*)

GAJOWNICEK: Kolbe is singled out for ill treatment by the guards. He is made to do useless work at running pace, even though he has severe tuberculosis and only one lung. (*one of the*

GUARDS *has brought in a bowl of watery-looking soup, while another has a tiny amount of bread.* KOLBE *staggers back in*)

GUARD: (*shouts*) Your food is here. (*All but one of the* PRISONERS *push each other to get there first.* PRISONER 2 *is still lying on the ground, where he has been pushed.* KOLBE *graciously allows each of the* PRISONERS *to go ahead of him to get to their food*)

PRISONER 1: Father, you must eat! We are all like skeletons here.

KOLBE: Every man has an aim in life. For most men, it is to return home to their wives and families. For my part, I give my life for the good of all men. (KOLBE *is finally served. He takes the small amount he has and gives it to* PRISONER 2. GUARDS *start to clear up and exit*)

GAJOWNICEK: People gather in secret to hear his words of love and encouragement. (PRISONERS *gather round* KOLBE *as he feeds the soup and bread to* PRISONER 2)

KOLBE: The real conflict is the inner conflict. Beyond armies of occupation and extermination camps, there are two irreconcilable enemies in the depths of every soul: good and evil, sin and love. And what use are the victories on the battlefield if we ourselves are defeated in our innermost personal selves? Love is the key. (*he continues talking to them silently*)

GAJOWNICEK: In a place where hunger and hatred reigns, Maximilian Kolbe opens his heart and speaks of God's infinite love. (PRISONER 1 *has come to stand alongside* GAJOWNICEK)

PRISONER 1: (*directly to the audience*) Every time I see Father Kolbe in the courtyard, I feel an extraordinary sense of his goodness. Although he wears the same ragged clothes as the rest of us, with the same tin can hanging from his belt, I forget his wretched exterior and I am conscious only of his inspired countenance and radiant holiness. (*he turns to join the others. Enter* KROTT *and* GUARDS, *angrily pushing* PRISONERS *away from* KOLBE)

KROTT: Line yourselves up for roll call! Quickly! Quickly! (PRISONERS *shuffle together in a line.* GUARDS *stand to attention behind the line.* KROTT *paces up and down the line, but speaks slowly and menacingly*) Three of your fellow prisoners have escaped from the camp. This is a very bad mistake. You know the rule. It means we have to kill some of you. You, you and you will be taken to the starvation bunker. (*points at three* PRISONERS. GUARDS *push the selected* PRISONERS *forward. They include* PRISONER 2)

PRISONER 2: (*falls to his knees shaking and crying*) Oh, my poor wife, my poor children. I shall never see them again. (KOLBE *kneels beside him and puts his arm round him*)

KROTT: (*screams at* PRISONER 2) Get up!

KOLBE: (*stands and speaks directly to* KROTT) Sir, I will take this man's place.

KROTT: (*looks at* KOLBE *in astonishment. Then with suspicion*) What is this? (*then shrugs his shoulders*) What difference does it make to us who dies? (*nods at the* GUARDS) To the bunker. (GUARDS *lead off the selected* PRISONERS, *including* KOLBE. PRISONER 2 *is left on the floor sobbing. The remaining* PRISONERS *exit.*

The stage now becomes the starvation bunker.
GUARDS *bring in* KOLBE *and the selected* PRIS-
ONERS *and throw them to the ground.* GUARDS
exit)

GAJOWNICEK: In their cell, Father Kolbe leads the men in
               prayers and songs.

(KOLBE *kneels and starts to recite prayers.* PRISONERS *join in*)

KOLBE/PRISONERS: Hail Mary, Mother of God, blessed art
                   thou above all women . . .

GAJOWNICEK: Fervent prayers sound in all the corridors.
               Soon men from other cells are joining in.

KOLBE/PRISONERS: Our Father, who art in heaven, hallowed
                   be thy name . . . (*enter* KROTT)

GAJOWNICEK: They are often so deep in prayer that they do
               not even hear when visitors come to their
               bunker.

KROTT: (*shouting over the top of the prayers*) Shut up!
               Stop your praying!

PRISONERS: (*moving towards him on their knees, hands
               outstretched*) Please give us food! We need
               some food! (KROTT *kicks one of them over
               onto the ground and exits*)

GAJOWNICEK: Father Kolbe does not beg, but helps raise
               the spirits of others. Two weeks pass in this
               way. By now, prayers are only being whis-
               pered because the men are so weak. (PRISON-
               ERS *are all lying on the floor, apart from* KOLBE
               *who is kneeling in the centre of them. He
               touches one on the shoulder to see how he is*)
               One after another they die, until only Father
               Kolbe is left. The authorities feel this has
               gone on for too long. They need the cell for
               other prisoners. (*enter* KROTT *with one*
               GUARD *who has a syringe.* KOLBE *crosses
               himself and offers his arm to the* GUARD. *The*

GUARD *gives him the injection*) Father Kolbe dies with a prayer on his lips, and an anticipation of heaven. (KOLBE'*s head slumps to one side, but he still looks calm and radiant. Exit* KROTT *and* GUARD) In that desert of hatred, he has shown love. His life and death are like a powerful shaft of light in the dark hellhole of that camp. In 1971, Maximilian Kolbe is beatified. Like his master, Jesus Christ, he had loved his fellow men to the point of sacrificing his life for them. (*takes a step forward*) I was that man who should have died: I am non-commissioned officer Franciszek Gajownicek. Now I know the meaning of that phrase: 'Greater love has no one than this: that he lay down his life for his friends.' (*pause. Exit solemnly*)

Special Services and Other Events

30. Cocktail Party

Aim: *To show how we live in a society with a pick'n'mix attitude towards religion – and how uncompromising the real gospel message is. This could also be performed at a normal Holy Communion service to emphasize the importance of the bread and wine.*

Cast: *Smooth-talking* BARMAN; *middle-aged couple* GEORGE *and* MILDRED; *flashy businessman* GORDON (*and optional friend*); TWO CHRISTIANS *of the charismatic variety; cynical regular drinker* DAVE; *radical Christian* RICHARD *and offstage* VOICE.

Props: *A long table, set at a 45-degree angle to the audience, and designed to look like a bar. On it are beer mats, towels, glasses, cocktail shakers and bottles of drinks. Also needed: bar stools, tables, chairs; Communion wine.*

(*The* BARMAN *is standing behind the cocktail bar. He is wiping the bar with a towel when* GEORGE *and* MILDRED *enter*)

BARMAN: Hi there! What can I get you?

MILDRED: Oh, well, I don't really know. I've never been to one of these religious bars before. What kinds of things do you sell?

BARMAN: Drinks for the discerning, madam. We're licensed to sell a wide selection of intoxicating religious ideas neatly blended together to form your very own personal philosophy. What's your poison?

MILDRED: (*looks around indecisively*) I don't know. What are you having, George?

GEORGE: Pint of agnostics, please. (BARMAN *starts to pull his pint*)

MILDRED: Agnostics? What's in that?

GEORGE: Well, no one really knows, love. But it's what everyone else at work has. (BARMAN *gives* GEORGE *his pint*)

MILDRED: Well, I've always been Church of England, I think . . .

BARMAN: (*sharp intake of breath, then tut-tuts*) You don't want to try that, madam.

MILDRED: Why not? I always have a little tipple every Christmas.

BARMAN: (*looks around to see if anyone is listening, then speaks quietly*) The truth is, madam, that we seem to be able to water down the Anglican beer as much as we like . . . and no one ever seems to notice! (*enter* GORDON *in trendy suit, with a friend if possible. He goes straight to the bar*)

GORDON: (*flashing a fiver*) I say, barman, can I have a couple of New Age cocktails when you're ready, eh? Good man!

MILDRED: Ooh, that sounds exciting! What's in that?

BARMAN: (*gets out his cocktail shaker*) Well, a bit of every-thing. (*putting in a dash from each bottle as he speaks*) Some earth-worship, a bit of meditation and a dash of Christian morality – that's your usual, isn't it?

GORDON: Er . . . yes. Actually, we're rather getting into aromatherapy at the moment, so can you make sure that cherry smells nice, eh?

BARMAN: See – you can have anything you like in this one.
           (*he puts the lid on and starts shaking*)

MILDRED: Oh yes. I'll have one of those, please, George.
           (GEORGE *stumps up the cash reluctantly as*
           BARMAN *pours* GORDON's *drinks and does
           another for* MILDRED. TWO CHRISTIANS *stagger
           across the stage leaning on each other drunkenly
           and singing worship songs at the tops of their
           voices before exiting.* GORDON *moves off with his
           drinks*)

GEORGE: What's up with them?

BARMAN: Oh, just ignore them. They've been on Holy
           Spirits all night. (GEORGE *and* MILDRED *go and sit
           at one of the tables. Enter* DAVE, *who wanders
           morosely up to the bar*) What's wrong with you,
           Dave?

DAVE: Well, you know, Ted. I've tried everything you've
           got, and I don't really like the taste of any of it.

BARMAN: What about that beer you tried last time?

DAVE: What – the Pentecostal pint? Did you see the size
           of the head on that? It was all froth and no doc-
           trine!

BARMAN: Bitter?

DAVE: You bet I am! Those charismatics have a lot to
           answer for!

BARMAN: How about the Methodist ale?

DAVE: (*shakes his head*) Not enough life in it for me. It
           didn't go well with the reincarnation chaser. Just
           give me a double sceptic, will you? (BARMAN
           *pours him a spirit which he knocks straight back
           as* RICHARD *comes to the bar*)

BARMAN: Anything else?

DAVE: No thanks. Once you've had one of those, all the
           others taste the same.

RICHARD: Listen, I've got some brilliant stuff here – you've got to try it! (*he gets out a couple of bottles of red wine*)

DAVE: Oh yeah?

RICHARD: In fact, everyone, the drinks are on me! Have a taste of this! (*he pours wine into* DAVE's *empty glass and starts to pour it into everyone else's as they gather round. General murmurs of approval from the assembled drinkers, who look at it, smell it, and are just about to drink it when . . .*)

BARMAN: (*looking at the label on the other bottle*) What is it? Communion wine? (*all freeze as voiceover comes from someone offstage*)

VOICE: This is my blood, shed for you and for many for the forgiveness of sins. Drink this in remembrance of me.

GEORGE: Er, no thanks, mate. I think this stuff's a bit strong for us. (*he and* MILDRED *leave*)

GORDON: (*still smelling the bouquet*) I say, it's a rather cheeky vintage, eh? How long has this been fermenting? (*he takes a sip*)

RICHARD: About two thousand years.

GORDON: (*nearly coughs it up again*) By Jove! I bet this costs a fair bit!

RICHARD: It costs you everything you've got. But it never runs out.

DAVE: (*taking a sip*) Hey, it tastes all right, this. Where do you get it from?

RICHARD: (*points out of a window*) It's that off-licence across the road.

DAVE: What? But isn't this the only drink they sell over there?

RICHARD: That's right. (*he holds up the bottle*) It's either this or nothing.

31. Keeping the Faith

Aim: *To show how many people view sport as their true religion – and how easily that faith can let them down. The script was originally written in 1992 and has been constantly updated since then to reflect recent events. This version dates from the 2002 World Cup (when, interestingly, commentators were hailing Sven-Goran Eriksson as a modern-day Messiah) and may need to be updated. It has also been adapted for club sides (worshipping Eric Cantona, Alan Shearer and others), for rugby fans (Martin Johnson), and could even be used to comment on the annual act of faith we place in Tim Henman to win Wimbledon. Obviously the name (David Beckham) can be replaced by other suitable options. It may also be appropriate to make it plain at some point during the occasion of your performance that this sketch is about* us *and* our *reactions, not about the celebrities themselves, who may or may not appreciate the 'worship' we give them.*

Cast: ONE *and* TWO, *both male football supporters wearing England football shirts, scarves – anything they can lay their hands on.*

Props: *As much England stuff as you can get; poster of David Beckham.*

(ONE *and* TWO *walk in dressed in football kit*)

ONE: (*speaking in the style of a religious revival meeting*)
         Brothers and sisters. You are joining us for a religious
         experience. Is that right, brother?

TWO: It surely is, brother.

ONE: We have come here to honour the Mighty One, the
         Everlasting One, the Great and Most Blessed, the
         Saviour of England's chances in World Cup qualifi-
         cation . . . . David Beckham. (*he unfurls the poster of
         Beckham. Both kneel and worship*)

TWO: Oh Mighty David Beckham! Oh gracious captain of
         England!

ONE: Every England match, we go to the tabernacle and
         worship the sacred turf he steps on.

TWO: We sing our chants: (*in choirboy style*) 'There's one
         David Beckham!'

ONE: The Ever-Faithful Beckham steps onto the pitch with
         his ten disciples – Seaman, Neville, Campbell,
         Ferdinand, Cole, Gerrard, Scholes, Sinclair, Owen
         and Heskey. [*or whatever the latest England team is*]

TWO: He surely does, brother!

ONE: We pray that he will grant us forgiveness when we
         doubt that he will one day win us the World Cup.

TWO: Praise his name! We ask that he would grant us eter-
         nal qualification for the European Championships.

ONE: Hallelujah! But most of all, we thank him for the 5–1
         victory over the evil powers and dominions they call
         . . . Germany.

TWO: Amen! And any who doubt his power shall be thrown
         into the kingdom of Scotland, where they never get
         past the first round and there is much wailing and
         gnashing of teeth.

ONE: There was a time when I did not believe. I was lost
         and without hope before the days of Captain
         Beckham. I followed England under Kevin Keegan.

TWO: Preach it, brother!

ONE: But then I saw the light! I saw him score in the last minute against Greece, and I felt the power of Beckham flow right into my heart! I saw him tuck away the penalty that beat Argentina, and I was overwhelmed with love for him.

TWO: I knew then that those fantastic crosses from the right wing . . . he did it for me!

ONE: Those supernatural free kicks which bend unerringly into the top corners of the goal . . . he did them all for me!

TWO: We feel the presence of David Beckham here with us this evening, giving us the strength to proclaim that the European Championships in 2004 will be ours.

ONE: We can feel that power helping us when we are down.

TWO: Helping us get over those bad times like when we were beaten by a freak Brazilian free kick in the World Cup quarter-finals.

ONE: (*rising to a crescendo*) The Ever-Faithful David Beckham. He will never let us down. He will always be there to save us from the Argentinas, the Nigerias and the Swedens of this world. He will grant us success in the European Championships and help us bring home the trophy from Portugal.

TWO: (*pause, looks at* ONE *and says matter-of-factly*) Well, unless it goes to penalties again. (*they freeze*)

32. Heart Failure

 Aim: *To show how a healthy spiritual life can have other good side effects. Every corny joke is hugely overplayed – the idea being that the audience's groans grow louder and louder. This is an adaptation of another sketch, the original script for which has long since disappeared. Thanks to the author, whoever you are, and apologies for taking liberties!*

Cast: *Brusque* DOCTOR; *worried* PATIENT; NURSE.

Props: *Piles of boxes; hunk of stale bread; packet of sliced Mother's Pride; another packet of bread; packet of crumpets; copies of the* Independent, *the* Guardian, *the* Sun, *the* Mail on Sunday, *the* Observer, *the* Mirror, *local newspaper (if it fits the joke!); cuttings of crosswords; bottle of milk which has gone off; hammer to test reflexes; bars of Galaxy, Fruit'n'Nut, Snickers, Boost, Milky Way and other chocolate bars; stethoscope; two chairs and table.*

(PATIENT *staggers on with a pile of boxes*)

DOCTOR: Yes? What seems to be the problem?

PATIENT: (*weakly*) I'm . . . er . . . having trouble with my relationships.

DOCTOR: Relationships? Which ones?

PATIENT: Well, all of them, really.

DOCTOR: Come on then, let's take a look. (PATIENT *gets one*

of the boxes out and hands it to the DOCTOR)
What's this one? Relationship with your wife?

PATIENT: Er . . . yes. (DOCTOR *picks out loaf of Mother's Pride*)

DOCTOR: Hmm, well, it looks as though you thought she was the best thing since sliced bread!

PATIENT: Well, I did, doctor. (*takes bread from* DOCTOR) When I first met her, I could tell she was her Mother's Pride. (*takes second loaf from the box and holds both up in turn*) I stuck with her through thick and thin, but . . . erm . . . it's all gone a bit (*bangs hunk of stale bread against the table*) stale between us.

DOCTOR: (*takes one loaf back*) Well, use your loaf, man! You could always have buttered her up!

PATIENT: I know, doctor. I'm afraid I just let it fester for so long that our marriage went a bit mouldy. (DOCTOR *drops loaf in disgust*) You see, the real problem was that I didn't really want her. I always fancied a bit of crumpet. (*produces packet of crumpets from box*)

DOCTOR: Oh well, that explains it, then. (*takes another box and pulls out lots of newspapers*) Who's this relationship with?

PATIENT: Oh, er . . . that's with my mum and dad. We've always argued with each other, ever since I was a teenager.

DOCTOR: Don't tell me (*holds up newspapers in turn*) – you wanted to be *Independent*, but because you were the *Sun*, they always wanted to be your *Guardian*.

PATIENT: That's right. (*holds up more newspapers in turn*) I always thought my mum was having an affair with another man when my dad went to church. There was always a different *Mail on Sunday* – I

know because I used to *Observer* in the *Mirror*!
And my dad didn't pay me too much attention.
When he came in from work every night, he'd
always just fall asleep in his armchair.

DOCTOR: Ah! You mean he liked to have his *Manchester Evening Snooze*? [*adapt for local newspaper, if possible*]

PATIENT: Yes, and all we've done is exchange (*pulls out crossword cuttings*) cross words ever since.

DOCTOR: Hmm, that sounds very serious. What about this one? (*he picks up another box*)

PATIENT: That's my relationship with my boss at work. (DOCTOR *takes out a milk bottle and looks closely at it*)

DOCTOR: Well, this doesn't look too bad at all. (*points at it*) He obviously thought you had a lotta bottle. Did he see you as the cream of the new recruits?

PATIENT: (*takes milk bottle*) Well, he did until I had this massive row . . . (*pours out milk, which is lumpy and obviously a few days old into box*) and then it all went sour between us. I tried to milk him for as much money as I could, but after that our relationship just evaporated.

DOCTOR: This isn't looking good, I'm afraid.

PATIENT: It's not terminal, is it?

DOCTOR: Well, let me test your reflexes. (*he gets out his hammer and taps* PATIENT *on the knee as he says each thing*) What do you say if your best friend needs someone to talk to?

PATIENT: (*as if it were an automatic response*) 'Sorry, I'm busy at the moment.'

DOCTOR: Or if your children want you to read them a story?

PATIENT: 'Go to bed – I'm watching the television.'

DOCTOR: No, I'm afraid you seem to have no feeling left

inside you at all. There must be someone you get on with.

PATIENT: (*offers a big box*) Well, there's this one.

DOCTOR: Who's this one with?

PATIENT: Er . . . well . . .

DOCTOR: (*looks inside box*) Oh, I see – you have a relationship with yourself! Quite a big relationship, if I may say so!

PATIENT: Well, I don't suffer from lack of self-esteem.

DOCTOR: (*pulls out bars of chocolate, holding up those mentioned in turn*) Yes, I can see you were quite sweet on yourself. You probably thought you were the best person in the Galaxy, didn't you? Didn't people think you were a Fruit'n'Nutcase?

PATIENT: (*also holding up chocolate bars in turn*) Well, people used to laugh at me, but I would ignore their Snickers behind my back and give myself a real Boost by telling myself I was the best thing in the whole Milky Way! I couldn't help it – I just had a real soft centre for myself!

DOCTOR: (*pours out the rest of the chocolate bars*) It was a very unhealthy relationship you had! Not a pretty sight! I'd say all this was a major blockage to your heart working properly! (PATIENT *suddenly starts shaking uncontrollably as if having a heart attack*) Nurse! Nurse! (NURSE *runs on quickly*) I think he's arresting! (PATIENT *slumps in his chair.* DOCTOR *and* NURSE *try to revive him, but don't succeed*) Quick – call the crash team!

NURSE: (*runs to side of stage and shouts*) Crash! Come quick!

DOCTOR: (*takes* PATIENT's *pulse*) No, don't bother – I think we've lost him. (DOCTOR *puts a stethoscope to* PATIENT's *chest*)

NURSE: Was it another relationship failure, doctor?

DOCTOR: Yes, his heart had gone completely cold! He just lost the will to love. A complete breakdown in all meaningful communication.

NURSE: But why did it happen, doctor?

DOCTOR: In very severe cases like this, there's only one cause. Heart failure. (*he reaches for a small box that hasn't been examined yet, opens it and turns it over. It is empty*) Ah! It's just as I thought: this was his relationship with God.

(*all freeze*)

33. In at the Deep End

 Aim: *To show how important it is for us to take that step of faith and commit ourselves to following Christ. Some may think that all they have to do is believe the right things, others may think that it is just about turning up at church, and others may think that they are not good enough to be Christians. What some may need to realize is that at some point they have to take the plunge – and that this decision is in their own hands.*

Cast: *Calm, assured* SWIMMING INSTRUCTOR, *who can be wearing jogging bottoms and a T-shirt which says 'Instructor'; nervous first-timer* KEVIN, *who can be wearing a ridiculous-looking swimming costume, arm bands, rubber rings and the like. Baptist churches may be able to stage the sketch at the edge of their baptistry!*

Props: *One chair; rubber rings; arm bands.*

(KEVIN *lies on the chair, pretending to do front crawl, while the* INSTRUCTOR *looks on*)

INSTRUCTOR:	(*as if for the hundredth time*) So . . . you've got that now? Kick with the feet and bring the arm over.
KEVIN:	Right. (*he tries it*)
INSTRUCTOR:	And you've got the hang of the breathing?

KEVIN: Yes. (*he tries moving his head to breathe as he brings each arm over*)

INSTRUCTOR: That's it! Great!

KEVIN: (*gets off the chair*) Well, thanks for teaching me how to swim. I feel a lot safer now. (*he holds out a hand to shake* INSTRUCTOR's *hand*)

INSTRUCTOR: Hold on! You haven't been in yet!

KEVIN: Well, that's OK. You've told me what to do.

INSTRUCTOR: Yes, but you actually need to experience what it's like in the water.

KEVIN: (*as if that had never occurred to him*) Do I?

INSTRUCTOR: Yes! You can't be a real swimmer until you've actually swum in the pool!

KEVIN: But I come to swimming lessons every week. Isn't that enough?

INSTRUCTOR: No, Kevin. Just being in the leisure centre doesn't make you a swimmer.

KEVIN: Well, I believe in swimming, and in everything you've taught me. Isn't that enough?

INSTRUCTOR: If you really believed it, there wouldn't be a problem about getting in, would there?

KEVIN: (*inches towards the pool and looks in*) But I just wanted to know the basics – you know, in case of emergencies. I'm not sure I want to get wet every time I come here. What about if I dipped a toe in?

INSTRUCTOR: (*shakes his head and speaks gently*) At some point you're going to have to take the plunge, Kevin. You know all there is to know about swimming on dry land. Now you need to put it into practice.

KEVIN: OK, OK. (*he starts preparing himself to jump in, then stops and cowers back behind the chair*) But I'm scared. I'm not a real swimmer like you. I'm not dedicated enough. I don't swim for half an hour before breakfast every day like you. And I don't revise my diving techniques before I go to bed.

INSTRUCTOR: Kevin, you only have to start with a few minutes of swimming every week. That'll help you become a better swimmer.

KEVIN: (*grasping at straws*) But I still have some questions about the buoyancy of water. I need to have absolute proof that the water will hold me up if I jump in. And I haven't resolved yet whether I believe more in breast-stroke or butterfly!

INSTRUCTOR: (*gently*) That's fine, Kevin. Lots of people have those kinds of doubts, but they get into the water anyway, in faith that they will float. And do you know what? I've never known anyone sink to the bottom.

KEVIN: Well, maybe I'm just not the swimming type. Can't I just stay here and watch other people swimming?

INSTRUCTOR: You can, Kevin. But I think you need to try it for yourself.

KEVIN: (*getting agitated*) Why do I need to do it myself? Give me one good reason why I can't just walk out of here and never set foot inside a swimming complex ever again!

INSTRUCTOR: (*slowly and deliberately*) Because it might just save your life.

34. The Full Treatment

 Aim: *To show how we often have unquestioning faith in doctors, yet are sometimes very sceptical of more spiritual ways of treating illnesses.*

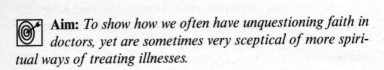 **Cast:** *Believer* SARAH *and doubting* PAUL *are a couple. The* DOCTOR *is an efficient professional.*

Props: *A dressing; a couple of chairs to represent a waiting area; a GP's desk and chair to represent his office (optional).*

(SARAH *drags* PAUL *on. He is holding his arm*)

SARAH: Come on! Get in here and stop complaining!

PAUL: Don't pull me, Sarah!

SARAH: Paul, you've injured your arm. You need to see a doctor. If you don't get treatment, it will just get worse.

PAUL: You know I don't believe in any of this medicine stuff.

SARAH: Look, we've tried everything else and it hasn't worked. We're just going to have to have faith that the doctor can do something. (*she sits down.* PAUL *starts pacing around*)

PAUL: But that's just it – I haven't got any faith in him. I'm not like you, Sarah. I don't go to hospital every week. I'm not a practising NHS patient and I've never committed my life into a surgeon's hands.

SARAH: That doesn't matter, Paul. The doctor accepts you into his surgery whatever you're like. And you know what it says in the Patients' Charter . . .

PAUL: Years ago people believed everything their doctors said, but we're more sophisticated these days. Some of them don't really know what's wrong with you. Sometimes their diagnoses are more like guesswork. So how can you believe they'll heal me?

SARAH: It does happen, Paul! I've seen it!

PAUL: Remember, I did come here once before hoping to get healed. When I had that infection.

SARAH: Yeah? So?

PAUL: Don't you remember what happened? I went forward into the consulting room, the doctor laid hands on me, talked some mumbo-jumbo and then said I'd be all right.

SARAH: Mm?

PAUL: Well, there was no instant healing then, was there? I had to keep taking this medicine for the next few weeks!

SARAH: Yes, well, sometimes he can do something straight away, and sometimes it takes a while for the healing to happen.

PAUL: No. Coincidence, that's all it was. You can't tell me that his diagnosis and those antibiotics did anything for me. It was just a natural process.

SARAH: Rubbish. Listen, I had a friend who we brought to this surgery with a dislocated shoulder. The doctor saw her and it was healed instantly. One minute it was all bent and twisted, the next it was all back in place.

PAUL: I'm sorry, Sarah. I just think it's all a lot of emotional hype. It's all in the mind, you know. (*enter* DOCTOR)

DOCTOR: OK, who's next?

SARAH: Come on, Paul. Let's go forward to the front of the surgery and see if the doctor can help.

PAUL: (*pause, then sighs*) OK – but I warn you, it won't work! (*they approach the* DOCTOR)

DOCTOR: Right. What seems to be the problem?

PAUL: It's . . . erm . . . it's my arm, doctor.

DOCTOR: (*feels it*) Yes, I think this arm could be broken.

SARAH: That's amazing, doctor! It's almost supernatural how you knew that.

DOCTOR: So I'll just put on a clean dressing, put your arm in plaster and then give you a sling.

SARAH: You see, Paul! He had a 'word' for you! And that's *so* relevant to your situation!

PAUL: (*slightly impressed*) OK, go on then. (*the* DOCTOR *takes a dressing and starts wrapping it around* PAUL's *arm. Before he can finish,* PAUL *tries to move his arm again*) Ow! It still hurts!

DOCTOR: But I haven't finished . . .

PAUL: (*starts to move away from the* DOCTOR) What a fraud! Right, I'm going to get this treated properly!

SARAH: What do you mean?

PAUL: I'm going to church to get someone to pray for me!

HEALING SERVICE

35. The Mask

Aim: *Many of us, both inside and outside the church, are plagued by low self-esteem, but rarely admit it. Tragically, that can lead many people to think of themselves as unworthy of God's love, but they put on some kind of 'front' to suggest that everything is fine – even with fellow Christians. A good way to express this dramatically is through the use of masks. This piece was developed from an anonymous poem entitled 'The Mask'. Because of the subject matter, it may work best during a service in which you have a team of people on hand to pick up the pieces and pray for those who would like to face feelings of inadequacy.*

Cast: NARRATOR; MAN; GOD. MAN *and* GOD *both can be either male or female. Both can be dressed similarly in black, or* GOD *can be dressed in white. It doesn't matter whether people realize that* GOD *is supposed to be God, as the poem works equally well if people assume that the character is simply someone else who will love them for what they really are.*

Props: *Three masks, each with a different expression – perhaps a neutral expression on one, a smiling face on another and a laughing face. It can be done with just one mask if that is all you have. Atmospheric music can also be played during the sketch.*

205

(MAN *walks into the centre of the stage, wearing his first mask, and drops his head*)

NARRATOR: Don't be fooled by me. (MAN *lifts head and looks at the audience*)

Don't be fooled by the face I wear.

For I wear a mask. (MAN *starts to walk around, looking as if he hasn't a care in the world*)

A mask that I'm afraid to take off. A mask that isn't me. (MAN *waves amiably to people as he passes them*)

Pretending is an art that's second nature to me. (MAN *starts to slow down, and raises his hands slowly to his head. He freezes in a pose that signifies despair*)

But don't be fooled. For God's sake, don't be fooled!

(*pause*)

I give you the impression that I am secure, (MAN *leaps back into life. He is now at church or at a party, shaking people's hands*)

That confidence is my name and competence is my game,

That the water is calm, and I'm in command, and that I need no one. (MAN *laughs heartily at a joke someone has made. He laughs so much that his body starts to shake and he brings his hand up to his mouth*)

But please don't believe. Please. (*the laugh dies and turns into a sob as he turns away from the people. His body is still shaking, but this time from the tears.* MAN *ends up on his knees, turned away from the audience. Pause*)

(*enter* GOD. *He approaches the front of the stage and looks at* MAN. MAN *hasn't seen him*)

Beneath my mask lies the real me. (MAN *starts to take first mask off slowly, with his back to* GOD *and side on to the audience. Underneath we catch a glimpse of a despairing face*)

In confusion, in fear, in loneliness. (MAN *sees* GOD *behind him*)

But I hide this. I don't want anyone to know this. (MAN *quickly puts his second mask on – or replaces his original mask – with his back to* GOD. GOD *turns away from him, respecting the fact that* MAN *is embarrassed*)

I panic at the thought of my weakness and fear being exposed.

That's why I create a mask to hide behind, (MAN *turns back to face* GOD *and checks that his mask is in place. He shakes hands with* GOD *and makes as if to move on*)

A nonchalant, sophisticated façade to help me pretend,

To shield me from the glance (GOD *looks straight at* MAN. MAN *is stopped in his tracks and freezes*) that knows,

But such a glance is precisely my salvation,

My only salvation.

And I know it. (MAN *is still frozen in fear.* GOD *approaches him*)

That is, if it's followed by acceptance, if it's followed by love. (GOD *puts his arm around* MAN. MAN *tenses up even more*)

It's the only thing that can assure me of what I can't assure myself –

That I'm really worth something.

But I don't tell you this. I'm afraid to. (MAN

suddenly pushes GOD *away.* GOD *ends up back in the position he was when he 'glanced' at* MAN)
I'm afraid your glance will not be followed by acceptance and love. (MAN *turns away angrily from* GOD)
I'm afraid that you'll think less of me, that you'll laugh at me. (GOD *tries to approach again, but* MAN *waves him away*)
And your laugh would kill me.
I'm afraid that deep down, I'm nothing, I'm no good, and you will see this and reject me. (MAN *crouches down again and takes off second mask. He puts on a third mask. Pause*)

And so begins the parade of masks, and my life becomes a front. (MAN *turns to the audience and starts gesticulating confidently, as if in conversation*)
I idly chatter to you in the suave tones of surface talk.
(GOD *watches* MAN *and looks at whoever* MAN *is talking to*)
I tell you everything that's really nothing,
And nothing of what's really everything.
Of what's crying within me. (GOD *approaches, with an arm outstretched.* MAN *dodges out of the way and continues talking to the audience*)
I'd really like to be spontaneous and genuine,
Just me.
But you've got to help me. (MAN *looks hesitantly at* GOD, *as if suddenly unsure of himself. Pause*)

You've got to hold out your hand, even when it seems like the last thing I seem to want or you

feel like doing. (GOD *slowly holds out a hand to* MAN. *This time,* MAN *takes it, hesitantly at first, still looking at* GOD)
Only you can reach the trembling child within the mask. (GOD *puts an arm around* MAN)
Each time you try to understand because you really care –
My heart grows wings with your sympathy and power of understanding. (GOD *holds* MAN *at arms' length so that he can look into* MAN's *face.* MAN *can't look at him*)
You can breathe life into me.
I want you to know that. I want you to know how important you are to me.
How you can be a creator of the person that is me. (MAN *finally looks at* GOD. *They hold that pose. Pause*)

Only you can break down the wall behind which I tremble; (GOD *lifts his hands to* MAN's *head to try to remove the mask*)
You alone can remove my mask;
You alone can release me from my shadow world of panic and uncertainty, from my lonely prison. (MAN *panics and moves* GOD's *hands away from the mask. He turns his back on* GOD)
It will not be easy for you.
A long conviction of worthlessness builds strong walls.
The nearer you approach, the more blindly I might strike back. (GOD *reaches out a hand towards the mask.* MAN *pushes his hand away violently*)
It's irrational, but I am irrational.
I fight against the very thing I cry out for. (GOD

grabs MAN's *hands and holds onto them.* MAN's
resistance fades)

But I am told that love is stronger than the
strongest walls;

And in this lies my hope.

My only hope. (GOD *turns the* MAN *round so that
they are facing each other again.* GOD *smiles at
him*)

Please, try to beat down those walls with firm
hands –

But gentle hands –

For a child is very sensitive. (GOD *removes the
mask.* MAN *looks around in astonishment, like
someone seeing for the first time.* GOD *smiles
again.* MAN *steps forward to look at the audience*)

Who am I?

You may wonder. (MAN *looks straight into the
audience*)

I am someone that you know

Very well.

36. Workmate

 Aim: *Most of us spend a huge amount of our time at work, yet few sermons are ever preached about how we relate to God in the workplace. It's good to be reminded that the promises of God apply just as much in the office as they do elsewhere, as – come Monday morning – we can easily forget that.*

Cast: *One* READER. *That person can use the lectern, or pretend to be doing a reading from the Bible in your church's normal way, or they can signal that this is something different by using the optional first line. The* READER *can, of course, easily use the script for this sketch.*

Props: *A Bible.*

READER: (*optional line*) An alternative Psalm 23:

     The Lord is my companion at work, I shall not get too stressed.

     He makes me pause by the photocopier,

     He leads me beside the water cooler, he restores my sense of perspective.

     He guides me in tough decisions for his name's sake.

     Even though I walk into the boss's office for a crucial meeting, I will fear no extra responsibilities,

For you are with me: your quiet voice and your
smile in the person who brings me coffee, they
comfort me.

You prepare spaces in my busy diary before me,

Despite the presence of those colleagues I find
difficult.

You give me a sense of value that my work alone
never can.

Surely goodness and love will follow me as I do
my job, all the days of my working life.

And I will work in the office with my Lord until
the weekend.

37. Southsea-Enders: Series I

Aim: Southsea-Enders *was so called because it was staged in Southsea, but the name can clearly be adapted to suit other locations. The episodes have been performed in school assemblies and morning services on successive weeks, but all three episodes could be performed within the same service with a suitable break between each. This series tackles various aspects of 'giving' from a child's perspective – (1) sharing things, (2) giving time and effort, and (3) giving to God.*

Cast: SPIKE SMITH *is a lovable but naughty ten-year-old;* JIM, *his friend, is a Christian; school bully* HARRIET 'SPOTTY' DAWKINS *is a freckle-faced girl in their class. It is funnier (and easier!) if all the children's parts are played by adults dressed as children – especially if they are trying to wear the uniform of the local school. Also: Spike's* DAD, *who is headteacher, and Spike's teacher* MRS HARRISON, *who are both firm but fair;* NARRATOR; *Spike's* GRANNY.

Props: Eastenders *theme music; school uniform and gym kit for* SPIKE, HARRIET *and* JIM; *breakfast things, including teapot and cups; table and chairs; sports bags; whistle; numbers to pin on runners' backs; tape of* Chariots of Fire *theme, and music for silly chase; exercise books; textbooks; enormous present.*

Episode One – Sharing

(Eastenders *theme music plays as* SPIKE *comes down to break-fast, wearing school uniform and carrying his sports bag*)

SPIKE: (*to audience*) Hello! My name's Spike Smith and
           I'm ten years old. I live here at number 25 Acacia
           Avenue and I go to the school just down the road
           – Acacia Avenue School. My dad's the head-
           teacher, but I'm in Mrs Harrison's class. She's all
           right, really. She let us do cooking last week, and
           we all got covered in flour and eggs and stuff.
           (DAD *enters*)

DAD: You're up early today, Spike. (*he sits down to
           breakfast*)

SPIKE: Well, Dad, today I've decided that I'm going to
           be really good. I'm not going to play football and
           get all muddy and . . . and I'll make you a cup of
           tea now, if you like.

DAD: (*taken aback*) Oh, well, that would be very nice.
           (SPIKE *exits to get tea*) He can be a little angel
           sometimes, can my boy Spike. He can be really
           naughty as well. (*he frowns*) Hmm, I hope he's
           not after something (SPIKE *returns with the pot of
           tea which he pours out*) Thank you, Spike. That's
           very nice of you. But . . . you're not after some-
           thing, are you?

SPIKE: No, Dad, honest. I just want to be good today,
           that's all.

DAD: Well, that's all right then. (*starts eating his break-
           fast*)

SPIKE: Er . . . but, Dad . . .

DAD: (*warily*) Ye-e-es?

SPIKE: You know it's my birthday next week . . . ?

DAD: I thought so! I knew this was too good to be true!

SPIKE: Well, you know that Robo-car Transformer [*or*

	insert name of latest must-have toy] that Jim's got . . . ?
DAD:	Ye-e-es.
SPIKE:	Well, can I have one for my birthday? Please, Dad . . . aw, go on . . . Jim got one for his birthday.
DAD:	Well, you carry on keeping out of trouble and I'll think about it. (*knock at imaginary door.* SPIKE *pretends to open it. It is* JIM, *who also has a sports bag*)
JIM:	Hi, Spike. Are you ready?
SPIKE:	Yeah, Jim. (*he collects his bag*) Bye, Dad! (*they start to walk to school.* DAD *exits*) Hey, guess what? I'm going to get one of those Robo-car Transformers like yours for my birthday. Dad said I was going to get one, but I have to be really good until then.
JIM:	Hey, that's really good, Spike! Oh yeah – did you remember it's sports day at school?
SPIKE:	Yeah – I've got my kit. (*he indicates his bag*)
JIM:	Well, I bet you win the running race, Spike, because you're really good at that. (HARRIET *approaches.* JIM *and* SPIKE *stop when they see her*) Oh no, Spike! Here's Spotty Dawkins!
SPIKE:	Spotty Dawkins! Oh no, Jim! She doesn't like me since I covered her in flour and eggs and stuff when we were cooking!
HARRIET:	Spike Smith! I want a word with you! (*she grabs his hair and jerks back his head*) I still haven't got you back for getting me into trouble in that lesson!
SPIKE:	Oh, er . . . I'm really sorry about that, Spotty.
HARRIET:	Did you call me 'Spotty'? You know I don't like being called 'Spotty'. My name's Harriet, remember?
SPIKE:	Er . . . oh yes, Harriet. I'm really sorry.

HARRIET: Huh. You will be sorry, Spike – I'm going to make sure you don't win that running race this afternoon. (*she lets go of his hair and runs off*)

SPIKE: Ow! I wonder what she meant by that, Jim . . . (*they exit*)

(*Enter* MRS HARRISON, *who blows her whistle*)

MRS HARRISON: Welcome to the Acacia Avenue School annual sports day. Can we have all the runners for the 100 metres running race here, please? Lane one is Spike Smith, lane two is Harriet Dawkins, and lane three is Jim Goodbody. (SPIKE, JIM *and* HARRIET *enter with their gym kit on, and numbers on their backs. They start warming up*) OK, on your marks . . .

HARRIET: Just remember, Spike – you're not going to win!

MRS HARRISON: . . . get set . . .

SPIKE: Oh yes I am, Spotty!

MRS HARRISON: GO!

(*Cue* Chariots of Fire *theme music.* SPIKE, JIM *and* HARRIET *all start running in slow motion.* SPIKE *gets off to the best start and is way ahead of the other two. After a few paces,* HARRIET *reaches out and grabs* SPIKE's *hair, pulling him over. He falls and hits the floor in slow motion, with his face contorted in agony.* HARRIET *races past in slow motion with delight on her face.* SPIKE *then grabs hold of her ankle and she trips over. She picks him up and punches him in the stomach and he retaliates . . . all in slow motion. Meanwhile,* JIM *wins the race*)

MRS HARRISON: (*blowing her whistle, which ends the music*

	and the slow motion) Spike Smith! Harriet Dawkins! What is going on?
SPIKE:	It was her!
HARRIET:	No it wasn't, Miss! It was him!
MRS HARRISON:	Harriet! Get over here! (*she takes* HARRIET *away and starts giving her a severe lecture*)
JIM:	(*to* SPIKE) Are you all right?
SPIKE:	No I am not! Oh, I really hate that Harriet Dawkins. I should have won that race! Aw, what will Dad say now? He'll kill me! I said I was going to be good today and now he'll blame me for getting into a fight with that Harriet 'Spotty' Dawkins. I'll never get my Robo-car Transformer now!
JIM:	Well, Spike, I've been thinking. Do you want to share mine?
SPIKE:	Yours? But you only got it last week – it's really new and expensive!
JIM:	I know, but, well, it wasn't your fault. It *was* Harriet who started that fight. And I was at church yesterday . . .
SPIKE:	Hmph! That's only for really sad people, that!
JIM:	Well, ours isn't! Ours is really good! Our Sunday Club leader was saying that Jesus likes us to share things with people who need them more than we do. Well, you want a Robo-car Transformer more than I do. So do you want to share it?
SPIKE:	Well, yeah! Thanks, Jim. And tomorrow I'm going to get that Spotty Dawkins back.
DAD:	(*enters*) Spike Smith! I want to talk to you! Get over here this instant!
SPIKE:	Aw no! It's Dad! (*all freeze. Eastenders theme music*)

Episode Two – Giving time and effort

NARRATOR: Last time, our hero, Spike Smith, was told he might get a Robo-car Transformer for his birthday if he was good. But he got into a fight with Harriet 'Spotty' Dawkins and thinks he won't get one now. His best friend Jim offered to let Spike share his instead. But now Spike is in real trouble because his dad, who is the headteacher, saw him fighting . . .

(Eastenders *theme music*. SPIKE, JIM, HARRIET *and* DAD *take up positions as before*)

DAD: Spike Smith! I just saw you fighting with Harriet Dawkins. How many times do I have to tell you not to get involved in fights? Just look at the state of you!

SPIKE: I'm sorry, but it was Harriet Dawkins' fault!

DAD: Was it indeed? Harriet Dawkins, get yourself over here! Did you hit Spike? Did you start the fight?

HARRIET: No Sir, it was . . . er . . . Jim!

DAD: Jim? Now, don't be ridiculous, Harriet. I saw you. Right, you can both do some extra home-work tonight. And you can forget all about having a Robo-car Transformer, Spike. (*he exits*)

HARRIET: (*glares at* SPIKE) Right, Spike Smith, just you wait! I'm going to get you again after school for telling Sir it was my fault. You big telltale! Just cos he's your dad! (*she exits*)

SPIKE: Aw no, Jim, she looked really mean! I think she meant that! Aw, Jim, I'm really scared! What shall I do? Shall I get my big brother to come and beat her up for me?

JIM: No, Spike! It's wrong to hit people back!

SPIKE: Well, how else am I going to stop myself from getting hurt?

JIM: Well, why don't you say sorry?

SPIKE: Me say sorry? What for? It was her that hit me!

JIM: Say sorry for covering her with flour and stuff, and for telling tales on her just now.

SPIKE: Oh! Do you think I should?

JIM: Yes, and while you're doing that, why don't you offer to help her with the extra homework your dad's going to set her, because you know she's no good at homework, and you're really good.

SPIKE: Help her with her homework? Why?

JIM: Because when Jesus talks about loving other people and giving things to them, he doesn't just mean giving things, like me letting you share my Robo-car Transformer, but giving people your time, even people you don't like very much.

SPIKE: I can't do that!

JIM: Well, it's worth a try, isn't it? If you don't, she'll probably hit you again!

SPIKE: All right, then. I'll try it. (*they exit*)

(*Enter* HARRIET, *looking mean*)

HARRIET: Right, Spike Smith, I'm waiting for you. This time I'm really going to pulverize you. (*she mimes what she might do to him*) I'm going to scratch your eyes out, and stamp on you, and tear your arms off, and . . . (*enter* SPIKE, *being pushed reluctantly towards* HARRIET *by* JIM) Here he is! Right, Spike – you're dead!

SPIKE: Hello Harriet! Er . . . nice day, isn't it?

JIM: Go on, Spike, tell her you're sorry!

SPIKE: I can't! (*fast instrumental music starts, and*

chase sequence ensues. SPIKE *runs around the church – if possible, around the congregation – pursued by* HARRIET *shaking her fists, and then* JIM. *There are lots of shouts of 'I'll get you, Spike!', 'Help me, Jim!' and 'Tell her you're sorry!' They go out of a door, or offstage, and reappear with* JIM *chased by* HARRIET *chased by* SPIKE. *They all run off again.* JIM *backs on slowly from one side,* SPIKE *from another, and they bump into each other. They both scream and run off the way they came.* JIM *re-emerges being chased by* HARRIET, *then* SPIKE, *until . . .*)

JIM: STOP! (*music stops.* HARRIET *runs into* JIM. SPIKE *runs into them both*) Harriet! Spike's got something to tell you!

HARRIET: (*grabs* SPIKE *by the hair*) Well, it had better be good!

SPIKE: I . . . er . . . well, Harriet, I . . . er . . . just wanted to say that . . . er . . . I'm sorry for telling tales on you, and for covering you in food, and . . . er . . .

JIM: Go on, Spike!

SPIKE: . . . and if you like, I'll help you with the extra homework that my dad gave you.

HARRIET: (*surprised*) Will you? (SPIKE *nods*) Oh! (*she lets go of his hair*) Right, well . . . er . . . come round tonight then, to my house (*turns to go, then turns back again*) and don't tell tales on me again!

SPIKE: Er . . . no, I won't, Harriet! (*exit* HARRIET)

JIM: There, you see! I said it would work. She's not as bad as you thought.

SPIKE: Well, I don't know if I really want to go round to her house, but I suppose I'll have to now.

DAD: (*enters*) Spike, is that you? Your tea's ready!

SPIKE: I had to see someone, Dad.

DAD: Well, get yourself inside, my lad. Your granny has come round for tea and to stay the night.

SPIKE: But Dad, I've got to go out somewhere tonight!

DAD: You're not going anywhere tonight! You can stay in and talk to your granny after tea while I wash up. And then you can do that extra homework! Remember, you promised to be good this morning!

SPIKE: (*to* JIM) But I've got to go to Harriet Dawkins' house tonight! Oh no, Jim! What shall I do now? (*all freeze.* Eastenders *theme music*)

Episode Three – Giving to God

NARRATOR: Our hero, Spike Smith, has been learning about God from his best friend, Jim. Jim has let Spike borrow his Robo-car Transformer, and Spike has offered to give Harriet 'Spotty' Dawkins his time and effort as he helps her with some extra homework. Spike has promised to go round to Harriet's house to help her, but now he's discovered that his dad wants him to stay at home and talk to his granny, who has just arrived for tea . . .

(Eastenders *theme music.* DAD, JIM *and* SPIKE *take up positions*)

DAD: Get yourself inside, Spike, and hurry up about it! (*exits*)

SPIKE: But Jim, what about going round to Harriet Dawkins' house tonight?

JIM: Well, tell you what, Spike – if you like, and if your dad lets me, I'll go and talk to your granny while you go round to Harriet's house.

SPIKE: Will you, Jim? That would be really good!

JIM: Yes, I will. But Spike, if you're going to Harriet Dawkins' house, I think that we should pray about it first.

SPIKE: Pray? I've never done that before!

JIM: Well, it's dead easy. You just talk to Jesus like you'd talk to anyone else, and say that you really need his help. When I give Jesus time and pray to him, things always seem to work out better.

SPIKE: So you think that if I asked Jesus now, he'd make it so I wasn't scared of Harriet, and I could be friends with her?

JIM: Yes. And you could make friends with Jesus too. Be his friend – just like you and I are friends.

SPIKE: Oh, right! So will you stay here with me now while I pray to Jesus?

JIM: Yes, of course I will! (*they both kneel, with eyes tightly closed and hands together*)

SPIKE: Dear Jesus . . . er . . . hello! My name's Spike Smith, and I'm a friend of Jim's. You probably know him better than you know me . . . er . . .

JIM: Go on, Spike! You're doing fine!

SPIKE: Er . . . Jesus, thank you to Jim for letting me use his Robo-car Transformer, and thank you that I can give Harriet Dawkins some of my time tonight. Jesus, I want to be your friend, and I'll give you whatever you like and I won't mind. And Jesus, please help me now, because I've got to go and help Harriet with her homework. Lots of love from Spike. Amen. Oh, and Jesus, please let it be OK for Jim to talk to my granny instead of me. Amen again.

JIM: Amen. You see, that wasn't so bad. Right, I'll go and talk to your granny then. Bye! (*exits*)

SPIKE: Bye! Right, I've got to be friendly to Harriet, be friendly to Harriet . . . (*he exits a different way, muttering to himself*)

(*The scene changes to* HARRIET's *house. She is sitting at a table surrounded by exercise books and textbooks.* SPIKE *knocks on the door*)

SPIKE: Spott . . . er . . . I mean, Harriet! Are you in?

HARRIET: Yes, I'm in. Get yourself in here, Spike Smith! (*he enters*)

SPIKE: Hello, Harriet. Are you having some trouble with the homework?

HARRIET: Yeah – I can't do these sums at all. (*shoves book under* SPIKE's *nose*)

SPIKE: Oh, that! That's dead easy! (*seeing* HARRIET's *reaction*) Erm, I mean that's quite hard, really. But you just take that away from that, and add that to that, and you get the answer. See? (*he shows her*)

HARRIET: Hmph. I'm not as clever as you, Spike. I wouldn't have got that.

SPIKE: Well, that was a bit difficult. This one is easier. You take that away here, and add it to this bit, and then you get the answer there. Do you understand?

HARRIET: Oh yeah! Yes, I think I can do it now. You should help me with my homework all the time. Weren't you scared of coming here, Spike?

SPIKE: Well, yes, but I asked Jesus to be my friend, and Jim said Jesus would be with me and help me not to be scared.

HARRIET: Jesus is your friend? Oh . . . well, you see, (*reluctantly*) I don't have many friends . . .

SPIKE: Why's that, Harriet?

HARRIET: I don't know. Maybe it's because I beat some of

them up. You're the first person to want to be friends with me.

SPIKE: Well, look, because we've finished this dead quick, I've still got time to go home and have tea with my granny. And Jim's at my house. Why don't you come round to our house for tea, and me and Jim can tell you all about being friends with Jesus?

HARRIET: Yeah! Could I?

SPIKE: Course you can! You see, because I prayed about it, Jesus gave me the time to come to your house and help you *and* get back to be with my granny for tea! (*they exit talking*)

(*The scene is* SPIKE's *house again, with* DAD, GRANNY *and* JIM *sitting round the table for tea. Enter* SPIKE *and* HARRIET)

SPIKE: Dad – can Harriet come for tea?

DAD: Yes, of course she can, Spike. But what took you so long?

SPIKE: Well, tonight I had to make two new friends. One was Jesus, and one was Harriet! And guess what, Jim? Harriet wants to become a friend of Jesus too!

JIM: That's great!

DAD: Well, do you know why I wanted you to come in and see Granny so quickly, Spike?

SPIKE: No, why?

DAD: Because she's got something for you!

GRANNY: (*producing enormous present*) It's one of those Robo-car Transformer things for your birthday!

SPIKE: Oh, thank you, granny! Thank you very much! (*all freeze.* Eastenders *theme music*)

38. Southsea-Enders: Series II

Aim: *This series tackles aspects of worship by comparing worshipping God, who never lets you down, to being fanatical about human heroes, who do. It can be performed even if you have not first done Series I.*

Cast: SPIKE SMITH *is a lovable but naughty eleven-year-old who is now a Christian;* HARRIET 'SPOTTY' DAWKINS *is a reformed school bully who has a teenage crush;* TRACEY *is similarly girly; the* BOY BAND – *including* LEAD SINGER – *are a typical set of good-looking boys who sing and dance together; the* LEADER *of the Sunday Club at church; extra Sunday Club children;* MRS HARRISON *is the school teacher; the* CHOIR *are a full gospel group;* NARRATOR.

Props: Eastenders *theme music; school uniform for* SPIKE *and* HARRIET; *chairs for Sunday Club; huge poster of* BOY BAND; *request from* HARRIET; *tapes of band singing; two 'beds' (or duvets and pillows laid out to represent beds); alarm clock; pyjamas/nightie; 'waking-up' music; make-up and mirror; exercise book and plants for photosynthesis project; guitar; choir robes; sheet music.*

Episode One – Telling God how brilliant he is

NARRATOR:
In the last series of *Southsea-Enders*, Spike Smith and his friend Jim were learning about giving. Jim gave Spike a chance to borrow his Robo-car Transformer, Spike gave some of his time to help the school bully Harriet 'Spotty' Dawkins, and Spike decided to give the rest of his life to God. Spike and Harriet have now become friends and go to the same Sunday Club at church.

(Eastenders *theme music. Enter* SPIKE, HARRIET *and other Sunday Club children who sit on chairs. They listen to the* LEADER, *who starts speaking quietly*)

SPIKE:
(*to audience*) Hello! My name's Spike Smith and I'm now eleven years old. I'm in the Sunday Club, and this is one of our leaders. She's dead good. Me and my new friend Spott . . . erm, I mean Harriet Dawkins, have been coming here every week and learning lots of things about God.

LEADER:
. . . so the reason we sing songs together is to tell God how brilliant he is. To say thank you for everything he's done. And to tell him how much we love him.

HARRIET:
Hmph. I know who I really love. (*unfurls huge poster*) I love all the singers in Boy Band. (*she kisses poster*)

SPIKE:
Urgh, not Boy Band! They're rubbish!

HARRIET:
No they're not! They're brilliant. I write to them all the time and buy their records and pin up their posters on the walls.

LEADER:	There you are. Harriet likes Boy Band, so she writes to them to tell them how brilliant they are. That's what we do when we worship God.
HARRIET:	Well, I'm going to see them tonight at a concert with my friend Tracey, and we're going to tell them we love them. They're better than God and church! (*she runs off*)
LEADER:	OK, that's it for today. See you all next week. (*all exit apart from* LEADER *and* SPIKE)
SPIKE:	So why do we need to tell God how brilliant he is? Doesn't he know already?
LEADER:	Well, yes, but it makes God happy when we tell him how special he is. It's like when someone tells you they love you. Doesn't that make you feel special?
SPIKE:	No one says they love me apart from my Auntie Ethel. And she gives me big slobbery kisses on the cheek.
LEADER:	Well, why don't you try something, Spike? Every night before you go to bed, why don't you tell God how brilliant he is? That'll make him very happy.
SPIKE:	Well, I don't think I'll have time tonight.
LEADER:	Why's that, Spike?
SPIKE:	I've got lots of homework to do. I've got to do a big project on photosynthesis for school.
LEADER:	Well, have you tried praying about it?
SPIKE:	No.
LEADER:	Well, look – God won't let you down. I'm sure if you made the time to worship him tonight, he'd help you finish the project on time. I'll see you next week, OK? (*they exit*)

(*Enter* HARRIET *and* TRACEY *in their best concert-going gear.*
HARRIET *is still holding her poster*)

HARRIET:	Ooh, Tracey! I can't wait for this! We're going to see Boy Band in concert!
TRACEY:	Yeah! (*she points at poster*) Aw, I think that one is dead fit!
HARRIET:	Oh no, the lead singer's better looking than him, I think. I'm going to see if I can get a date with him.
TRACEY:	You? Why should he want a date with you?
HARRIET:	Because I'm his biggest fan! You wait! I'm going to give him a message at the stage door here. (*goes to 'stage door' and pretends to hand something over*) Excuse me! Could you give this to the band, please?
TRACEY:	You've got no chance, Harriet!
HARRIET:	Well, come on! It's nearly time for the concert to start! Let's see if we can get near the front! (*if possible, hoards of other screaming girls rush to the front of the stage.* HARRIET *and* TRACEY *join them. Enter* BOY BAND. *Either they sing a well-known song by a famous boy band, or something like the following, with a dance routine*)
BOY BAND:	We're a Boy Band, we're a Boy Band! We look so cool, but our lyrics are bland. No hair out of place, cute looks on our face. We'll sing this tune until you can't stand . . . . . . it any more. We're a Boy Band, we're a Boy Band! Our stomachs are flat and our skin is tanned. We dance in time, and we always mime. We'll sing this tune until you can't stand . . .

... it any more. (LEAD SINGER *then takes piece of paper from his pocket*)

LEAD SINGER: I've got a bit of a request here. It's from someone called Harriet Dawkins. Is she here?

HARRIET: (*screams*) It's me! I'm over here!

LEAD SINGER: She's sent me a little note saying: 'Can we meet for a date?' Well, what d'you think, lads? (*they chortle*) It says: 'I'll meet you round the back of Acacia Avenue School in Southsea tomorrow at 10.00.' Right, well, I'll be there, Harriet! (*he winks at the rest of the band*)

HARRIET: (*to* TRACEY) He's going to be there! I don't believe it! I've got a date with him!

TRACEY: Do you think he was serious?

HARRIET: I'm sure he was! Oh, wait until I tell that Spike Smith! This is better than God or Sunday Club. I definitely prefer worshipping Boy Band! There's nothing they could do now to stop me loving them. I bet they're going to go on for ever and ever ...

LEAD SINGER: ... Oh yes, and there is one other thing we wanted to announce to all our fans. We're splitting up.

HARRIET: Aarrghh! Oh no! (*freeze*. Eastenders *theme music*)

Episode Two – God won't let you down

NARRATOR: In last week's episode of *Southsea-Enders*, Spike Smith was learning about worshipping God. But his friend Harriet 'Spotty' Dawkins was only interested in worshipping her heroes, Boy Band. She handed in

a note to the lead singer who said on stage
he would meet her for a date. But then the
group announced they were splitting up . . .

(Eastenders *theme music. Two beds are strategically posi-
tioned on stage for later. Enter* HARRIET, *crying her eyes out.
Enter* SPIKE *in T-shirt and shorts*)

SPIKE: Harriet! What's the matter? What hap-
              pened at the concert?

HARRIET: It's awful, Spike!

SPIKE: What's awful? Were they not very good?

HARRIET: (*stops crying immediately as she leaps to the
              defence of her heroes*) Don't be stupid,
              Spike – they were brilliant! But they'll
              never do another concert again!

SPIKE: What? Are they splitting up? (HARRIET
              s*tarts crying again, even louder, nodding her
              head*) Oh dear.

HARRIET: But there is one good thing, Spike. (*starts
              smiling*) I've got a date with the lead singer!
              (*screams*) I can't believe it! Me and him on
              a date together!

SPIKE: Are you sure?

HARRIET: Yes, he said he was going to meet me
              behind the school at 10.00 in the morning!

SPIKE: But Spott . . . (*she hits him*) I mean, Harriet
              – we've got to hand in our project about
              photosynthos . . . phattysonath . . . about
              plants to Mrs Harrison at 10.00!

HARRIET: Don't be silly, Spike! The Boy Band are
              more important than some stupid project.
              (*sighs*) Maybe they'll write a song for me.

SPIKE: You don't think he was just . . . just joking,
              Harriet, do you? (*she gives him a withering
              look*) Well, it's bedtime now, Harriet. I'll

see you tomorrow. (SPIKE *pretends to open a door to go into his house and goes to his bed.* HARRIET *sighs wistfully and goes off to put her nightie or pyjamas on.*)

SPIKE: Now, what was I going to do before I went to bed? My Sunday Club leader said that if I worshipped God tonight and asked him to help me with my project, he would. I need to tell him how brilliant he is. (*he kneels by the bed as* HARRIET *reappears in her nightie/pyjamas and kneels by her bed*) Dear God, I think you're really brilliant!

HARRIET: (*holding out poster*) Boy Band! I think you're really brilliant!

SPIKE: Thank you, Lord Jesus, for everything you have done for me. For being my friend even though you are king of everything.

HARRIET: Thank you, lead singer, for all those records you made for me. For being my friend even though you're a big superstar!

SPIKE: Thank you for answering my prayers. And please help me tomorrow morning when I do my project.

HARRIET: Thank you for asking me out on a date. Please help me tomorrow morning, 'cos I'll be really nervous.

SPIKE: I know you won't let me down. I really love you and I'll do anything for you. Amen.

HARRIET: I know you won't let me down. I really love you and I'll do anything for you. (*she kisses the poster. They both get into bed and pretend to be asleep. Cue lively waking-up type music – e.g. 'Wake Up Boo!' by the Boo Radleys.* SPIKE *jumps out of bed first and looks at his alarm clock. He is late. He tries to put his trousers over his shorts and falls over.* HARRIET *stretches and falls back to sleep. Then she suddenly realizes and leaps out of bed.* SPIKE *is struggling into his school shirt and tie.* HARRIET *brushes her hair and starts putting it into plaits, then rushes off to get changed.* SPIKE *gets an exercise book out and starts working frantically, writing, sticking bits of plants in it, screwing some pages up and starting again.* HARRIET *reappears in her best skirt and top, tries to put on some lipstick, but does so very badly.* MRS HARRISON *starts to walk past the front of the stage, so* SPIKE *runs up to her as* HARRIET *goes to wait for the lead singer. Music ends*)

SPIKE: Miss, Miss! I've finished my project!

MRS HARRISON: Hello, Spike! Let's have a look, then. (*she flicks through it*) Hmm, yes, this looks very impressive, Spike. This must have taken you some time to do.

SPIKE: Thanks, Miss! (*she wanders off with it*) And thank you, God! I knew you wouldn't let me down! (*exits*)

HARRIET: (*looks at her watch*) Well, he's only 15 minutes late. That's all right. He's probably very busy being a pop star . . . (*wandering around*) He did say he'd be here. (*checks her face in a small mirror*) He wouldn't let me down, would he? Not the lead singer of Boy Band! (*enter* MRS HARRISON)

MRS HARRISON: Harriet Dawkins! What are you doing hanging around out here? And what are you doing with all that make-up on?

HARRIET: (*feebly mutters*) I'm . . . erm . . . waiting to

go on a date with the lead singer of Boy
Band, Miss.

MRS HARRISON: You should be handing in your photosynthesis project! Where is it?

HARRIET: Erm . . . I haven't done it, Miss.

MRS HARRISON: Right, you can come with me, Harriet!
You're in big trouble!

(Eastenders *theme music as* MRS HARRISON *marches* HARRIET
off)

Episode Three – Real worship

NARRATOR: In last week's episode of *Southsea-Enders*,
Spike Smith discovered that God wouldn't
let him down after he helped Spike finish
his photosynthesis project on time. But
Harriet Dawkins discovered that her
heroes, Boy Band, had let her down. Not
only were they splitting up, but the lead
singer didn't turn up for a date with her.
She also got into trouble for not doing her
project at all. It is now a week later, and
Spike is in Sunday Club . . .

(Eastenders *theme music. Sunday Club is set up as before.*
SPIKE *is there listening to the* LEADER, *but there is an empty
chair where* HARRIET *usually sits*)

LEADER: Spike, do you know where Harriet is?

SPIKE: No. I've hardly seen her at all since the
other day. She said she was going out on a
date with someone from Boy Band, but I
don't think he really meant it. I think she's
very upset.

LEADER: So, did you do what I asked you to?

SPIKE: Yes. I made sure I worshipped God. I told

him every night before I went to bed how brilliant he was. And God helped me with my homework, like you said!

LEADER: That's great, Spike!

SPIKE: And I made up a song as well! Can I sing it to you?

LEADER: Well . . .

SPIKE: Aw, go on! I can play it on the guitar as well! (*he picks up a guitar*)

LEADER: Erm . . . well, OK.

SPIKE: (*starts to sing, completely out of tune, while strumming a random tune on the guitar*)
God, I think you're really brilliant,
And I've been learning to worship you every night.
God, I think you're really brilliant,
And you're a much better hero to have than any Boy Band.
Because you never let us down;
Well, you never let me down, anyway.
So, God, I think you're really brilliant,
And you let yourself get killed for all the wrong things I do,
And you answer my prayers.
So, God, I think you're really brilliant,
And I want to learn even more about you
. . .

LEADER: Yes, yes, that's very good, Spike!

SPIKE: I've got another twelve verses to go yet!

LEADER: It's OK – I think I get the idea! And it's real worship, because you're saying exactly how you feel about God.

SPIKE: My dad said it sounded a bit out of tune.

LEADER: Well, that doesn't *really* matter, Spike. Real worship can be a bit out of tune. Listen, if you're really keen on worshipping God, why don't you join the choir?

SPIKE: The choir? They don't use guitars, do they?

LEADER: No, thank goodness . . . But you could sing. You've got a really (*searches for the right word*) powerful voice.

SPIKE: OK.

LEADER: Come with me, then, Spike, and we'll ask if you can join. (*they exit*)

(*Enter* HARRIET, *looking depressed*)

HARRIET: It's not fair! I really thought I had a proper date with the one from Boy Band, but he let me down. And I got into trouble from Mrs Harrison for not doing my project – I've got to stay behind after school every night this week!

SPIKE: (*enters in choir robes*) Harriet! Where have you been?

HARRIET: (*laughing at* SPIKE) What's that you're wearing?

SPIKE: I'm joining the choir!

HARRIET: What? You? You can't sing!

SPIKE: Well, I'm learning.

HARRIET: Hmph. Well, I suppose you were right, Spike. I was a bit silly worshipping Boy Band, wasn't I? I've torn down all my pictures of them from my bedroom now.

SPIKE: It's much more exciting worshipping God, you know.

HARRIET: Yeah, I know God does things that are really exciting, but being in church isn't as exciting as being at a Boy Band concert, really, is it?

SPIKE: Well, Harriet. Wait until you hear what

we're singing! (CHOIR *in robes are assembling behind him*) Do you want to sing it with us?

HARRIET: It can't be better than Boy Band's number one single, can it?

SPIKE: Here. (*gives her a copy of the music*) Listen to this. (CHOIR *sing up-tempo gospel number – such as 'I Love Him' from the film* Sister Act, *or 'Oh Happy Day!' – complete with harmonies, clapping and dancing.* East-enders *theme music*)

39. Southsea-Enders: Series III

 Aim: *This series takes a look at peer pressure. Again, it can be performed without having staged Series I and II.*

Cast: SPIKE SMITH *is a lovable but naughty twelve-year-old Christian;* HARRIET 'SPOTTY' DAWKINS' *is a reformed school bully who is now his friend; Spike's* DAD *is firm but caring; the* TRENDY BROTHERS *are two immaculately dressed eighteen-year-olds who wear sunglasses, similar clothes and do everything together;* NARRATOR.

Props: Eastenders *theme music; suitcases; bucket, spade, teddy bear, rubber ring, shorts and Bible; four chairs; 'Summer Holiday' tape and tape of car starting up; towels; sunglasses; cigarettes; cans of beer; romantic film soundtrack; boxes of popcorn; 'trendy' clothes for* SPIKE.

Episode One – Feeling left out

NARRATOR: In the last series of *Southsea-Enders*, Spike Smith learned that God wouldn't let him down when he helped Spike with his photosynthesis project. But Harriet 'Spotty' Dawkins discovered that her heroes Boy Band had let her down because they split up. It is now the school holidays . . .

(Eastenders *theme music. Enter* SPIKE *with his suitcase*)

SPIKE: Hello! My name's Spike Smith, and I live here at number 25 Acacia Avenue. I'm twelve years old now, and I'm really excited today because we're going on holiday! Me and my dad are going to Clacton-on-Sea for a whole week, and Dad said Harriet Dawkins could come too. (*enter* DAD)

DAD: Are you ready yet, Spike? We're going soon, and Harriet's here now. (*he exits as* HARRIET *enters, dragging a huge suitcase behind her*)

HARRIET: Ooh, Spike! I'm really looking forward to going to Clacton-on-Sea! I'm going to make lots of sandcastles and swim in the sea and everything!

SPIKE: Why have you got so much stuff, Harriet?

HARRIET: Well, I need lots of different outfits for the beach, just in case I meet a big hunk.

SPIKE: Oh, I think it's soppy, all that boyfriend and girlfriend stuff and kissing . . . urrgghh! (*enter* DAD)

DAD: OK, Spike. Are you ready?

SPIKE: I've just got to make sure I've got everything before we go. (*he opens suitcase and throws out suitable props*) I've got my bucket and spade, my rubber ring to go swimming with, and Walter my teddy bear, and my shorts. (*he holds up Bible*) Do you think I should take this, Dad?

DAD: Yes, take your Bible. You'll want to read that while you're away, won't you?

SPIKE: Dad . . . there's something else I want to take on holiday with me.

DAD: What's that, Spike?

SPIKE: Can I take God on holiday with me?

DAD: Yes, of course you can.

SPIKE: Well, I'm not sure if there's room in the car for him, you see, with me and you and Harriet and all the luggage . . .

DAD: Spike! I think God will come anyway! He doesn't need to go to Clacton-on-Sea by car. He's all around you!

SPIKE: Oh. (*innocently*) But didn't you say before that Clacton was a God-forsaken place? What does that mean?

DAD: (*embarrassed*) Never mind that now, Spike. Get into the car, will you? (*he lifts* SPIKE's *case into the back of four chairs, which are set up on stage to represent the car. He then tries to lift* HARRIET's *case, which is a real effort. They mime getting into the car. Cue sound effects of car starting up, then music such as 'Summer Holiday' by Cliff Richard starts.* DAD *mimes driving, while* SPIKE *and* HARRIET *point at things out of the window.* DAD *turns round to check if they are OK, and* SPIKE *notices that they are about to crash and points it out. They all lurch to one side, then the other. The car finally screeches to a standstill. Music ends*)

SPIKE: Is this it?

DAD: Yes, this is Clacton.

SPIKE: Can we go down to the beach straight away, Dad . . . please!

DAD: Well, OK then. You go to the beach, and I'll park the car and join you in a minute. (HARRIET *and* SPIKE *get out of the car with their cases, and* DAD *mimes driving away*)

HARRIET: Come on, Spike! Let's find a good place to sunbathe! (SPIKE *and* HARRIET *take the towels out of their suitcases and lie on them, pretending to soak up the sun. Enter the* TRENDY BROTHERS.

They do a trendy walk which involves them strutting and clicking their fingers. They come to a halt and stand posing at the front of the stage)

SPIKE: (*stands*) Look at them, Harriet! They look interesting!

HARRIET: (*also stands*) Phwoargh! Hey Spike! They look really hunky!

SPIKE: Maybe we can make friends with them. (*goes up to* TRENDY BROTHERS) Hello! Who are you?

TRENDYS: (*in unison*) Hi! We're the (*they pause and run their fingers through their hair every time they say the word 'trendy'*) Trendy Brothers and we're really (*fingers through hair*) trendy!

TRENDY 1:   Who are you, pipsqueak?

SPIKE: My name's Spike Smith, and this is my friend, Harriet!

TRENDY 2:   Hi, Harriet! (*she lets out a girlish giggle*)

SPIKE: What is being (*tries to run fingers through his hair in a similar way, but ends up looking stupid*) trendy, then?

TRENDY 1:   (*laughs*) Well, you wear all the latest clothes, and you look really cool, like we do . . .

TRENDY 2:   (*sees* SPIKE'S *open suitcase*) . . . and you don't bring teddy bears on holiday with you! (*picks up teddy bear by the ear*)

SPIKE: But that's Walter! (TRENDY 2 *kicks teddy into audience*)

TRENDY 1:   (*puts his arm round* SPIKE) Look, kid – you're too old for teddy bears. You don't have them if you want to look (*hand through hair*) trendy.

HARRIET: (*trying hard to get noticed*) I don't have any teddy bears!

TRENDY 2:   If you want to be (*hand through hair*) trendy, you wear these (*gives* SPIKE *sunglasses*) and you walk like this, (*does trendy walk*) looking really cool, and people think you're a really good person to be with.

SPIKE: What, like this? (SPIKE *tries trendy walk and fails miserably, again looking stupid*) Gosh – will people really like me better if I walk around like this?

TRENDY 1: Not if you have this (*holds up Bible*) on holiday with you. You don't go to church, do you? That would be very untrendy!

SPIKE: Er . . . no, of course I'm not . . . er . . . it's Harriet's!

HARRIET: What?

SPIKE: Yeah! Harriet is a friend of Jesus. She's a Christian and she reads the Bible. I don't. I've never even *heard* of Jesus.

HARRIET: Spike!

SPIKE: Oh, shut up, Harriet! You and your soppy Christianity. Hey guys, why don't we go and be (*tries to run his hands through his hair*) trendy somewhere else and make some more friends?

TRENDY 2: Yeah – clear off, sad person! (*exit* TRENDY BROTHERS *doing trendy walk, with* SPIKE *stumbling along behind as he tries to copy them*)

HARRIET: But Spike – you can't just stop being a friend of Jesus when you like. And you shouldn't be telling lies about being a Christian! Come back, Spike! (*enter* DAD)

DAD: I've parked the car now, Harriet . . . where's Spike?

HARRIET: He went off with some older boys, Mr Smith!

DAD: He did what? Harriet – I thought I could trust you to look after him. You are older than him, after all!

HARRIET: I'm sorry, Mr Smith!

DAD: You will be sorry, Harriet Dawkins. If any-thing's happened to my Spike, don't think you'll be staying in Clacton with us! (*all freeze. Eastenders theme music*)

Episode Two – Following the crowd

NARRATOR: In last week's episode of *Southsea-Enders*, Spike Smith, his dad and Harriet Dawkins went on holiday to Clacton-on-Sea. Spike went off with some older boys who called themselves the Trendy Brothers. Spike pretended he wasn't a friend of Jesus to impress them. Spike's dad was angry with Harriet for letting Spike go off with them . . .

(Eastenders *theme music. Enter* TRENDY BROTHERS, *doing trendy walk, followed by* SPIKE *who hasn't quite mastered it yet.* SPIKE *is wearing trendier clothes, but doesn't look quite right*)

TRENDYS: Hi! We're the (*hands through hair*) Trendy Brothers, and we're really (*hands through hair*) trendy!

SPIKE: And I'm a (*tries to run his hand through his hair*) Trendy Brother as well now. Now I've got my (*hand through hair*) trendy clothes and my sun-glasses, I'm bound to make lots of friends!

TRENDY 1: Hey, Spike – do you smoke?

SPIKE: Erm . . . (*thinks carefully*) Not unless I'm on fire.

TRENDY 2: No, cretin – do you smoke cigarettes?

SPIKE: Oh! No, I don't, thanks very much.

TRENDY 1: (*gets out packet*) Well, we do. It's really (*hair*) trendy to smoke. (*he passes a cigarette to* TRENDY 2 *and lights up*)

SPIKE: Oh. Well, I'll have one, then. (*he watches what*

the others do and tries to copy them. SPIKE *ends up coughing violently*)

TRENDY 2:   (*flicking ash off the end of his cigarette*) It's good, isn't it?

SPIKE: (*eyes watering and wheezing*) Yes, it's really good . . .

TRENDY 1:   Hey, Spike – have you got a girlfriend?

SPIKE: A girlfriend? No, I don't like girls very much. They don't play football very well and they're always giggling . . .

TRENDY 2:   But it's really (*hair*) trendy to have a girlfriend! We have lots!

SPIKE: Oh. How do I get a girlfriend, then?

TRENDY 1:   It's really easy. You just tell a girl how (*hair*) trendy you are, and then ask her to come out on a date. (*enter* HARRIET, *looking for* SPIKE)

TRENDY 2:   Look – here comes a girl now. Why don't you try it? (*pushes* SPIKE *towards her*)

SPIKE: But I'm not even sure I want a girlfriend! (*bumps into* HARRIET) Oh, er . . . hello Harriet!

HARRIET: Spike! Your dad's really worried about you . . . (*stares at his clothes*) What are you wearing?

SPIKE: (*looks nervously back at* TRENDY BROTHERS) I'm really (*hair*) trendy and I want to take you out on a date!

HARRIET: A date? With you? (*looks at* TRENDY BROTHERS) Are they coming?

SPIKE: Erm . . . yes, I think so.

HARRIET: (*flutters her eyelashes at* TRENDY BROTHERS) OK. See you later at the cinema! (TRENDY BROTHERS *strut off.* HARRIET *waits until they exit, smiling at them, then grabs* SPIKE) Now, you're coming back with me so your dad can check you're OK. (SPIKE *tries to take another drag of his cigarette and coughs again.* HARRIET

	grabs it and throws it away) And you can stop putting that thing in your mouth straight away!
SPIKE:	But it's trendy!
HARRIET:	No it's not! It's stupid. And you're only doing it because those other boys say you should. Now come on! (HARRIET *drags* SPIKE *off*)

(*Scene changes to a cinema – four chairs in a row. Enter* SPIKE *with* TRENDY BROTHERS)

SPIKE:	But I've never had a girlfriend before – I don't know what to do!
TRENDY 1:	Here. Have a drink of this. (*gives him a can of beer*) That will make you feel less nervous.
SPIKE:	(*drinks, then immediately spits it out*) What is that?
TRENDY 2:	Hey – it's really (*hair*) trendy to drink beer.
SPIKE:	Oh. (*drinks more, winces, but gulps it down*) Mmm, yes, that's very nice. (*enter* HARRIET *in her best dress*)
HARRIET:	Come on, then, Spike. Let's see this film. (*she walks past and goes to sit down on the end chair.* SPIKE *looks at her and drains his can of beer. He gives it to* TRENDY 1, *who goes to drink some and discovers there's none left*) Come on, it's starting! (SPIKE *sits down next to* HARRIET, *and* TRENDY BROTHERS *take the other two seats. Lights are dimmed and film music starts – a soppy love theme. All four characters grab boxes of popcorn from under their seats and stare as if glued to the screen. In complete synchronization, each takes one bit of popcorn from their box, raises it to their mouth and eats it, then another piece, and so on – all the time gazing straight ahead. After a while,* SPIKE *looks at* HARRIET, *then at* TRENDY BROTHERS, *who encourage him to*

get on with it. SPIKE *yawns massively, putting his arm round* HARRIET. *She turns to look in horror at* SPIKE's *face. He has his eyes closed and has puckered his lips towards her as if expecting a kiss. Music stops*)

SPIKE: (*opens his eyes and looks at her*) Harriet – do you want to be my girlfriend? (*all freeze.* Eastenders *theme music*)

Episode Three – God looks at the heart

NARRATOR: In the last episode of *Southsea-Enders*, Spike Smith had made friends with some older boys called the Trendy Brothers. They said he should smoke cigarettes, drink beer and have a girlfriend if he wanted to be trendy. He took Harriet 'Spotty' Dawkins to the cinema . . .

(Eastenders *theme music.* SPIKE, HARRIET *and* TRENDY BROTHERS *take their places on the four chairs which represent the cinema.* SPIKE *puts his arm round* HARRIET *and goes to kiss her*)

SPIKE: Harriet – do you want to be my girlfriend? (*enter* DAD)

DAD: Spike! What are you doing here? You should have been home hours ago!

SPIKE: Dad!

DAD: And what do you think you're doing with your arms round poor Harriet?

SPIKE: Erm . . . (*he removes his arm*)

DAD: (*picks up beer can and cigarette packet*) And whose are these?

TRENDYS: (*look at each other, then in unison point at* SPIKE) His!

DAD: Right – you're coming straight home, Spike! And don't think I'm letting you stay up late

	while we're in Clacton again! (*grabs* SPIKE *by the ear*)
TRENDY 1:	Ha, ha! You could never be a (*hair*) trendy person, Spike! Not with your dad telling you what to do all the time!
TRENDY 2:	Yeah – go back to Daddy, Spike!
DAD:	Come on, Spike! (*pulls him offstage*)
SPIKE:	Ow! Let go – it hurts! (*they exit*)
TRENDY 1:	What a wimp! I never thought he'd make a (*hair*) Trendy Brother anyway! Come on, let's go! (TRENDY BROTHERS *do trendy walk to get offstage.* HARRIET *follows*)
HARRIET:	Erm . . . excuse me! What about me? Yoo-hoo! (*they exit*)

(SPIKE *wanders back on stage, taking his trendy clothes off to reveal his usual clothes underneath*)

SPIKE:	Hmph. I got into a lot of trouble from my dad. I was only trying to be trendy. Now I've got to stay in every night while we're on holiday. And I've ruined everything with Harriet. I didn't really want her to be my girlfriend. I only asked her because those Trendy Brothers said it was a good idea.
HARRIET:	(*enters*) Spike? Can I come in?
SPIKE:	Harriet!
HARRIET:	I just came to tell you that . . . well, I can't be your girlfriend . . .
SPIKE:	(*immediately*) Oh good!
HARRIET:	. . . I know it's hard for you to understand, but, well . . . you're not really my type, and . . . (*realizes*) whaddaya mean, 'Oh good'?
SPIKE:	Well, I only asked you because I thought it was trendy to have a girlfriend.
HARRIET:	Thanks very much!

SPIKE: I've been really silly, haven't I? I've just been doing all these things because everyone else does.

HARRIET: Well, Spike. Do you remember what our Sunday Club leader told us before we came on holiday? She said that God doesn't look at what we're like on the outside. He looks inside us, at our hearts. So it doesn't really matter what you wear.

SPIKE: So I don't need to look trendy?

HARRIET: No. And you don't need to drink and smoke just because other people do.

SPIKE: Good. Because I didn't really like the taste of those cigarettes. And that beer made me feel all funny inside. I suppose I should say sorry to God, really, shouldn't I, because I said before that I didn't believe in him. (HARRIET *nods.* SPIKE *gets on his knees.* HARRIET *does too*)

SPIKE: Dear God. I've been very silly, and I want to say sorry for it all. I've not been a very good friend to you, Jesus, by saying that I don't believe in you, and by not telling the truth. Please forgive me and help me to start all over again being your friend. Lots of love, Spike Smith, 25 Acacia Avenue.

HARRIET: Amen!

SPIKE: Oh yes, Amen as well. (SPIKE *and* HARRIET *open their eyes and look at each other*)

HARRIET: Listen, Spike. You know how I don't want to be your girlfriend now? Well, that's because we're only twelve. But . . . well, maybe, when we're older . . . maybe we could get married and have lots of children and . . .

(SPIKE *looks in horror at the audience as* HARRIET *rattles on.* Eastenders *theme music*)

40. The Lord's Army

 Aim: *When things seem to go right, we can often forget that it was God – not us – who was behind that 'success'. God made sure Gideon wouldn't miss that when he asked him to fight the Midianites.*

Cast: GIDEON, *who confidently leads an* ARMY *around the church; voice of* GOD, *perhaps amplified from off-stage or shouted from a balcony.* GIDEON *and the* ARMY *can all be dressed in the appropriate Old Testament costume, or they can wear modern-day soldiers' fatigues. There needs to be quite a few members of the* ARMY *to start with, but this could be an ideal sketch to perform with lots of children, as all they do is repeat what* GIDEON *sings.*

 Props: *Swords, or sound effects of battle in progress.*

(GIDEON *and his* ARMY *come marching on very confidently. They march around the church singing loudly in the style of US soldiers . . .*)

GIDEON: (*sings*) We are in the Lord's army!
ARMY: (*sing*) We are in the Lord's army!
GIDEON: Midianites will have to flee!
ARMY: Midianites will have to flee!
GIDEON: Thirty thousand men with me,
ARMY: Thirty thousand men with me,

GIDEON: Will help God grant us victory!

ARMY: Will help God grant us victory!

GIDEON: We are in the Lord's . . .

GOD: (*shouts*) Gideon!

GIDEON: (*shouts*) Squad halt! (*they do. He speaks*) Yes, God?

GOD: Gideon, are you *sure* that I will help you defeat the Midianites?

GIDEON: Oh, yes. Definitely!

GOD: Well, just so that you remember it was me and not your army who helped you win the fight, why don't you leave behind all the ones who are scared?

GIDEON: OK. (*to the* ARMY) Anyone who is scared can go home. (*some of the* ARMY *run away screaming*) Oh dear. (*starts marching again and sings less convincingly*) We are in the Lord's army!

ARMY: We are in the Lord's army!

GIDEON: Midianites will have to flee!

ARMY: Midianites will have to flee!

GIDEON: Just ten thousand men with me,

ARMY: Just ten thousand men with me,

GIDEON: Will help God grant us victory!

ARMY: Will help God grant us victory!

GIDEON: We are in the Lord's . . .

GOD: (*shouts*) Gideon!

GIDEON: (*shouts*) Squad halt! (*they do. He speaks*) Yes, God?

GOD: Gideon, are you *really* sure that I will help you defeat the Midianites?

GIDEON: Oh, yes. Definitely!

GOD: Well, just to make sure that you remember it was me and not your army who helped you win the fight, why don't you leave behind all the ones who kneel down to drink from this water?

GIDEON: (*more reluctantly*) OK. (*to the* ARMY) Squad, drink water! (*all* ARMY *apart from one person kneels down and pretends to drink water. Only* ONE *person pretends to lap it like a dog.* GIDEON *stares, then says in a not too convincing voice*) OK, squad. All those who knelt down to drink, go home. (*all except* ONE *go, grumbling that it was a waste of time.* ONE *looks around and is disconcerted to discover that he is the only person left with* GIDEON. GIDEON *smiles weakly and points at* GOD. *He starts marching again, this time more reluctantly, and sings in a less convincing voice with frequent baleful looks at* GOD) We are in the Lord's army!

ONE: We are in the Lord's army!

GIDEON: Midianites will have to flee!

ONE: Midianites will have to flee!

GIDEON: Just three hundred men with me.

ONE: Just three hundred men with me.

GIDEON: (*suddenly cheerful and marches more vigorously*) God *will* grant us victory!

ONE: God *will* grant us victory!

GIDEON: We are in the Lord's . . . (*he looks at* GOD, *expecting an interruption, but it doesn't come*) army!

ONE: We are in the Lord's army . . . (*they both march off. We hear the sound of a battle, swords hitting swords, people dying and panic among the Midianites.* GIDEON *and* ONE *reappear, looking triumphant and waving their swords*)

GIDEON: We are in the Lord's army!

ONE: We are in the Lord's army!

GIDEON: Midianites – they had to flee!

ONE: Midianites – they had to flee!

GIDEON: Just three hundred men with me!

ONE: Just three hundred men with me!

GIDEON: God *did* grant us victory!

ONE: God *did* grant us victory! (*they march off happily*)

41. Pharisee Investigations plc

 Aim: *The report in John's Gospel of Jesus' healing of the man born blind and the investigation by the Pharisees sounds hilarious. Miracles don't get any simpler than this, but the Pharisees still can't seem to find a reasonable explanation for what's happened, and even resort to asking the man's parents whether they have the right man. Perhaps we also sometimes have difficulty seeing God at work in our daily lives.*

Cast: *Two narrators,* ONE *and* TWO; *a* SPIV *dressed in pin-striped suit and with a pair of sandals strapped inside his jacket;* CROWD *(can be any size);* PHARISEE 1 *and* PHARISEE 2, *who can be dressed in first-century Palestinian costumes, or as Sherlock Holmes/Inspector Clouseau-type figures;* BLIND MAN, *who is in rags;* MUM *and* DAD, *who are made up to look very elderly.*

Props: *Sandals; magnifying glasses; stethoscopes; clip-board; eye chart; tape of* Pink Panther *music.*

(ONE *and* TWO *stand on either side of the stage*)

ONE: In first-century Palestine

TWO: There were a lot of shady people about. (*enter* SPIV, *who looks carefully around and opens his coat to reveal some sandals to* TWO)

SPIV:	Psst! Wanna buy some sandals for the desert? Only five denarii the pair? (TWO *shakes head*)
ONE:	People followed all sorts of crazy ideas and religions. (*enter* CROWD *who approach* SPIV *fervently*)
CROWD 1:	We have heard about the power of 'The Sandal'.
CROWD 2:	We believe it can supernaturally keep sand from injuring our feet!
CROWD 3:	We have come to worship 'The Sandal'!
SPIV:	Not bloomin' likely, mate! Unless you've got five denarii to spend . . . (*exits, pursued by* CROWD)
TWO:	People needed someone who could keep an eye on things.
ONE:	Make sure no one was led astray by dodgy prophets,
TWO:	Mysterious Messiahs,
ONE:	Or harebrained healers.
TWO:	They needed the help of . . .
ONE:	(*melodramatically, as he points to the back of the church*) Pharisee Investigations plc! (*cue* Pink Panther *music. Enter* PHARISEE 1 *and* PHARISEE 2 *from the back of church. They start examining items around the church with magnifying glasses. They can also hold stethoscopes against the heads – or hearts – of people in the congregation as* ONE *or* TWO *continue. Music stops*)
TWO:	They can solve your spiritual dilemma!
ONE:	A quick word from Leviticus and they'll soon know whether you've had a genuine spiritual experience,
TWO:	Or been fooled by a fake. (PHARISEE 1 *signals to* PHARISEE 2 *that the person he has just examined is loopy*)

ONE: Today's investigation is a tricky one.

TWO: This man claims he was blind,

ONE: But that now he can see! (PHARISEE 1 *and* PHAR-ISEE 2 *reach the front of the church.* CROWD *bring* BLIND MAN *on. They throw him onto his knees in front of* PHARISEES)

ONE: The man explained:

TWO: Someone called Jesus had rubbed mud onto his eyes, (BLIND MAN *rubs his eyes.* PHARISEE 2 *gets out a clipboard and starts taking notes*)

ONE: And told him to go and wash them in the Pool of Siloam. (BLIND MAN *mimes washing in a pool.* PHARISEES *shake their heads and* PHARISEE 2 *writes something on his clipboard*)

TWO: They checked whether he could see. (PHARISEE 1 *brings out optician's eye chart*)

PHARISEE 1:   What's that?

BLIND MAN: (*looks puzzled*) I don't know.

PHARISEES: (*in unison, waggling their fingers at the* BLIND MAN) Aha!

PHARISEE 2:   So! Conclusive proof that you are, in fact, still blind!

BLIND MAN: You're holding a card with lots of letters on it. It says: (*he reads it out perfectly*) F, D, G, T, O, I, E, S, H, L, N. I just don't know what it's called. (PHARISEES' *shoulders slump*)

PHARISEE 2:   Oh dear.

ONE: They accused him of never being blind. (PHAR-ISEES *point fingers at* BLIND MAN *accusingly*)

PHARISEE 1:   Close your eyes. (BLIND MAN *does so*) What happens?

BLIND MAN: I can't see!

PHARISEES: (*together*) Aha!

PHARISEE 2:   So! Conclusive proof that you were never blind!

BLIND MAN:	(*opens eyes*) But now I can!
PHARISEE 2:	Oh dear.
TWO:	They called in his mum and dad. (*enter* MUM *and* DAD, *who are very old*)
ONE:	And asked whether this man was their son. (PHARISEES *point at* BLIND MAN *and shake their heads*)
TWO:	Maybe he was an imposter!
PHARISEES:	(*together*) Aha!
PHARISEE 2:	So! Conclusive proof that you were never blind!
DAD:	He's not an imposter! He's my little boy! And he was born blind!
PHARISEE 2:	Oh dear. (MUM *and* DAD *shuffle off*)
TWO:	They asked him about Jesus.
ONE:	And the man said he was a Jewish prophet.
TWO:	But the Pharisees said that a real Jew wouldn't have healed him on the Sabbath.
PHARISEES:	(*together*) Aha!
PHARISEE 2:	(*as if that decided the matter*) So! Conclusive proof that he cannot have healed you at all!
BLIND MAN:	But he *did*!
PHARISEE 2:	Oh dear.
ONE:	They realized that Jesus must have been a man. (PHARISEES *look inspired*)
TWO:	That all men are sinners.
ONE:	And that sinners cannot perform miracles.
PHARISEES:	(*together*) Aha!
PHARISEE 2:	(*again, as if that decided the matter*) So! Conclusive proof that he cannot have healed you at all!
BLIND MAN:	(*as frustration mounts*) But it *was* a miracle!
PHARISEE 2:	Oh dear.
TWO:	There was just *one* possible explanation left.

BLIND MAN: (*relieved that the penny has finally dropped*) At last!

ONE: The blind man must be lying to make Jesus look good. (*they wag their fingers at the* BLIND MAN *again*)

TWO: Because he was one of his disciples.

PHARISEES: (*together*) Aha! (PHARISEE 2 *goes to speak again, but* PHARISEE 1 *gets there first*)

PHARISEE 1:   So! Conclusive proof that he cannot have healed you at all! (BLIND MAN *goes to speak, but is beaten to it by* PHARISEE 2)

PHARISEE 2:   I think that concludes our investigation. Get out, please! (*he picks up the* BLIND MAN *by his clothes and pushes him offstage as he protests*)

PHARISEE 1:   Another successful investigation, brother Pharisee!

PHARISEE 2:   I think so, brother Pharisee! (*they shake hands and walk off to the back of the church*)

TWO: So, remember.

ONE: If you have a supernatural happening,

TWO: If you need to find a reasonable explanation,

ONE: Come to Pharisee Investigations plc.

TWO: They have a 100 per cent record

ONE: Of getting it wrong.

42. Silly Sammy and Clever Carl

 Aim: *This parable has been told and retold so many times that we may have become over-familiar with it. It is good, therefore, to remind people that it is not about being 'wise' in the conventional sense of being clever or intelligent, but simply about obeying what Jesus says. As the Bible reminds us elsewhere, God chose people whom the world considers foolish to shame the wise. The rhythm of the rhymes should dictate the pace of the sketch.*

 Cast: *Narrators* ONE *and* TWO; CLEVER CARL, *who can be dressed in bowler hat and pinstriped suit;* SILLY SAMMY, *who can be dressed in the most ridiculous clothes you can find. Others can become their wives, builders, or 'the storm', pouring water from watering cans, or throwing buckets of water (use confetti for fake water).*

 **Props:** *Umbrella; sun cream; pieces of paper made to look like banknotes; large Bible with the title* 'How to Build Your Foundations Properly' *on the front cover; watering cans; buckets of water; a sturdy roof (made out of wood, corrugated iron or perhaps the roof from a doll's house); a flimsy roof (made out of newspaper); sandpit and boulder (optional).*

(ONE *and* TWO *stand on either side of the stage*)

ONE: The story we would like to tell,

TWO: Is one that Jesus told as well.

ONE: It starts with men in Galilee,

TWO: They are as different as·could be. (*enter* CLEVER CARL *and* SILLY SAMMY)

ONE: Clever Carl knows what to do, (CARL *steps forward*)

TWO: He's sensible and brainy too. (CARL *taps his finger on the side of his head to signify 'brainy'*)

ONE: He thought before he dressed today, (CARL *tips his hat to the audience*)

TWO: And gives advice on what to say.

ONE: He earns good money, has no debt, (CARL *produces some banknotes*)

TWO: Brings his brolly when it's wet. (CARL *produces a rolled-up umbrella and holds out his hand to see if it is raining*)

ONE: He reads the paper, knows a lot, (CARL *puts the umbrella down*)

TWO: And puts on sun cream when it's hot. (CARL *produces some sun cream from his pocket and holds it up*)

ONE: Silly Sammy's not so bright, (SAMMY *blunders forward, nearly tripping himself up*)

TWO: He never plans anything right. (SAMMY *grins inanely at the audience*)

ONE: He grabbed the first clothes he could find, (SAMMY *indicates his clothes, and shrugs his shoulders*)

TWO: At school was always miles behind.

ONE: He can't find work, and he's in debt, (SAMMY *turns out his pockets. They are empty*)

TWO: Brings his sun cream when it's wet, (CARL *passes* SAMMY *the sun cream.* SAMMY *suddenly realizes it's raining*)

ONE: Can't read, so brainy he is not,

TWO: And brings his . . . brolly when it's hot. (*either* CARL *gives* SAMMY *the umbrella, or* SAMMY *produces his own umbrella – which has lots of holes in it.* SAMMY *then indicates that he is very hot)*

ONE: Both these men have plans to build

TWO: Homes to make their families thrilled.

ONE: Clever Carl knows what to do, (CARL *starts making calculations on his fingers)*

TWO: He'll build something smart and new. (CARL *mimes sawing wood)*

ONE: He pictures it inside his head,

TWO: The walls, the roof, his comfy bed. (CARL *indicates where he wants to put each of those items)*

ONE: He knows exactly what he's planned,

TWO: He wants to build it there . . . on sand. (CARL *points to one side of the stage. If a sandpit is available, it could be used to denote the beach)*

ONE: 'Foundations – no, I don't need those,' (CARL *mimes brushing aside suggestions that he should put any foundations down)*

TWO: Says Clever Carl as his house grows.

ONE: 'I'm building my house cheap and quick, (CARL *mimes hammering nails)*

TWO: I'm not like Sammy. He's quite thick!' (CARL *looks across to* SAMMY *and freezes)*

ONE: But Silly Sammy knows his plight,

TWO: He needs help to get it right. (SAMMY *picks up a really heavy book, entitled 'How to Build Your Foundations Properly'. He is holding it upside-down)*

ONE: He asks some men what he should do,

TWO: To build a proper home for two. (SAMMY *pretends to be showing the book to an expert, as if he is seeking clarification of a detailed point. He realizes that the book is upside-down and turns it the right way round)*

ONE: He gets instructions, plans with care, (SAMMY *nods his head, as if agreeing with the expert)*

TWO: Decides to lay foundations there. (SAMMY *looks over at the other side of the stage. If a large boulder is available, it could be used to denote the rock*)

ONE: Clever Carl got quite a shock, (CARL *looks surprised as* SAMMY *goes over to the boulder*)

TWO: Sammy was building . . . on the rock. (SAMMY *puts his foot on the boulder and puts his book next to it*)

ONE: 'It takes years to dig that deep,' (CARL *mimes making fun of* SAMMY. *He finishes his house and starts sunbathing*)

TWO: Says Carl. 'The rock is hard and steep.'

ONE: Sammy works for many days, (SAMMY *mimes digging carefully into the rock*)

TWO: Keeps checking what the manual says. (SAMMY *has the book open next to him and looks back at what it says*)

ONE: When Silly Sammy's finally done,

TWO: Carl's beach-side home still has more sun. (SAMMY *collapses exhausted next to the boulder*)

ONE: But suddenly . . . a drop of rain! (ONE *starts to pour watering can over* CARL)

TWO: They'll have to go inside again. (TWO *starts to pour watering can over* SAMMY. CARL *and* SAMMY *both retreat into their 'homes' –* CARL *under his flimsy roof, and* SAMMY *under his sturdy roof*)

ONE: It rains and pours all day and night, (*empties watering can over* CARL'S *roof*)

TWO: There's floods and winds. What a sight! (*empties watering can over* SAMMY'S *roof*)

ONE: All round Carl there's lots of water, (*picks up bucket of water*)

TWO: The waves come close, the beach gets shorter. (*picks up bucket of water*)

ONE: There's no foundations – remember that? (*throws bucket of water at* CARL *and his flimsy roof*)

TWO: The floods rush in. It falls down flat. (CARL *falls over as his roof disintegrates*)

ONE: Sammy's house is safe and sound. (TWO *empties bucket of water onto the top of* SAMMY's *roof. The water runs down either side and onto the floor, but* SAMMY *remains dry*)

TWO: His work secured it on the ground.

ONE: He brings Carl inside to dry, (SAMMY *indicates for* CARL *to join him.* CARL *shelters under* SAMMY's *roof*)

TWO: And tells him he was daft to try

ONE: To build a house upon the sand, (SAMMY *wags a finger at* CARL)

TWO: With no foundations to grip the land.

ONE: Silly Sammy may not be brainy,

TWO: But he was right when it got rainy.

ONE: He's the wise man in our tale, (SAMMY *steps out from under his roof, holding his big instruction book*)

TWO: And Jesus said: 'You cannot fail

ONE: If you follow what's in this book.' (SAMMY *rips off the title to reveal that it is a Bible underneath*)

TWO: You'd be wise to take a look. (SAMMY *holds up the book*)

ONE: But if you ignore his commands,

TWO: Your life is built on shifting sands.

43. A Cup of Tea and a Slice of Fellowship

Aim: *To show how rarely we talk about how we're really feeling – even with people who would be happy to hear about it.*

Cast: DAVE, JANE *and* RACHEL *can be any age, but the sketch works best for teenagers or students if they look as though they are that age themselves.*

Props: *The lines in bold italics need to be pre-recorded onto tape to represent their thoughts, with enough space for the lines which will be delivered 'live' (it works best with minidisc, with a sound operator playing each pre-recorded line as it comes up). Also needed: cups of tea.*

(DAVE *and* JANE *enter from opposite directions with cups of tea. It is coffee time after a church service, youth group or Christian Union meeting)*

DAVE: Hi, Jane! I haven't seen you for a while! How are you?

JANE: (*they freeze each time the tape plays*) ***Well, I'm feeling pretty fed up. I've been really ill for the last few days, and I didn't feel like coming today at all . . . but Dave won't want to know about that.*** (*unfreeze*) I'm fine, thanks, Dave. How are you?

DAVE: ***Well, I'm having a terrible time wondering if I'm*** *going to get a job because I don't think my qualifications are good enough . . . but Jane doesn't want to hear about my problems.* I'm fine, yes. (*awkward pause. They both study their tea intently*) So . . . erm, how are you getting on with that lad you're going out with?

JANE: *We're not speaking to each other.* Oh, erm . . . all right, yeah! How's your love life?

DAVE: *The girl I had my eye on just started going out with my best friend, and I'm not pleased.* Well, you know, I'm just happy being single, you know . . . (*enter* RACHEL) Oh, hiya, Rachel. How's everything going?

RACHEL: *I've just had this big row with my mum on the phone, and I feel pretty upset about it, really.* (*she starts out as if to tell them how she really feels*) I'm feeling a bit . . . you know . . . (*pulls herself together quickly*) erm . . . fine, actually.

JANE: How's your mum these days?

RACHEL: *A pain in the neck.* Not too bad. (*another awkward pause*) What did you think of it tonight, then?

DAVE: *Well, I felt really challenged about my attitude towards money, because I hardly ever give any of it to God's work, and I should do, really.*

JANE: (*enthusiastically*) *It was brilliant, yeah! It really helped me realize that I don't need to worry about the future and I can trust God. I really needed to hear that.* (DAVE *and* JANE *look at each other, then speak at the same time in a fairly noncommittal way*)

DAVE/JANE: Yeah, it was all right, wasn't it?

DAVE: (*to* RACHEL) Are you . . . er . . . doing anything later, then?

RACHEL: *Well, I really wanted to sit down and pray with someone about this friend of mine who is really close to becoming a Christian.* No, nothing really. Why do you ask?

DAVE: *I thought I might come round and pray with you about this friend of yours who is really close to becoming a Christian.* No reason, really. (*looks at* JANE) I suppose you'll be at your boyfriend's house?

JANE: *No chance.* Er . . . yeah, probably, I suppose.

DAVE: Well, it's been really good sharing like this with you.

JANE: Yeah, it's good to have friends you can really talk to.

DAVE: Right. See you next week then.

RACHEL: See you. (*they all freeze just as they are about to go their separate ways. The final pre-recorded line is all three of them speaking together*)

ALL: *I just wish we knew each other a bit better.*

44. Deep, Meaningful Relationship

 Aim: *To remind us how easy it is to delude ourselves into thinking that sex before marriage is no big deal.*

Cast: *It is easier if the actors* ADAM *and* KATE *are already a couple – or at least comfortable with cuddling fairly intimately! Although the sketch can be performed in a youth group or student setting, teenagers themselves are likely to find it difficult to perform without embarrassment.*

Props: *A bed; a kettle. The kettle boils on cue only because in rehearsals you test it using different quantities of water! Needless to say, please be very careful with boiling water on stage and ensure it cannot be tipped over and there are no trailing flexes.*

(*Enter* ADAM *and* KATE, *laughing. They are students/youngsters who have just returned from a Christian Union/youth club talk*)

KATE: Thanks, Adam. It was really good of you to walk me home. Listen, are you sure you wouldn't like to come in for some coffee?

ADAM: OK, I think I will. (*he sits on the bed.* KATE *puts the kettle on*)

KATE: It was good tonight, wasn't it? (*she sits on the bed next to him*)

ADAM: Oh, the old 'relationships' talk. Well, I've heard it all before. I got that sort of problem sorted out quite early in my Christian life.

KATE: Really? (*looks away in concern*)

ADAM: (*breezily*) Yes, it's simply an act of the will not to give in to your bodily desires.

KATE: (*embarrassed*) But Adam . . . sometimes it's not that easy to do that. You see, sometimes I . . . well, I don't know, I think I get too emotionally involved with the lads I go out with, and . . . well, I want to show my affection.

ADAM: (*sounds interested, despite what he's saying*) Oh yes?

KATE: I know it sounds terrible because I'm supposed to be a Christian, but sometimes it just seems OK when you're in a deep, meaningful relationship. And then I feel really dirty and I think I've really let God down. But I do so much want to live my life for him. (*she is close to tears*)

ADAM: You shouldn't let yourself feel so guilty about it. (*puts his hand on her shoulder. She looks at him*) Look, I went . . . you know, a bit too far not so long ago, but because I repented straight afterwards, God forgave me and took away that guilt. God can forgive you too if you let him.

KATE: Well, yes, but . . .

ADAM: And you heard what the speaker said tonight. Of course sexual sin is bad, but it's just as bad as things like pride and dishonesty. Don't let it get to you. (*he strokes her face*)

KATE: But when Jesus talks about looking at someone lustfully being just as bad as adultery . . . well, I know quite a few good-looking blokes. When I want to show my affection for them and hug and kiss them, is that wrong?

ADAM: No, of course it's not wrong. You just like to show

your feelings for your friends physically. It's quite understandable – I do it myself. (*he puts his arm round her*) Look, you shouldn't set yourself such high standards. God sets standards, but he realizes we can't keep them, so don't feel condemned every time you break them. God forgives you every time, you know.

KATE: Yes, I suppose so.

ADAM: And remember what the bloke said tonight? God created sex, so it's a good thing and we should enjoy it!

KATE: (*looks sharply at him*) In marriage!

ADAM: Yeah. So don't worry so much about it!

KATE: (*smiles weakly*) No, I won't. Look, Adam, it's really good of you to be so honest about sex and relationships. Is there any way I can thank you?

ADAM: Oh, I'm sure I can think of one . . . ! (*he pushes her back on the bed with his arms round her and kisses her or buries his head in her neck. The kettle boils without them noticing*)

45. Comedy Club

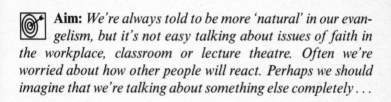

Aim: *We're always told to be more 'natural' in our evangelism, but it's not easy talking about issues of faith in the workplace, classroom or lecture theatre. Often we're worried about how other people will react. Perhaps we should imagine that we're talking about something else completely . . .*

Cast: JASON *and* BECCA *are pleasant, happy people;* LUKE *is very uptight, and comes across as excessively serious-minded.*

 Props: *None.*

(JASON *and* BECCA *enter, laughing uproariously as if they've just heard the funniest joke in the world. They slap each other on the back, and start to fall on the floor laughing. Enter* LUKE)

LUKE: (*staring at them*) What is it? What's so funny?

JASON: (*still laughing*) You won't believe it! We've just heard the funniest thing . . . (*he collapses into fits of giggles again*)

LUKE: (*curious*) What? Tell me what's so funny!

BECCA: Oh, it's this bloke . . . (*laughing so hard she can't get the words out*) He's just so funny!

LUKE: Which bloke?

JASON: (*points back the way they've come*) This bloke! He's a comedian!

LUKE: Friend of yours, is he?

BECCA: Yeah. That's right! Oh, Luke, you've got to meet him! He's great!

LUKE: (*now suspicious*) Hang on! Is this the bloke you told me about before?

BECCA: Probably!

LUKE: Ah, but hang on! Don't you all go to that comedy club together? You read out his jokes to one another, and ask him to tell you more?

JASON: (*just about recovered*) That's right! And, I have to tell you, Luke – he's funnier than ever!

LUKE: Well, you know what I think. For people who like comedy and that sort of thing, it's OK. If it works for them, that's fine. But you shouldn't force other people into accepting your type of humour.

BECCA: (*looks at* JASON *and shrugs her shoulders at* LUKE) Fine. But you're the one missing out.

LUKE: I mean, there's all sorts of different types of comedians, aren't there? There's your traditional one who relies on mother-in-law jokes, then there's your alternative comedian, and that's not to mention visual humour . . . How do you know that your comedian is the best?

JASON: Well, he just makes us laugh, that's all, Luke. Maybe you should go along to the comedy club with us once in a while. Just to see what it's like.

LUKE: Oh no. You're not getting me to that comedy club again. Last time I went it was really boring. They had hard seats, but I still fell asleep during the opening monologue.

BECCA: Whatever.

LUKE: I'm fine as I am, thank you. I can make myself laugh. I don't have to join your club.

JASON: OK, that's fine. But can I just tell you one small joke that the comedian said . . . ?

LUKE: This isn't one of your testimonies about how the power of laughter changed your life, is it?

JASON: Well, yeah . . .

LUKE: I don't want to hear it! They're always the same. You always say it was the comedian who made you laugh. Well, I think it was just coincidence that you happened to laugh just as he got to the end of his joke. (*accusingly*) That's all it is. Pure coincidence.

BECCA: (*pleasantly*) OK, fine. We'll leave you alone, shall we? But give us a call if you ever want to know more about this comedian, won't you? (*exits with* JASON. *She whispers something in his ear and they both start laughing again*)

LUKE: (*looks around to make sure they are gone*) Right. I can make myself laugh. (*deliberately*) Why did the chicken cross the road? To get to the other side! (*gestures to himself to start laughing, but nothing happens*) Erm . . . guys? (*he follows* JASON *and* BECCA) Where did you say that comedian was playing next?

46. Salty Towers: Cana Branch

 **Aim:** *You might not get away with this kind of riotous farce at some weddings . . . but at others it might be just the thing! It would also be suitable for a family service focusing on Jesus' miracles.*

Cast: MR SALTY, MRS SALTY, CARLOS *(all in 1970s costumes)*, MR GOLDBERG *and* MRS GOLDBERG, *who could be played by the bride and groom themselves,* MARY *and* JESUS, *and assorted* WEDDING GUESTS, *all in first-century Palestine costumes.*

Props: *See* 'Salty Towers: Bethlehem Branch' *for a description of the set, although a proper front door is not as vital for this sketch; phone; napkins; doorbell; crate of empty wine bottles; coins; crate of 'full' wine bottles (or a cardboard box which contains enough broken glass to sound like a crate of wine bottles breaking); bottle of sherry; bottle of meths; glasses; jug of water; some kind of red food colouring to put at the bottom of the empty wine bottles to make it appear as though the water is turning into wine.*

(MR SALTY *and* MRS SALTY *stand behind the counter.* MR SALTY *is on the phone.* MRS SALTY *is sorting out some napkins)*

MR SALTY: Yes, that's Salty. S-A-L-T-Y . . . Well, it should have been here by now! I've got a

270

hotel to run here! (*slams phone down*) I
don't believe it! How many times have
those wine merchants let us down? It'd be
quicker to tread the grapes myself!

MRS SALTY: (*not looking up*) Not with the state of your
feet, dear . . .

MR SALTY: (*starts pacing up and down the hall*) I put in
that order for 30 crates of Jerusalem
Liebfraumilch last Friday! I wouldn't
mind, but it was supposed to come by reg-
istered camel the very next day! (*he picks up
a crate of empty bottles and puts it next to
the front door*) I've got these empties for
them to collect too. (*looks at his watch*)
What time is this wedding party due?

MRS SALTY: (*still not looking up*) Any minute now. Can't
you just send Carlos to the off-licence?

MR SALTY: (*incredulously*) Send Carlos to the off-
licence? This is a Jewish wedding, for goodness sake! They're not just coming for some
cucumber sandwiches and a glass of sherry
– they've invited 200 guests to come and
get riotously drunk every night for a whole
week!

MRS SALTY: Just a suggestion . . .

MR SALTY: It's the biggest wedding there's ever been in
Cana, and you think we should just send a
Spanish half-wit out to buy a couple of
bottles of Galilean plonk and hope they
won't notice? (*pause*) It's worth a try . . .
Carlos!

CARLOS: (*comes rushing on*) Qué?

MR SALTY: (*helping* CARLOS *put on his coat while he
tells him*) Nip down to Caesar's Wine
Shop and see what you can get for a couple

	of denarii . . . (*gives him money as doorbell rings*)
CARLOS:	(*looks at money incredulously, then at* MR SALTY *again*) Qué?
MRS SALTY:	(*goes to answer the door*) That'll be them . . .
MR SALTY:	(*pushing* CARLOS *off in a different direction*) Go on then – or we'll be toasting the bridesmaids with the oxtail soup.
MRS SALTY:	(*opens the door and invites* MR GOLDBERG *and* MRS GOLDBERG, *the bride and groom, into the hall, along with assorted* WEDDING GUESTS) Ah, Mr and Mrs Goldberg – welcome to the Cana branch of Salty Towers.
MR SALTY:	Good wedding was it? Rabbi didn't go on too long, then?
MR GOLDBERG:	(*grasps* MR SALTY *warmly by the arms and kisses him on both cheeks*) Ah! This was a splendid wedding, and we are looking forward to a good party, with some of your excellent wine!
MR SALTY:	Wine! Ah, yes, well . . . we are very orthodox on this side of the Sea of Galilee, and the local Pharisees are very strict. Perhaps we could interest you in our alcohol-free selection . . . ?
MR GOLDBERG:	Pah! If there's no wine, there's no party. Perhaps we should conduct our festivities elsewhere . . . (*makes as if to go*)
MR SALTY:	(*gets in the way*) Ha, ha, well, then again, for *special* occasions like this, I'm sure we can bend the rules.
MR GOLDBERG:	I should think so too!
MRS SALTY:	Well, perhaps if you'd like to come this way, we've got some nibbles in the drawing

room before we sit down to the main meal
. . . (*leads* MR GOLDBERG, MRS GOLDBERG
and WEDDING GUESTS *off towards the bar*)

MR SALTY: (*shouts after them*) Yes, I think we've got
some pork scratchings in there!

MRS SALTY: (*returning*) Don't be so insensitive! You
know they don't eat animals with cloven
hooves.

MR SALTY: (*under his breath*) You should be quite safe
then, dear. (*out loud*) I'm just going to
check the cellars again, in case there's a
bottle of Syrian Rosé lurking behind the
water tank. (*he exits. Doorbell goes again.*
MRS SALTY *opens it. It is* MARY *and* JESUS)

MARY: We're with the wedding party.

MRS SALTY: Oh, do come in. I'm Mrs Salty. (*goes behind
the counter and looks at checklist*) And you
are . . . ?

JESUS: Jesus-bar-Joseph. And this is my mother,
Mary.

MRS SALTY: Well, we're delighted to see you – if you'd
like to come through here with the others
. . . (MRS SALTY *leads* MARY *and* JESUS *towards
the drawing room, but they are stopped by*
MR SALTY *approaching, covered in dirt and
cobwebs, clutching a couple of bottles*)

MR SALTY: What about this? (*holding up a sherry
bottle*) Chef uses it in the trifle, but they
won't notice once they've had a couple of
glasses. Then we give them this. (*holds up
another bottle, which* MRS SALTY *takes and
looks at*)

MRS SALTY: This is methylated spirits!

MR SALTY: Well, it's only until Carlos gets back . . .

MRS SALTY: (*stands aside and lets* MR SALTY *see* MARY *and* JESUS *behind her*) Can I introduce you to two of your guests?

JESUS: Bit of trouble on the wine front?

MR SALTY: (*stares blindly for a few seconds, opening and shutting his mouth like a goldfish*) Er . . . no . . . no, not at all, we were just discussing what we could strip the wallpaper with . . . erm . . . will you excuse me a moment? (*he exits towards the kitchen*)

MRS SALTY: I do apologize for my husband. It's been a bad time for him, what with the psychiatric treatment . . . (*they exit. Enter* CARLOS *furtively with a crate of wine*)

CARLOS: Meester Salty? Meester Salty? I bring wine. Ees lots of wine. Meester Salty? (*he shrugs his shoulders, picks out one of the bottles and takes a swig, holding the crate in the other hand. He keeps drinking and looking towards the bar.* MR SALTY *enters from the other side, sees* CARLOS *and approaches him with his fist ready.* CARLOS *doesn't see him*)

MR SALTY: Carlos! (CARLOS *leaps up in the air and drops the whole box of wine and the bottle he is holding on the floor. There is the sound of lots of glass breaking.* MR SALTY *and* CARLOS *stare at the box, then at each other, then at the box.* MR SALTY *is making audible sounds of anguish, then speaks through clenched teeth*) Was that the wine from the off-licence? (CARLOS, *who still has wine in his mouth, nods unhappily.* MR SALTY *starts to advance on* CARLOS *and follows him around the hall, fist clenched*) You stupid Spanish nitwit! (MR GOLDBERG *enters.* MR SALTY *immediately leaves* CARLOS *and becomes the charming host*)

MR GOLDBERG: Mr Salty! We're as dry as the Sinai desert in here! What's happened to this wine?

MR SALTY: (*leaping in front of the crate of broken bottles*) Ah, yes, just coming up, Mr Goldberg! (MR GOLDBERG *exits.* CARLOS *tries to edge away, but* MR SALTY *chases him again*) What's that in your mouth? Have you still got some wine in there? (CARLOS *shakes his head frantically and starts to run faster, but* MR SALTY *catches him, gets a glass from the counter, puts it on the floor, then turns* CARLOS *upside down and starts shaking*) Right – spit it out! Come on – if the only bit of wine in this hotel is in your greasy mouth, I'm having it! (CARLOS *struggles frantically, but eventually deposits the contents of his mouth into the glass. Enter* MRS SALTY *and* MRS GOLDBERG)

MRS SALTY: Now, if you just want to put your veil in the cloakroom . . . (*they stand watching, horrified, until* MR SALTY *turns round and sees them and stops shaking* CARLOS)

MR SALTY: Right – now, that's what you do if a guest has a fish bone stuck in their throat. (*he puts* CARLOS *back down again*) Ah, hello, Mrs Goldberg – just doing a spot of staff training . . . OK, run along, Carlos – we'll teach you to lay the table tomorrow! (*confidentially to* MRS GOLDBERG) He's from Barcelona! (CARLOS *staggers towards the counter to get his breath back.* MRS SALTY *escorts* MRS GOLDBERG, *who is still staring at* MR SALTY, *off left.* MR SALTY

	picks up the glass of wine and strides off towards the bar) Mr Goldberg! I've got some of that wine for you . . . (*enter* JESUS *and* MARY)
MARY:	I'm sure they've run out, love.
JESUS:	Well, why do you want to involve me? I'm not here to do party tricks!
MARY:	I've got faith in you! (*to* CARLOS) Hey, you, wine waiter!
CARLOS:	Qué? (*he looks round, puzzled*)
MARY:	Listen, (*pointing at* JESUS) whatever he tells you to do, do it! (*she winks at him*) I'll leave it to you. (*she exits*)
CARLOS:	Qué?
JESUS:	Oh, Mum! You are embarrassing sometimes! (CARLOS *looks enquiringly at* JESUS) OK. (*he looks around and sees the crates of empties at the door. He puts them on the counter*) Right, fill these bottles with water and then serve them to the groom.
CARLOS:	Qué? Water?
JESUS:	Yes. But don't tell anyone I told you to do it.
CARLOS:	(*tapping the side of his nose conspiratorially*) I know nothing! (JESUS *exits.* CARLOS *goes into the kitchen to get a jug of water.* MR SALTY *backs on from the bar with* MR GOLDBERG *pursuing him*)
MR SALTY:	. . . I am sorry, Mr Goldberg. It must have been Chef who ordered bacon-flavoured crisps.
MR GOLDBERG:	Well, we're still waiting for some proper wine. All I've had so far is one glass, and that was far too warm! And since when did Beaujolais Samaria have bubbles in it?

(*enter* CARLOS, *with a jug of water. He starts pouring it into the bottles. As he does so, he suddenly realizes what is happening and smiles*)

MR SALTY: Er . . . yes, I'm just going to get some more wine now . . . (MR GOLDBERG *exits back into the drawing room again.* MR SALTY *turns round, sees what* CARLOS *is doing and stares*)

CARLOS: Ah, Meester Salty. Ees plenty wine for everybody. Everything is all right! (*starts humming to himself*)

MR SALTY: What are you talking about, you blithering idiot? That's water you're pouring into those bottles!

CARLOS: (*wags a knowing finger at* MR SALTY) Si, Meester Salty, ees very special water! (*he picks up a bottle and goes to take it into the drawing room*) Ees for the happy couple!

MR SALTY: (*gets in the way*) Oh no it isn't! I've a hotel full of guests here expecting to get steaming drunk, and you want to give them Perrier! They'd get more drunk on wine gums! (CARLOS *tries to pass him, but* MR SALTY *catches him, picks him up and puts him over his shoulder.* CARLOS *tries desperately to stop the bottle spilling*) You're not going anywhere near those wedding guests with that! (*he starts to spin* CARLOS *round. Enter* MRS SALTY *and* MRS GOLDBERG *again.* MR SALTY *turns to face them and, for a moment, is nonplussed*) Er . . . yes, and if there's a fire alarm, this is the best way to carry somebody out of the building . . . (*he puts* CARLOS *down again.* MRS GOLDBERG *stares at him again*)

MRS SALTY: I *do* wish you'd stop playing with Carlos
               and get on with seeing to our guests. (*she
               glances at the crate of wine bottles on the
               counter*) Oh, I see he managed to get some
               wine, then. (*she picks up a bottle, which is
               obviously wine rather than water*)

CARLOS: (*rubbing his neck ruefully*) *Si*, Mrs Salty.

MRS SALTY: (*calling*) Mr Goldberg! Would you like
               some wine?

MR SALTY: (*moves to counter and snatches bottle off*
               MRS SALTY *without looking at it*) Has every-
               body gone stark raving mad? You're not
               giving this to Mr Goldberg! (*enter* MR
               GOLDBERG)

MRS SALTY: *What* is wrong with you today? (*snatches
               bottle back and gives it to* MR GOLDBERG)
               Here you are, Mr Goldberg. Sorry for the
               delay.

MR SALTY: (*incredulous*) Wh-what is wrong with me?
               Well, perhaps I've missed something – has
               Chateau Tap Water circa AD 30 become
               some kind of vintage in the last 20
               minutes? (*he grabs the bottle and walks over
               to stand next to* CARLOS) Or maybe we
               should just change our licence – 'Salty
               Towers, established AD 12, licensed to sell
               intoxicating H_2O on and off the premises'!
               (CARLOS *pinches the bottle back, gives it to*
               MRS SALTY, *who gives it to* MR GOLDBERG)

MRS SALTY: What *are* you talking about?

MR SALTY: (*covers his face with his arms*) Right, well
               that's it! I'm as good as out of business!

MR GOLDBERG: (*pours wine and takes a sip*) Mmm! (*sips it
               again and swirls it around his mouth
               expertly*) Hey, this is good wine! In fact,

	this is some of the best I've ever tasted! Where d'you get this stuff?
MR SALTY:	(*peers out from between his fingers*) What?
MR GOLDBERG:	Hey, most people, they give you the best wine first and leave the worst till last. But you, my friend, have done it the other way round!
MR SALTY:	(*staring incredulously*) B-b-but . . .
MRS SALTY:	Well, thanks for saying that, Mr Goldberg – shall we share it with your other guests? (MR GOLDBERG *and* MRS GOLDBERG *go into the drawing room.* MRS SALTY *looks* MR SALTY *up and down*) Do pull yourself together. (*she takes crate of wine into the drawing room*)
MR SALTY:	W-wha . . . ? What did you do?
CARLOS:	Qué?
MR SALTY:	H-how did you do that? Can you do it again?
CARLOS:	(*spreads his arms out wide*) Meester Salty, I know nothing!

(MR SALTY *chases* CARLOS *out*)

47. Living Water

 Aim: *Water is a significant Christian symbol, nowhere more so than at baptism. Jesus spoke about the living water, and this sketch aims to show how important it is to share that water with others.*

Cast: VIOLA *and* PETUNIA *are dressed in flower outfits – the more extravagant the better – and treat their colourful blossoms and luscious greenery as if they were fashionable clothes. They talk like fashion victims.* DAFFODIL *is also dressed in a flower outfit, but has dried-up leaves and withered flowers.*

Props: *Watering cans.*

(VIOLA *and* PETUNIA *enter from opposite sides, both carrying watering cans*)

VIOLA: Petunia, darling! (*kisses her on the cheek*) You look absolutely stunning!

PETUNIA: Viola, sweetie! You're too kind. These are just some old summer blooms from last year. They're not my best display.

VIOLA: And your leaves! They're so green! How do you keep them like that?

PETUNIA: Plenty of moisturizer, dear. At my age, you start to show the creases unless you're watered every day. (*she motions for* VIOLA *to water her*)

280

VIOLA: (*realizes*) Oh darling! Absolutely! More water needed here. We can't have your lovely green leaves drying out! (*she waters* PETUNIA, *who sighs contentedly*)

PETUNIA: Thank you, sweetie! My roots don't absorb as much as they used to. What about you, sweetie? (*feels her flowers*) Mmm, gorgeous petals there, love. Really gorgeous!

VIOLA: Oh yes, well, I absolutely swear by my mud bath. I really do!

PETUNIA: The one you put on your face?

VIOLA: No, dear. The compost heap I stand on in the garden!

PETUNIA: Ah! And you keep that . . .

VIOLA: . . . well watered, dear, yes. Can't have my lovely compost drying out, can we? (*she motions to* PETUNIA *to water her*)

PETUNIA: Oh no, love. That's right! (*she waters* VIOLA *with her watering can*) How does that feel, sweetie!

VIOLA: Fabulous, darling! Do you know, that gardener is so good to us, isn't he? What a sweetheart! He gives us water whenever we want it! I feel privileged to be part of his special rockery! (DAFFODIL *crawls in*)

PETUNIA: Oh, darling, don't look now, but here comes one of those horrible plants from the other end of the garden!

VIOLA: Oh dear, sweetie. Look at the state of him. He really has let himself go, hasn't he? Look at those dried-up leaves and that wilting flower!

DAFFODIL: (*panting*) Please . . . please, can you help me? I need some water. I'm going to die unless I get some water. (PETUNIA *and* VIOLA *both hide their watering cans behind their backs*)

PETUNIA: Well, you'll have to go and see the gardener, I'm afraid, sweetie!

DAFFODIL: But you've already got water! The gardener gives us plenty to go round, but you lot stand under the sprinklers all day!

VIOLA: Oh, you poor little flower. You don't seem to understand! Petunia and I need every drop of water we can get! Imagine if we had some kind of blemish on our leaves or our petals started dropping off. We'd be an embarrassment to the whole rockery!

PETUNIA: We're trendsetters, you know. What we're wearing this season will be worn all over the garden by the summer!

DAFFODIL: Please! Just a drop . . . (PETUNIA *and* VIOLA *studiously ignore him. He dies*)

VIOLA: Oh dear, Petunia. There seems to be a dead plant in our topsoil.

PETUNIA: I know. I blame the gardener. I mean, why can't he come and water some of these flowers occasionally?

VIOLA: Did you say 'water', sweetie?

PETUNIA: Oh yes, rather, sweetie! (*they both take their watering cans and start watering each other heavily, to their obvious mutual delight. Ad-lib until offstage*)

48. Misconceptions of God

Aim: *Schoolchildren, especially those in secondary school, are sometimes the hardest people to perform to, not least because they often start from the standpoint of simply not believing in God (or not caring either way). You can be halfway through a detailed exposition of the fruits of the Spirit before you realize that they have already dismissed Christianity because they think science has disproved the creation story. This sketch aims to meet them at the most basic level – what do they think God is like? Because teenagers can also remain resolutely unimpressed with anything half-hearted, the actors – in particular the one playing the professor – must come across as completely zany, over the top and beyond embarrassment.*

Cast: *The mad* PROFESSOR HAROLD VON CLEVER-TROUSERS, *who is dressed in a white coat, bow tie and hair sticking out on the top and sides of his head; his* DAD, *who is dressed exactly the same, but looks much older; and* ONE, TWO *and* THREE.

Props: *Computer or laboratory equipment (optional); beer glass; policeman's helmet and truncheon; false white beard; jigsaw puzzle box; school books; walking sticks.*

(*Enter* PROFESSOR HAROLD VON CLEVER-TROUSERS, *who can*

start working on a computer or fiddling with test tubes. ONE, TWO *and* THREE *stand with their backs to the audience*)

HAROLD: (*in a mock German accent*) Ah-ha! Ladies and gentlemen, velcome to my laboratory, vere I haf just made ze most fantastic discovery! It is, how you say, a 'Eureka!' moment! I haf just discovered somezink vich has been troubling ze human race since ze dawn of civilization! It is somezink about God! Now, you may not believe in ze God at all, or you may zink you know all about him. (*he looks carefully at the audience and strokes his chin*) Yes, zis vill be an interesting experiment! Some of you may zink zat ze God is like zis – zat he is only around to stop us having fun because he doesn't like us having ze good time, ja? Zat he is some kind of cosmic policeman . . . .! (*exits*)

(ONE *pretends to pull a pint of beer into glass and gives it to* TWO)

ONE: There you go, mate!

TWO: (*lifts pint and begins to drink*) Cheers! (TWO *is just about to drink it when* THREE *runs on in policeman's helmet, waving a truncheon*)

THREE: 'Ello, 'ello, 'ello! Is that a pint of beer I can see? You are having too much fun! (*hits* ONE *and* TWO *with truncheon*) I think you had better leave this 'ere pub and come along to a boring church service with me! (*leads* ONE *and* TWO *off*)

TWO: Aw – God! You always spoil my fun!

HAROLD: (*comes on wagging his finger*) Now, zat is not vot ze God is like at all. He does not vant to spoil your fun. Maybe you zink zat ze God is something like ze Father Christmas or ze tooth fairy zat you grow out of. Perhaps you zink that he is a bit childish, and zat he wants us all to be childish too . . . (*exits*)

(TWO *and* THREE *hold hands on either side of* ONE *and look lovingly into his eyes. All three of them skip along soppily*)

TWO/THREE: (*singing together in children's voices*) 'Gentle Jesus, meek and mild. Look on me a little child ...' (*they sit at* ONE's *feet, and he pats them on the head*)

HAROLD: (*comes on shaking his head*) Now, zis is not right either. Perhaps zere are some of you who zink zat God is a bit like a nice old man who gives out presents, but is out of touch with vot is going on zese days ...! (*exits*)

(TWO *has put on a white beard and walks slowly, like an old man.* ONE *runs up to* TWO *like a child*)

ONE: God! Can I have £100 to buy some trainers? [*or current must-have gadget*] Aw, please, God! Go on ...!

TWO: (*puts hand to his ear*) What did you say?

ONE: (*shouts*) Can I have £100 to buy some trainers?

TWO: Trainers? What on earth are they? And what's all this music you listen to these days? It's all thump-thump-thump – there's no melody! I'll tell you what I have got for you. All the children like these – it's a jigsaw puzzle of your local post office!

ONE: (*sarcastically*) Oh great! Thanks, God!

HAROLD: (*comes on tut-tutting*) Ah, now zis vill not do! Zis is not correct! God is not like ze policeman, not like ze childish friend, and not like ze old man. Now, some people, zay only turn to God when zay really need him, when zay have ze crisis – even if zay say zay do not belief in him. Zay think he is a soft touch, and zay can get away vis it ....! (*exits*)

(TWO *walks around in hysterically distraught state, clutching school books*)

TWO: Oh, this is terrible! I've got all this GCSE course-
            work to do for tomorrow. I'm never going to get
            it finished in time! I'm going to get into real
            trouble for this. I need someone to help. (*flash of
            inspiration*) God! That's it! God will help me.
            Dear God, I don't believe in you, but I really need
            your help . . . (*enter* THREE)

THREE: Hello! (*takes school books from* TWO) Physics, is
            it? Don't worry. I'll do it. You go away and enjoy
            yourself. And if you have anything else you'd like
            me to do, just say.

TWO: Thanks God! (*runs off*)

HAROLD: Zis is not right! God is not like zis! Now, some
            people, zay zink of God only as ze philosophical
            idea, like zis!
            (THREE *and* ONE *walk on stroking their chins*)

THREE: . . . and, of course, the quintessential question is
            whether God represents the totality of life itself
            in both the benevolent and malevolent aspects of
            the universe.

ONE: Well, it all depends on whether one is talking
            purely in the spiritual realm or in the physical
            sense . . .

HAROLD: (*shaking his head again*) Zis is wrong, because zay
            are zinking of God as just an idea or a force
            within ze universe, and not as a real person! Now,
            ze final way zat some of us zink of God is zis: zat
            he only lives in ze church.
            (ONE *and* TWO *walk together towards where* THREE
            is standing. THREE *dons the white beard again*)

TWO: So, I've been feeling a bit religious recently, and I
            think I'd better talk to God. Where do you think
            he is?

ONE: (*thinks for a second*) Er . . . church. That's it! That's
            where God lives. Oh look, here's a church now.

THREE: (*shakes their hands*) Hello. Welcome to church. I'm God. You'll find hymn books on the left and Bibles in the pews. And you'll need to start looking a bit more miserable, please.

(ONE *and* TWO *go past* THREE, *kneel and adopt very pious and serious poses*)

HAROLD: Many people zink zay can do vot zay like outside church, but once zay come inside, zay have to be all serious and respectful to ze God. Now zis is complete poppycock. Because if God is God, he can see vot zay are doing outside church also! Now, imagine zat you are God, and people are zinking ze wrong zing about you all ze time – maybe zere are a lot of rumours about vot you might be like, but no one can be sure. Vot would you do? (*he invites some responses*) Send a postcard? Draw a picture of yourself? No, no. You vould come and show yourself in person. Zat is vot ve belief happened viz Jesus Christ. Now, vot does it mean ven ve say ze 'Son of God'? Let me show you. Haf any of you ever met my father? My dad? (*if there is some response,* PROFESSOR *should ask what he looked like. If none . . .*) Vell, you might zink zat you vould haf a good idea vot my father vas like because you had met me, ja? Let me introduce you to my father, Professor Harold von Even-Cleverer-Trousers! (*enter* DAD, *who shuffles on with a stick*)

DAD: (*in the same ridiculous accent*) Hello everyone, I am Harold's father – Professor Harold von Even-Cleverer-Trousers!

HAROLD: Now, if you vanted to know vot my dad vas like, you may look at me, ja, and haf a pretty good guess. (*grabs* DAD *and pulls him towards himself*)

So, just as ze little Harold is part of ze big Harold, so it is ze same wiz God! Zank you very much! You haf been, as zay say, a lovely audience! (*they exit*)

49. Hats Off!

Aim: *To show how many of us are often unthinking slaves to the latest fashions and easily succumb to peer pressure. Hats can be seen as a substitute for trainers, or haircuts, or even certain attitudes we choose to hold only because our friends do. Devised in a drama workshop by Top Cat Theatre Company.*

Cast: *Five people (though can be done with four or more than five).* ORPHAN *and* HAT SELLER *can be in initial line-up or can be separate actors. The cast may want to practice saying 'hat' (or another word) in as many ways as possible to convey different kinds of meanings before attempting this.*

Props: *Lots of different kinds of hats; long coat with hats pinned to the inside; 'hungry and homeless' sign; money; newspaper with 'Hats Off!' headline (optional).*

(*Enter* ONE *wearing a small hat*)

ONE: (*pleased with himself and pointing at the hat*) Hat! (*enter* TWO *with a slightly bigger hat. They stand in a line facing the audience*)

TWO: (*smugly, as he points at his hat*) Hat!

ONE: (*impressed as he points at* TWO's *hat*) Hat! (*points at his own, slightly shamefacedly*) Hat?

289

TWO: (*feeling superior as he points at* ONE's *hat*)
                    Hat! (*enter* THREE *with a much wider-
                    rimmed hat than* TWO's. *He joins the line-up*)

THREE: (*even more smugly as he points at his hat*)
                    Hat!

ONE and TWO: (*impressed as they point at* THREE's *hat and
                    measure the size of it with their hands*) Hat!
                    Hat! (*feeling inferior as they consider their
                    own smaller hats*) Hat?

THREE: (*sees* ONE's *and* TWO's *hats, and chuckles
                    slightly*) Hat? Hat! (*he draws his hand
                    around the rim of his to check its enormity*)
                    Hat!! (*enter* FOUR *with the most gigantic hat
                    to join the line-up. His is also tall and
                    includes all sorts of fruit and flowers*)

FOUR: (*in the most smug voice of them all*) Hat!!!

ONE, TWO and THREE: (*as their jaws drop*) Hat!!

FOUR: (*enjoying the attention and illustrating with
                    his hands how tall the hat is*) Hat! Hat! Hat!

ONE: (*shaking his head as he considers his own
                    hat*) Hat?

TWO: (*sympathizing with* ONE) Hat!

THREE: (*peering intently at* FOUR's *hat*) Hat!

FOUR: (*catches sight of the other hats for the first
                    time, laughs and ridicules them in turn*) Hat!!
                    Hat?! Hat?? (*enter* FIVE, *without a hat at all,
                    whistling a tune and seeming pleased enough
                    with life.* FIVE *joins the line-up.* FOUR *catches
                    sight of* FIVE *first and nudges* THREE. *They
                    stare at* FIVE. THREE *nudges* TWO, *who also
                    looks, then* TWO *nudges* ONE)

ONE, TWO, THREE and FOUR: (*accusingly as they all point at*
                    FIVE) HAT!!! (FIVE *holds head in hands in
                    shame. All freeze*)
                    (ONE, TWO, THREE *and* FOUR *all exit. Enter*

HAT-SELLER, *who is wearing a long coat, and* ORPHAN *who is holding a sign saying: 'Hungry and homeless'.* FIVE *sees the orphan, feels sorry for him, and starts to delve into a pocket for some money. The* HAT-SELLER *approaches* FIVE *and opens his coat – to reveal a massive array of different kinds of hats pinned inside*)

HAT-SELLER: (*persuasively*) Hat??

FIVE: (*pauses in the act of giving money to the* ORPHAN, *turns to* HAT-SELLER *and gasps at all the hats.* FIVE *points at each hat in turn*) Hat! Hat! Hat! (*she looks back at the* ORPHAN *and pockets her money.* ORPHAN *exits*)

HAT-SELLER: (*pointing out all the hats he has to sell*) Hat! Hat! Hat! Hat! Hat!

FIVE: (*indecisively*) Hat! Hat! Hat! (*then impulsively grabs one*) Hat! (*she gives him the money. Exit* HAT-SELLER *as* FIVE *tries on new hat.* FIVE *is pleased with it*) Hat! (*exits*)

(ONE, TWO *and* THREE *all enter, still wearing their hats, and looking puzzled. They have lost* FOUR)

ONE: (*using his hands to illustrate an enormous hat*) Hat? Hat?

TWO: (*shakes his head*) Hat.

THREE: (*pointing in the direction* ONE *has come from*) Hat? Hat?

ONE: (*shakes his head*) Hat. (*they end up lining up in the same positions they occupied before. Enter* FOUR, *this time without a hat at all. He can be reading a newspaper with the headline 'Hats Off!' to make the point clearer.* ONE, TWO *and* THREE *all gasp and point as he walks past them*)

FOUR: (*casually indicating his absence of head-wear*) Hat!

THREE: (*looks at* FOUR, *considers his own hat and throws it off his head*) Hat! (*he rubs his hands and looks pleased with himself*)

TWO: (*grabs his hat and flings it to the floor quickly as if he can't believe he'd ever been wearing one*) Hat! (*he flicks his hair out of his eyes, as if enjoying the feeling of liberation*)

ONE: (*sees what has happened to the others, but has to wrestle for a moment or two with thoughts about what happens if he removes his hat. In the end, he takes it off and throws it away too*) Hat! (*he nods to himself, as if knowing it was the right decision. Enter* FIVE, *still wearing new hat, and stands in line next to* FOUR *again. In a precise replay of what happened earlier,* FOUR *catches sight of* FIVE *first and nudges* THREE. *They stare at* FIVE. THREE *nudges* TWO, *who also looks, then* TWO *nudges* ONE)

ONE, TWO, THREE and FOUR: (*accusingly as they all point at* FIVE) HAT!!! (FIVE *holds head in hands in shame again. All freeze*)

CHURCH ANNIVERSARY

50. St X's, This Is Your Life

Aim: *If you go to the kind of church that is likely to celebrate the anniversary of when it was first built, you may want to use this as part of your celebrations. Inevitably, this will be something of a do-it-yourself sketch, as you will have to fill in the blanks or add details from your own church's history. Some examples have been included below to give you some ideas.*

Cast: *Depends on the history of your church, but you will definitely need smartly dressed* PRESENTER *and a* CHURCH. *Ideally, that person should be given a costume that looks like your church – perhaps a large rectangular box with stained-glass windows and other features painted on, which can be attached to string and dangled from that person's shoulders. If your church has a spire or tower, you can make one for* CHURCH *to wear like a hat.*

Props: *Again, this will depend on the history of your church and the scenes you create, but you will definitely need a microphone, a big red book, and a tape of the music from the TV programme* This Is Your Life.

(PRESENTER *enters holding microphone a big red book with 'This Is Your Life' on it, as* CHURCH *looks studiously in the wrong direction*)

PRESENTER: Well, we're here to honour one of the most historic buildings in [*name of town/city/village*]. Today is a very special day for this building – this is its [*suitable number*]th birthday. We're just going to surprise it now. (*taps* CHURCH *on the shoulder*) Excuse me . . .

CHURCH: (*turns, realizes that* PRESENTER *has the 'This Is Your Life' book and covers mouth with hand in shock*) Oh my goodness! I don't believe it!

PRESENTER: You thought you were here today just to stand in [*name of street*] and look majestic. But we have a surprise for you . . .

CHURCH: I never expected anything like this . . . (*to audience*) You all knew about this, didn't you!

PRESENTER: Because today, [*name of church*], on your [*number*]th anniversary . . . this is your life! (*Cue* This Is Your Life *music.* CHURCH *and* PRESENTER *move onto stage to suggest they are now in a TV studio with the audience as the studio audience*)

PRESENTER: Yes, [*name of church*], this is your life. You've been standing here, watching over [*name of town/city/village*] for [*number*] years, with your handsome structure, your elegant spire and your well-built interior [*or suitable description*]. Today members of [*name of church*] past and present get to pay their respects to what has been a fantastic building to worship in. We're going to look back at selected highlights from your life. And, first of all, do you remember this voice?

ARCHITECT: (*offstage*) You cost me £5,000 [*or appropriate figure*], but you've been worth every penny!

PRESENTER: Yes, it's the original architect and founder of [*name of church*], it's [*name of architect/founder*] (*enter* ARCHITECT)

CHURCH: I haven't seen you for almost [*number*] years!

PRESENTER: [*name of architect/founder*], let's ask you: why did you build a church?

ARCHITECT: [*details of why church was built*]

PRESENTER: But not everyone was keen, is that right?

ARCHITECT: [*details of any opposition to church being built, or necessary fundraising*]

PRESENTER: Thank you very much, [*name of architect*]! (ARCHITECT *exits*) So, how did you celebrate that foundation stone being laid?

CHURCH: Well, we had a full choral service here! (CONDUCTOR *enters with a baton and taps it on an imaginary music stand. He conducts an imaginary choir in a short burst of singing – either on tape, or using a real choir*)

PRESENTER: Now, your early years involved . . . [*fill in detail of early years of church and neighbourhood*] And, of course, that involved more building work, didn't it?

CHURCH: That's right!

PRESENTER: Go on, then, show us your medieval/Victorian/Edwardian/Georgian/modern extension.

CHURCH: (*showing the audience an extension*) It's just there. I think you can just about see the join.

PRESENTER: But you could easily have disappeared

during the Second World War. What happened then?

CHURCH: Well, it was incredible. There were bombs dropping all around me. People looked at me and saw there were fires all around, and they didn't think I'd last out the night. But somehow I was spared.

PRESENTER: Yes, let's just relive that night now. (NAZI AIRMAN *zooms onto the stage, making aeroplane noises and throwing balls as if they are bombs at* CHURCH. CHURCH *dives to the left and right like a goalkeeper to catch them and throw them away. Cue* The Dambusters *music.* NAZI AIRMAN *gives up in disgust and flies away*) Yes, that's right. All the shops around here were just heaps of rubble, but you survived!

CHURCH: Ah, well! Maybe it was by divine intervention!

PRESENTER: In [*insert year*], you opened a church hall. That building is now used by the nursery/mother and toddler group/scouts and guides. And do you remember this voice?

PREVIOUS VICAR: (*offstage*) That church hall was my idea!

PRESENTER: Yes, we've brought him back to be with you here today. He was vicar here from [*insert year*] to [*insert year*]. It's the Reverend [*insert name*]! (*enter* PREVIOUS VICAR)

PRESENTER: What do you remember from your time here?

PREVIOUS VICAR: [*shares some of his memories, briefly*]

PRESENTER: And, of course, more recently, I believe you've had a bit of cosmetic surgery?

CHURCH: (*slightly embarrassed*) Yes, that's right! I was looking a bit shabby, so I've had my spire repaired and some of my older parts refurbished [*or give details of appropriate repairs*]. I still need some work on my flanks, though.

PRESENTER: Well, you're looking great for your age! And I believe you're throwing a party to celebrate your [*insert number*]th birthday!

CHURCH: Yes, that's right! A children's party with a bouncy castle, face painting, displays of archive material [*or appropriate details*]. It's my free gift to the whole parish, and it's happening today!

PRESENTER: But, tell us [*insert name of church*], you're not just here to look good, are you?

CHURCH: That's right. I'm really here to help lives change.

PRESENTER: And although you are the building, it's the people around us are the ones who actually make up [*name of church*] itself.

CHURCH: And they're the ones who'll be writing the history of [*name of church*] in the future.

PRESENTER: So, it only remains for me to say: (*looks at audience and holds out 'This Is Your Life' book*) 'People of [*name of church*], This is Your* Life.' (*theme music*)

Subject Index

Numbers in brackets refer to sketch numbers.

Giving your life to Jesus:

Healing:

History of your church:

Holy Spirit:

Humility:

Insecurity:

Jesus, the life of:

Jesus, the death of:

Jesus, the power of:

Jesus, the resurrection of:

Jesus, the Son of God:

Jesus, the teaching of:

Love:

Materialism:

50 Sketches for all Occasions

by Michael Botting

A rich collection of sketches from a variety of sources –
including teachers, ministers, drama group leaders and
theatre companies – to provide something for almost
any occasion.

Whether you are looking to liven up your Christmas or
Easter services, provide an opportunity for outreach, or
simply illustrate a talk, this resource with its index of
themes and Scripture references is sure to help.

If you have never used drama before, the introductory
section provides vital clues to all you need to know,
including:

- visibility and audibility
- basic mime techniques
- the use of minimal props and equipment
- involving children

Two books by David Burt...

50 Sketches about Jesus

Picture the scene: Jesus preaching at Wembley
Stadium; a paparazzi photographer in Bethlehem;
Mary cooking spaghetti hoops on toast; the wise men
shopping in Harrods. Strange? Maybe. Funny?
Certainly. But every sketch here highlights a truth
about Jesus of Nazareth that is relevant to life today.

There's something here for all levels of expertise, and
all ages. Fully indexed by themes, occasions and Bible
references, this is an ideal resource for churches and
other groups who wish to communicate old truths in
fresh ways.

25 Sketches about Proverbs

The book of Proverbs in the Bible has long been a
source of wit and wisdom for people of various ages,
races and cultures. So what better resource could we
have for creating funny but poignant sketches about
everyday life? From subjects as diverse as betrayal,
bullying, laziness and loneliness, there is something
here for everyone! Ideal for seeker-friendly services
and all-age worship.